Digitizing collections

Strategic issues for the information manager

Digital Futures Series

Series Editors: Marilyn Deegan and Simon Tanner

Digital Futures: strategies for the information age
    Marilyn Deegan and Simon Tanner ISBN 1-85604-411-4

DIGITAL FUTURES SERIES
Series Editors: Marilyn Deegan and Simon Tanner

Digitizing collections
Strategic issues for the information manager

Lorna M. Hughes

facet publishing

© Lorna M. Hughes 2004

Published by
Facet Publishing
7 Ridgmount Street
London WC1E 7AE

Facet Publishing (formerly Library Association Publishing) is wholly owned
by CILIP: the Chartered Institute of Library and Information Professionals.

Lorna M. Hughes has asserted her right under the Copyright, Designs and
Patents Act 1988 to be identified as Author of this work.

First published 2004

British Library Cataloguing in Publication Data
A catalogue record for this book is available from the British Library.

ISBN 1-85604-466-1

Typeset in 10/14 pt New Baskerville and Zurich by Facet Publishing
Production.
Printed and made in Great Britain by MPG Books Ltd, Bodmin, Cornwall.

Contents

Series Editors' introduction

The Digital Futures series began its life in the book *Digital Futures: strategies for the information age* by Marilyn Deegan and Simon Tanner. What became obvious in writing this first book was that no single work can cover in great depth all the issues facing librarians and other information workers as they engage in digital activities. Thus the Digital Futures series idea was born, to enable further volumes to explore in detail the major topics that concern our digital information age.

Written by leading international experts, each book in the Digital Futures series will examine some of the key strategic and practical issues facing libraries and other cultural institutions in the rapidly expanding world of digital information. We welcome this latest volume, by Lorna M. Hughes, as a valuable and insightful addition to the series. The next volume in the series will be a collection of essays written by experts on the difficult issues that surround digital preservation.

Anyone interested in contributing to the Digital Futures series is invited to contact the Series Editors at marilyn.deegan@qeh.ac.uk and simon.tanner@kcl.ac.uk.

Marilyn Deegan
Simon Tanner

Introduction

This second book in the Digital Futures series had its origins in intense discussions between the author and Series Editors about what staff in memory institutions need to know about the strategies and practical issues involved in putting digital collections of cultural materials online. *Digitizing Collections* is intended primarily for librarians, archivists and museum professionals, as well as for students of these subjects, and introduces the idea of digitizing collections with a view to creating digital surrogates of cultural heritage materials that will become valuable resources for the whole user community.

Presented here is an overview of the many reasons for digitizing collections: improving access to collections for all users; contributing to preservation activities by protecting fragile originals from excessive handling; raising the profile of the institution; and creating leverage for funding for future digitization activities.

Included are chapters outlining the many aspects involved in developing a digitization plan or policy, accompanied by suggestions for further reading and resources for expert guidance on all topics.

The book is divided into two sections. The first part deals with the strategic decisions that will precede a digitization initiative:

- the advantages and economics of digitization
- developing selection policies and criteria for digitization
- managing the intellectual property and copyright questions that may arise

- assessing the institutional framework and developing strategies for risk management
- the benefits of a collaborative approach.

The second part takes the reader through the many complex issues involved in running a digitization project, with an emphasis on case studies from digitization initiatives in cultural heritage institutions around the world. The chapters in this section discuss:

- developing a project plan and identifying funding opportunities
- managing a digitization project
- the digitization of rare and fragile collections.

The final chapters are devoted to an analysis of case studies illustrating the digitization of text, image, and audio and moving image materials.

There is a focus throughout on the economic and financial implications of making the significant investment required for digitization. The theme of understanding and managing the risk factors in digitizing collections underlies many parts of the book, as does that of developing sustainable resources that can be used over the long term. Most importantly, there is an analysis of strategic considerations that must be taken into account before starting a digitization project. Digitization requires a significant investment, and it is important to assess realistically what the costs and benefits are likely to be: these costs and benefits will not be solely financial, but will include, among other features, time, opportunity costs, institutional prestige, staff training and morale. One of the most important aspects of developing a digitization policy or plan is the evaluation of whether digitization is actually the right strategy at all: whether this is the right collection, the right time to digitize, or the right project plan. Advice on when not to digitize is given in the book, as well an overview of the evaluative criteria that will inform these decisions. One of the important tools that can inform such a decision is the development of accurate cost models and of prototype projects, and the book presents a detailed overview of both topics.

Above all, this book will help the project manager to formulate the right questions for assessing all of the components that go into developing a digitization project.

Lorna M. Hughes

Acknowledgements

I am enormously grateful to Marilyn Deegan and Simon Tanner, who planned the original proposal and outline for this book with me, and who have both subsequently committed a great deal of time, effort and encouragement throughout the course of this project. Both have provided the benefit of their tremendous insight and experience at every stage of developing this manuscript. I would like to thank them for all their input, and their willingness to overcome our geographic challenges by taking every opportunity for a planning meeting whenever our paths crossed, in locations as disparate and interesting as Oxford, New York, the Hague, Dublin (Ohio), and Newark Airport.

I was fortunate to have two extremely accomplished research assistants who worked with me on several parts of the book, Antje Pfannkuchen and Brian Beaton.

I would like to thank my colleagues in the Humanities Computing group at NYU, for their support, input and endless patience throughout the completion of this project: Gary Shawver, Matthew Zimmerman, Carlos Garcia, Eduardo Lage Otero, Nicola Monat-Jacobs and Anthony Policano. I would also like to thank Vincent Doogan and Marilyn McMillan for all their encouragement.

I am extremely grateful to Emma Taylor, Neil MacBride, Phil Galanter, Jane Del Favero, and Allan Dawson, John Price Wilkin and John Unsworth for reading and commenting on various sections. I would especially like to thank Charles Oppenheim for undertaking an especially helpful review of the section on copyright. All errors and omissions throughout the book remain, of course, my own.

Discussions with many other colleagues and friends over the years have influenced many of the ideas in this book. I would especially like to thank Jean Anderson, Christian Kaye, Des O'Brien, Steve Chapman, Allen Renear, Thornton Staples, Bruce Altschuler, David Hoover, Catherine Owen, Martha Wilson and the Franklin Furnace team, Jerry McDonough and Harold Short for insights too numerous to mention. I would also like to acknowledge my colleagues on the *NINCH Guide to Good Practice in the Digital Representation and Management of Cultural Heritage Materials*: David Green, Seamus Ross, Ann Gow, Celia Duffy, Maria Economou, Ian Anderson, Kathe Albrecht, Morgan Cundiff, LeeEllen Friedland, Peter Hirtle, Katherine Jones, Mark Kornbluh, Joan Lippincott, Michael Neuman and Richard Rinehart.

Thanks to Allison Coudert and Gordon Weiner for all their support and for setting me on the right path.

Rebecca Casey, Lin Franklin and all at Facet Publishing have been extremely supportive and patient with me, and I thank them for all their encouragement in writing this first book.

And, finally, my heartfelt thanks to my family, who have been extremely understanding and encouraging throughout this project: Kirk Stewart, Christine Hughes, Gregor Hughes, Nicola Docherty and Iona Hughes. I couldn't have done it without you.

Part 1
Strategic decision making

1

Why digitize?
The costs and benefits of digitization

Introduction

> The conversion of all sorts of cultural contents into bits and bytes opens
> up a completely new dimension of reaching traditional and new audiences
> by providing access to cultural heritage resources in ways unimaginable a
> decade ago.
>
> (Mulrenin and Geser, 2001)

Over the last three decades, cultural heritage institutions (libraries,
archives and museums) have integrated technology into all aspects of
their mission and services. The first part of this chapter looks at these
developments, and introduces case studies illustrating the wide range of
reasons that an institution might consider digitization of its collections.
The second part of the chapter will examine some of the new economic
challenges and service paradigms associated with digital collections.

The potential of digitization

The libraries, museums and archives of the world are filled with materials recorded in many 'analogue' formats. These include paper and
all its variants, for example vellum, papyrus, birch bark, wood and
other substrates. Images can be represented on paper or canvas, as
well as many surrogate forms including negatives, glass plates, and

microfilm and microfiche. Sound and moving image have been stored on film, videotape, audiocassette and LP records. Despite this variety of formats and playback devices with which it is associated, analogue information has three consistent qualities. Firstly, it is tied to a physical medium, meaning that analogue content is linear, bounded and fixed (Delany and Landow, 1994). Secondly, it is temporal, or bound to a sequential representation that is pre-determined by the author. Finally, it degrades when copied.

Digitization is the process by which analogue content is converted into a sequence of 1s and 0s and put into a binary code to be readable by a computer. Digital information also has common characteristics and qualities, regardless of whether the content is stored on DVD, CD-ROM or other digital storage media: it can be linked to other materials to create multimedia; it is not dependent upon spatial or temporal barriers, or hierarchies; it can be stored and delivered in a variety of ways; and can be copied limitless times without degradation of the original. Digital data can be compressed for storage, meaning that enormous amounts of analogue content can be stored on a computer drive, or on a CD-ROM. Digital content can be browsed easily, and can be searched, indexed or collated instantly. Most importantly, it can be linked to a whole 'web' of other content, either locally or globally via the internet.

The expansion of global computer networks and high-speed access to the internet has led to a proliferation of digital content, delivered to increasing numbers of computer users worldwide. There is a growing demand for immediate access to rich content and easily accessed, up-to-date information from news and media organizations. The development of 'digital libraries', a concept also known as the electronic library, the virtual library and the library without walls (Raitt, 2000), has preceded and anticipated much of this demand. Much of this development was anticipated by the work of visionary thinkers such as Vannevar Bush, articulated in his 1945 essay, 'As We May Think', where he famously posited the 'Memex' machine:

> Consider a future device for individual use, which is a sort of mechanized private file and library. It needs a name, and, to coin one at random, 'memex' will do. A memex is a device in which an individual stores all his

books, records, and communications, and which is mechanized so that it may be consulted with exceeding speed and flexibility. It is an enlarged intimate supplement to his memory.

(Bush, 1945)

The history of computing since Bush anticipated the notion of the scholar having access to infinite quantities of information at the desktop is one of rapid technological advances. These have led to a sea change in the accessibility, affordability and ease of use of computing and networked digital information. From mainframe computers of the 1940s, which were costly, labour intensive and maintained centrally by large organizations, via the introduction of micro and mini computers in the 1970s and 1980s, to the development of improved, inexpensive processors and memory which influenced the personal computing revolution of the 1990s, these changes have dramatically affected the way we live and work. In addition, access to networked computers, the internet, interactive materials and multimedia have created a technological infrastructure which has caught the popular imagination. These technological developments, and their rapid uptake by a large community of technology users, have underpinned the development of 'Digital Collections' and what we have come to call 'the digital library'. This is defined by the Digital Library Federation as follows:

Digital libraries are organizations that provide the resources, including the specialized staff, to select, structure, offer intellectual access to, interpret, distribute, preserve the integrity of, and ensure the persistence over time of collections of digital works so that they are readily and economically available for use by a defined community or set of communities.

(Greenstein, 2000)

Digitization in libraries, archives and museums

The use of technology has become a core part of the institutional mission of museums, archives and libraries around the world. Computer-based systems are now considered essential for many operational aspects of such Memory Institutions. These include collections management, as in the use of administrative databases and online catalogues; exhibit planning, including the management of loaned objects such as administering paperwork for insurance and transit; and user services and outreach, including the provision of online catalogues and reference materials, as well as public service websites with general information about mission, collections and services.

In addition to the use of technology for administrative purposes, more institutions are unleashing the 'added value' of their collections by developing digitization initiatives. Collections can be made accessible, via digital surrogates, in an enhanced format that allows searching and browsing, to both traditional and new audiences via the internet. Institutions of all sizes have seen such services multiply since the development of the world wide web in 1989. Consequently, many have become 'hybrid institutions', with a mission to manage both analogue and digital cultural resources, and to support and anticipate the demands of their patrons for both traditional and new resources. However, the dichotomy of preserving access to the resources such as the traditional card catalogue for some users, while also providing access to high-resolution images of key collection items and managing digital assets, is straining resources at some institutions (W. Arms, 2000).

There has also been significant growth of various national and international digitization projects in the last ten years, as libraries and universities all around the world have funded major initiatives to showcase their rich cultural and scientific heritage. Early pioneers included the Library of Congress in the USA (http://lcweb2.loc.gov/), the Bibliothèque Nationale de France (www.bnf.fr/), and the British Library (www.bl.uk/). The critical role that digitization plays in cultural heritage initiatives was recognized in the European Union's eEurope 2002 Action Plan (European Commission, 2000), aimed at stimulating European initiatives to realize opportunities created by the advent of digital technologies, and summarized by DigiCULT (Digital Heritage and Cultural Content) as endorsing the view that:

Digitisation contributes to the conservation and preservation of heritage and scientific resources; it creates new educational opportunities; it can be used to encourage tourism; and it provides ways of improving access by the citizen to their patrimony.

(DigiCULT, 2003)

It is easy to find similar testimonials to the potential of digitization from other sources around the world, from which it is clear that there are enormous benefits to be reaped by both the custodians and users of cultural heritage materials by the free delivery of cultural heritage collections at the click of a mouse. However, such statements are not the hollow pronouncements and promises of ten or 15 years ago, when early experimentation with desktop technologies and remotely accessible materials for instruction and research gave senior administrators in libraries and universities, as well as funding agencies and government departments, ideas that new technology would save millions of hours of teaching time and increase academic productivity, based on the assumption that a CD-ROM of a term's coursework could replace instructors and face-to-face classes. Such claims raised expectations unreasonably, and many enthusiastic 'early adopters' of digital technologies discovered at great expense that there are hidden costs and pitfalls to developing and using digital content. However, thanks to a period of extensive trial and error, experimentation and testing, a critical mass of digital content has been developed over the last two decades. This content, and the extensive experience of the practitioners and experts responsible for its creation, provides us with a valuable understanding of the digitization process, and its costs and benefits. This wealth of experience will realistically inform future project development, and provide information managers with the ability to assess accurately the potential of digitization for their collection, institution and patrons.

The most important lesson learned is probably that there are no short-term cost savings to be realized by digitizing collections. Such initiatives may save money in the long term, but start-up costs are not to be underestimated. Furthermore, technology has a short life cycle, which means expenditure in replacing systems after (an average of) three years, as well as significant investment required for staff to learn the latest systems and applications, which usually have a steep learning curve. Dealing with technologies that have such a short life cycle also means that the 'long term' – and the demand to see savings and returns on an initial investment – may come around sooner than anticipated. There can also be a problem with the available technologies. Systems developments are generally market led, not led by the needs of scholarship and research. Generic applications developed for business are often all that is available (unless an expensive custom system is commissioned), and this can create frustrations with limitations of the technology. More significantly, the proliferation of digital data, coupled with the short life cycle of technology, has created a preservation problem for the future (discussed in the section on preservation in Chapter 7). There is also a concern about presenting access to a surrogate copy of the original, which can never truly be a satisfactory substitute for the artifact itself. The concerns that critics like Robert Hughes have expressed about slides and reproductions, which 'destroy the sense of uniqueness and scale of the originals, and their physical presence', are equally applicable to digital images, which are that they are simply: 'an image of an image, not the thing itself but a bright phantasm, a visual parody whose relation to the original and actual work of art is the same as that of a shrunken head to the human being' (Hughes, 1992). The question is further complicated by the question of the authenticity of digital data – we know that digital data can be manipulated, copied and altered with ease. How can such content ever be an acceptable substitute for the 'real' materials? How can institutions ensure that patrons understand the electronic materials they see have not been in any way manipulated – that they are seeing what the custodian of the originals deems to be a true representation of the original (A. Smith, 1999)? Most importantly, the lesson learned from earlier projects is that institutions must not neglect other activities when allocating resources for the establishment and maintenance of digitization services; the impact of a digitization programme on the institution's other public service activities must be considered as a factor in informed decision making, and in keeping in perspective the investment made.

Advantages of digitization

In recent years, a growing understanding of the costs of digitization, in terms of both time and financial resources, has placed a greater focus on developing digitization initiatives and programmes that will realize tangible and strategic benefits for the institution and its users, rather than opportunistic or short term projects that are limited in their scope or focus. Consequently, it has been necessary to articulate clearly the concrete benefits of running digitization projects at the outset. The best way to do this is to focus on developing resources that push the boundaries of what is possible in research or access by placing a focus on not merely transforming 'pen to pixels', but on developing projects that support the type of work that cannot be done in an analogue format. Digitization is a complex process, and there are concrete benefits to be realized from many types of digitization projects. These can be summarized as access, support of preservation activities, collections development, institutional and strategic benefits, and research and education. These themes are outlined in more detail below.

Access: broader and enhanced, to a wider community

The primary, and usually the most obvious, advantage of digitization is that it enables greater access to collections of all types. All manner of material can be digitized and delivered in electronic form, and the focus of the content that is selected for digitization varies across institutions. Some institutions have followed a policy of creating an electronic image of every item in their collection and placing it on their website. The National Gallery in London is one organization that has done so (www.nationalgallery.org.uk/). Other institutions, such as the British Library (www.bl.uk/), have chosen to put only the 'greatest hits' of their collections online. Another approach is to collect electronic images based around exhibition themes, or educational modules, and the Metropolitan Museum of Art in New York (www.metmuseum.org/) is among the organizations that have chosen this option.

Digital materials can be made available to a broader audience than those who have the resources or ability to travel to see the analogue collections, and access can be expanded to non-traditional audiences such as lifelong learners. Audiences can access the collections for often unanticipated and broad-ranging research interests – for example, historical materials may be used for local history or genealogical research, which has been one of the main attractions of the digitized records of the National Archives and Records Administration (www.archives.gov/). Activists and advocacy groups may access audio recordings of US Supreme Court proceedings, which are available via the Oyez project, developed by a professor of political science at

Northwestern University (www.oyez.org). The Gertrude Bell Archive at the University of Newcastle (www.gerty.ncl.ac.uk/) found that its collection of maps and photographs of areas around the borders of Iraq, as mapped out by Miss Bell in the 1920s, may have been of tremendous interest to a whole new audience in the spring of 2003 (Buchan, 2003).

Whatever the audience, their access to the materials is enhanced by the advantages of the digital format. With the application of the right technological tools, and careful attention to the design of the user interface, it is possible to search, browse and compare materials in useful and creative ways. Patrons may scroll or browse through thumbnails of the materials in image catalogues, including images of materials that were previously inaccessible, such as glass plate negatives, or oversized or fragile materials. Digital images or texts can be integrated with, and linked to, other materials, to provide an 'enriched' archive of materials. Examples of this approach include the Blake and Rossetti Archives at the University of Virginia's Institute for Advanced Technology in the Humanities (IATH; http://jefferson.village.virginia.edu). Both integrate searchable collections of images, texts, commentaries and glossary materials, as well as advanced imaging applications to 'zoom in' on manuscript images.

Access can be provided to materials in all formats. The National Gallery of the Spoken Word (NGSW; www.ngsw.org/), a collaborative project based at Michigan State University, is creating a significant, fully searchable online database of spoken word collections spanning the 20th century, and will be the first large-scale repository of its kind. NGSW provides storage for these digital holdings and public exhibit 'space' for the collections. These include the Vincent Voice Archive, recordings of the spoken word and sounds, originally collected by G. Robert Vincent, who began recording voices in 1912 at the home of US President Theodore Roosevelt. He went on to amass the largest private collection of recordings of voices, believing that there was no substitute for hearing the actual voice – which can transmit meaning and inflections that cannot be conveyed by the written word. When he retired in 1962, he donated the recordings to MSU. He also donated his time and assisted in cataloguing the entire collection, meaning that the recordings have accurate and detailed catalogue entries. The collection houses taped speeches, performances, lectures, interviews, broadcasts, etc. by over 50,000 people from all walks of life, from Abbott and Costello to Graf Ferdinand von Zeppelin.

Another example of online access to multimedia resources for the remote user is The Experience Music Project in Seattle (www.emplive.com/), a collection of materials promoting and illustrating the history of popular music. Materials from the museum's collection are presented alongside interactive, audiovisual tools, interviews with contemporary musicians, a sound-lab, and an ever-changing selection of content from the permanent collection.

Supporting preservation

Developing a digital surrogate of a rare or fragile original object can provide access to users while preventing the original from damage by handling or display. This was the motivation behind the digitization of many priceless artifacts, most famously the Beowulf Manuscript at the British Library which is too fragile for use or consultation by scholars without special permission. The Library carried out high-resolution imaging of the original, which created digital images that can be subject to advanced imaging analysis including ultra-violet and x-ray photography. This has had the dual benefit of increasing scholarly understanding of the original while protecting the original. The multi-site Making of America project was similarly inspired, in their case by making digital copies of brittle copies of 19th-century journals accessible online. This is a common motivation for digitization. Often, the fragile condition of collections prevents their use. Digitization is not a substitute for traditional preservation microfilming, however. The digital format is too unstable, and issues related to the long-term preservation of digital media have not yet been resolved (see Chapter 8 on rare and fragile materials and the section in Chapter 7 on preservation for more on these topics).

Collections development

The provision of digital materials can overcome gaps in existing collections. Primarily, there is an opportunity for collaborative digitization initiatives to allow the re-unification of disparate collections. It is often the case that materials that were originally part of a complete collection are now held in far-flung locations, and there is a growing desire to present at least a 'virtual' sense of what the entire collection would look like. Many projects have been motivated by the goal of virtually 're-unifying' such materials.

One example is the Arnamagnaean Institute (AMI; www.hum. ku.dk/ami/aminst.html) at the University of Copenhagen. This project is making a web-accessible catalogue of medieval Icelandic manuscripts, and proposes to use this catalogue to achieve a 'virtual reunification' of the two halves of the Arnamagnaean collection, which is now divided between Reykjavik and Copenhagen. The AMI is also planning a full digitization of all manuscripts in its possession, and the catalogue records will link to these images as they become available (Driscoll, 1998).

Similarly, the Canterbury Tales project (www.cta.dmu.ac.uk/projects/ctp/) plans to develop CD-ROMs containing digital images, and transcriptions, of all extant manuscripts of the books of the *Canterbury Tales*, regardless of where the original resides. This will facilitate a unique comparative analysis and collation of the *Tales*. In addition to the advantages of seeing the folio pages in comparison with each other, the texts can be searched, browsed and collated to examine different usages of words in the different manuscripts.

Digitization is also a means of creating resources that can be re-purposed for unforeseen uses in the future. Changing research trends may alter the demand for items in a collection: the development of new fields of study (such as the study of popular culture) means that collections once perceived as ephemeral, or of low research value are now heavily researched. Similarly, collections of items that were once in high demand are now banished to offsite storage for lack of use (Price and Smith, 2000). Ephemeral materials – including magazines, pamphlets, badges and the like – may also be fragile, so digitization is especially advantageous for maintaining access to such materials. For example, at the University of Bournemouth the library and the University's media studies department are starting a project to digitize and make accessible their copies of *TV Times*, a guide to independent television programmes in the UK from 1956 to 1985. A magazine that was once perceived as a disposable weekly purchase to help households plan their television viewing selections is now a valuable record – in some cases the only remaining record – of programmes, cast lists and production information. It is sometimes the only record of particular programmes made by independent television in the UK (see www.bournemouth.ac.uk/library).

Furthermore, libraries are increasingly under pressure to provide access to materials in response to user requests, and are transitioning policies from collecting material 'just in case' someone will need it, to one of developing relationships which allow the library to deliver material from elsewhere 'just in time' to answer a user's needs. Providing access to digital material from many sources and places can facilitate this shift to on-demand delivery (Deegan and Tanner, 2002).

Institutional and strategic benefits

There is no doubt that digitization programmes can raise the profile of an institution. Projects to digitize priceless national treasures or valuable scholarly materials, if done well, can bring prestige to the whole institution. Raising the profile of an organization by showcasing digital collections can be a useful public relations exercise. Digital collections can also be used as leverage with benefactors and funders by demonstrating an institutional commitment to education, access and scholarship. Certain funding opportunities exist for digitization, and it may be expedient for an institution to use them as an opportunity to accelerate a digitization programme (this is discussed in more detail in Chapter 6). Internally, there can be benefits in several areas. Access to digital catalogues improves collections management in general, by creating detailed records about the collections. Online catalogues also provide detailed information about collections to users, or even by including browsable digital images in alignment with the catalogue entries. By thus enhancing services there may even be a reduction in costs of certain types, for example, delivering heavily used materials such as short loan collections online.

Developing digital projects can have long-term benefits for the institution, although it may take many years to realize these benefits fully. Such initiatives may create an opportunity for investment in the technological infrastructure, and can create an opportunity to develop the overall technological skills base among staff. Staff themselves will benefit from access to digitization programems that give them an opportunity to learn about new technologies. If managed correctly, internal digitization units can provide a tremendous opportunity for staff development. One institution that is now realizing such benefits is the New York Public Library (NYPL; http://digital.nypl.org/), where an initiative established to support digital projects is now providing programmatic support for the whole organization. NYPL's Digital Libraries Program was developed to support the NYPL Visual Archive (which was formerly known as ImageGate). The project dealt with over 600,000 images from all four research collections of the NYPL, including many different types of visual materials, such as printed ephemera, maps, postcards and woodprints. In order to support this undertaking, major investments in staff, technology and infrastructure were made. In particular, a team of almost 30 staff was developed, covering a broad scope of expertise in all aspects of digitization and technology infrastructure, including databases, web publishing and high-resolution imaging, as well as metadata and library standards. Now that the team is in place and fully equipped, and has completed some of the earlier projects, they are able to support additional projects and initiatives for the whole institution (Bickner, 2003).

Many funding opportunities are contingent on collaborations and partnerships between several institutions, so this can be an excellent opportunity to develop strategic liaisons with other institutions. Such initiatives are often developed under the auspices of a national digital library programme. For example Denmark's Electronic Research Library (DEF; www.deff.dk) is creating a portal for Danish research libraries. This will provide access to all the information resources managed by the individual libraries via a national infrastructure, with a common user interface and access system, enabling cross searching of all collections. This is a major undertaking, but it has led to a great deal of investment in the infrastructure of Danish research libraries, and the technological upgrading of library systems. Added benefits will include the negotiation and acquisition of 'national licences' for electronic journals and information databases; the provision of funding for the digitization of selected collections; a retro-conversion of paper-based catalogues; and development of the Danish Research Database and initiatives for electronic publishing.

Research and education

Digitization of cultural heritage materials can have tremendous benefits for education. Many institutions present educational 'modules' on their websites, presenting 'packages' of educational material based around their collections. Museums have been particularly successful in this respect, as most organizations have in-house educational departments, which have been charged with developing materials that will exploit the potential of technology for delivering educational resources to all levels of learners. The Hunterian Museum at the University of Glasgow boasts that its digital collections are used by schoolchildren 'from Barra to Brooklyn' (www.hunterian.gla.ac.uk/). The New Museum of Contemporary Art's Virtual Knowledge Project (www.newmuseum.org/) is an outreach programme that facilitates online discussions between museum staff, artists and schoolchildren around themes of contemporary art. Similarly, the Minneapolis Institute of Arts (www.artsmia.org) has put digital images of 5000 works from their collection online (out of 100,000 objects in the whole museum). These are organized thematically to allow in-depth study of key ideas and concepts, such as 'modernism' and 'myths and legends in art', using items from the museum's collection to develop teaching packs. This sort of outreach has become an essential way for many museums to fulfil their obligation of 'public education' in many parts of the USA, where a combination of budget cuts in school districts and security concerns have all but ended school visits to museums in many urban areas.

The advantages to academic research and advanced scholarship are equally impressive, and the potential of networked technologies to create a dynamic reading and scholarly environment is driving digitization initiatives at many institutions. John Unsworth has posited that networked digital information can support the fundamental elements of scholarship, the 'scholarly primitives', which he suggests are the ability to do the following with research materials: discovering, annotating, comparing, referring, sampling, illustrating and representing. These activities are basic to scholarship and common to all eras, disciplines and media. All are activities that can be enhanced considerably in scholarship that is based on digital information, and in particular, networked digital information (Unsworth, 2000). While the fundamental aspects of scholarly methodologies are still in place, there are assumptions that digital materials can be 'read' in new and creative ways, and that because of this, production and delivery paradigms for scholarly materials are shifting. No one model of electronic delivery is definitive; indeed, the nature of the format allows many representational models for different types of information, data and content. Both publishers and academics are starting to think about new ways to represent scholarly information. Digital library systems, which customize information upfront and create a dynamic reading/browsing/studying environment, can facilitate these goals, and also develop new and shifting paradigms in the relationship between scholars, users, publishers, cultural institutions and libraries. These changes in relationships work on many levels. The user is able to engage with the source materials in what has become known as an 'enriched' fashion: it is possible to not just read text or view an image on the screen, but to browse, search, annotate and compare materials. Digital collections offer flexible and interactive access to the materials, and enable new scholarly imperatives.

Another example of the potential to change the essentials of scholarship is the Chopin 1st Editions Project, based at Royal Holloway College, University of London. This project is developing an online variorum edition of Chopin's work, and is using this to analyse the creative history of Chopin's music. The variorum could also be used by performers to create their own editions by combining elements from a range of different sources.

Digitization can also be the first step in conducting advanced research on historical materials. Ancient documents present a prime candidate for digitization because of their historical import, combined with centuries of exposure and degradation. At the Rochester Institute of Technology, an important site for research into the digitization of ancient documents has emerged in a collaborative project between the Xerox Digital Imaging Technology Center and the Chester F. Carlson Center for Imaging Science. Their primary mission has been an effort to enhance and clarify ancient writings, with a particular emphasis on the Dead Sea Scrolls (www.cis.rit.edu/research/dir.shtml). This project has developed a purpose-built imaging software and digital camera station. Electronic sensors and digital image processing are combined to permit multispectral analysis. Multiple digital images of a single scroll are recorded at different wavelengths of light. The images are recorded by an electronic camera, which converts the light intensity in each section of the image into an electrical signal to be read by a computer. To aid in capturing the different wavelength ranges, coloured glass filters are placed over the camera before making the exposure. After the images are gathered, they are processed with software developed by the Xerox Corporation. The software permits the images to be analysed and combined in different ways. In many instances, this two-part technique of imaging and processing has revealed characters no longer recognizable to the human eye, granting translation scholars access to material not seen in thousands of years. The project has also conducted research with other fragile ancient documents, written on clay, papyrus or vellum. Some of the material consists of long scrolls, while other material consists of small pieces of documents, often numbering in the thousands. High-resolution scans are made and then manipulated by a variety of applications, including histogram and threshold adjustments, combined with hue and saturation manipulations following the initial scan. Experimentation of this nature is revealing ways in which advanced digital imaging, and digital cameras capable of reading a spectrum from the ultra-violet to the infra-red, can reveal characters in the otherwise unreadable manuscripts, increasing the overall accuracy of translation and interpretation.

Integration of technology: a case study of an incremental approach

Although there are many reasons to adopt computer technology in cultural heritage institutions, no one reason will predominate, and it is important to emphasize that most institutions will integrate many different technology-based projects over a long period of time. Some of these projects will overlap, some may ultimately contribute to an institutional 'digital library', while others may become known as 'legacy projects', leaving preservation concerns and headaches for future caretakers. Certain priorities will take precedence at different stages in an institution's history, and these initiatives may or may not be consistent with what technology is available at the time. Consequently, it is instructive to look at the history of digitization at one organization to see that reasons for digitization can be pragmatic and can change over time to adapt to funding and other considerations.

Established in the early 19th century, the UK's National Gallery of Art (www.nationalgallery.org.uk/) in London contains over 2000 works, including some of the most important European paintings in the world. Artists such as Botticelli, da Vinci, Titian, Rembrandt, Monet, Renoir and Van Gogh are well represented within the collection. To assist with its various conservation efforts, the National Gallery established a Scientific Department in the mid-20th century. The Department has since become an important site for conservation research, and more recently, the home of the Gallery's digitization efforts. Over the last decade, projects have included the development of scanning and photographic equipment capable of highly accurate colour images, as well as a colour separation system, which can print the images on a conventional four-colour press.

Initially, digitization efforts at the National Gallery were implemented to create archival colour records of paintings within the collection. These records could then be used for regularized comparison, often five or ten times a year, to monitor deleterious change within the works, particularly light-induced changes in pigment. With this goal in mind, the Scientific Department implemented the VASARI project in the late 1980s, a system for acquiring high-resolution digital images to facilitate a surface analysis of paintings. The system included a high-resolution monochrome camera, an accurate positioning system, a light projector containing a set of filters, image-processing software and a workstation. By the early 1990s, the Scientific Department had become interested in moving from mere digital acquisition to publication, resulting in a project known as MARC (at the National Gallery, MARC is an acronym for Methodology for Art Reproduction in Colour, and has nothing to do with the MARC standard for MAchine-Readable Cataloguing!). The primary results of the MARC project were the creation of a digital camera more portable than the system used for the earlier VASARI project, and the development of a colour separation system for four-colour printing. Yet by the mid-1990s, network access to the images generated by the VASARI and MARC processes, often over one gigabyte each, remained unrealized. Since that time, the Department has been conducting research into various file formats and worked to develop a network image viewer and central indexing system. Ultimately, standard JPEG and TIFF formats were selected.

In addition to the aforementioned series of projects, the National Gallery has realized the potential for systematic digitization and is currently creating digital surrogates of its entire collection. The digital images will be incorporated into a larger database of the Gallery's entire holdings, which can be used to record and manage the collection by curators, conservators and scientists alike. However, the Gallery's digitization efforts are not solely aimed at an internal audience. In the early 1990s, the Gallery was one of the first galleries to have computers for public use, in the Micro Gallery of the Sainsbury Wing, as well as making their collections available on CD-ROM. In the summer of 2000, every painting within the National Gallery's permanent collection was made available on the web and in 2002, the Scientific Department collaborated with a private firm to develop an innovative image enhancement technique for visitors to the site. The technique, resulting in high-definition scans which may be zoomed in on minute details, allows viewers extremely close access to prominent paintings within the Gallery's collection (including, in the summer and autumn of 2003, a beautiful representation of Raphael's 'The Madonna of the Pinks', prominently displayed on the Museum's home page). To deter copyright infringement, a discreet logo is embedded within each of the images. Eventually, this technique will be available for paintings throughout the permanent collection (for more information, see www.nationalgallery.org.uk/about/press/2003/zoom.htm).

The impact of digital collections on institutions

The development of digital collections and the proliferation of such content through the global 'information explosion' (Gill and Miller, 2002) are changing the way that information is used and managed. The 'digital library', the 'online archive' and what Martha Wilson of Franklin Furnace has called the 'desktop museum' (see www.franklin-furnace.org/ and Wilson, 2001), are enabling new paradigms for scholarship and access. In order to capitalize on these developments, new strategic visions and economic models are emerging, as administrators start to examine the way that digital collections can be managed and funded for the long term. The challenges of the digital age are moving memory institutions into new business models, and developing institutional enterprises around digitization. However, this transition is not from one static and identifiable paradigm to another static paradigm (S. Smith, 1998). Instead, the rapidly changing technology is facilitating a period of experimentation and evaluation of new models for scholarship and access, and an examination of new funding models.

Those who are developing and managing the technology do so in the hope that new technologies will enable the extension of the reach of research and education, an improvement in the quality of learning, and new methods of scholarly communication (A. Smith, 1999). Digital collections have enormous potential for changing the way that information is used, and for developing new ways of preserving, collecting, organizing, propagating and accessing knowledge (Witten and Bainbridge, 2003). At many institutions, electronic 'spaces' are seen as a resource to augment learning. As more and more libraries devote space to computer terminals, and museums develop kiosk systems, the physical presence of technology in memory organizations cannot be ignored. At the University of Hertfordshire, a new Learning Resource Centre provides a large space for computers in the library, equating and integrating student and faculty computing needs with information needs. A similar space is being built at Glasgow Caledonian University, incorporating library collections, computers and teaching space. These developments suggest that administrators have seen that the creation of a digital library or online archive enables the creation of new space even if the institution cannot buy any more physical space.

At one extreme, this idea has led to the notion of the 'virtual campus', the idea that the physical campus is no longer required when 'learners' can have access to all the content they need via an electronic library. Institutions such as the University of Phoenix – an entirely virtual campus offering extended education modules – attracted an enormous amount of attention in the mid 1990s (not coincidentally, also the years of the dot.com boom and bust), and many administrators were beguiled by the prospect that universities and libraries could package and sell academic content (their 'product') via online teaching materials. While there is a tremendous amount of potential for distance education, the reality is that the technology available at this time doesn't fully support such initiatives, and that the business plans of many such initiatives overestimated the market for such resources. The failure of Fathom.com, a high-profile for-profit online education initiative based at Columbia University but incorporating a number of prestigious partners including the British Library, is one such example indicating that reports of the demise of the physical campus were much exaggerated.

Nonetheless, there have been significant changes in the delivery of scholarly content, shifts in the relationship between content creators and users, and shifting paradigms in the 'delivery chain' of published materials. Notably, we see a shift from the traditional model of a publisher creating material, which is bought by a library and then distributed to users. Now, there are many different delivery models, such as from publisher to service provider (such as JSTOR) who creates an aggregate resource to which libraries subscribe. Users of the library are then able to access this material. This model raises questions about the provision of long-term access to such resources, as we see a movement away from the system of libraries purchasing, storing and preserving books and journals on paper (Guthrie, 2001). There are also changes in the relationships between scholars, users, publishers and cultural institutions and libraries (Deegan and Tanner, 2002). For example, scholars are investigating whether self-archiving of their research (including making available pre- and post-print publications) might resolve some of the difficulties associated with academic publishing. These archives could be published on their own websites, maintained by their employing university (Oppenheim, 2002).

Observation of such developments indicates that there is a role for a carefully managed institutional repository of electronic information that allows active engagement with electronic resources. Though faculty, librarians, archivists and curators all create electronic content that can become part of a digital library, it will only be through developing an understanding of how to properly manage this content that the economic potential of electronic information will truly be realized and understood. Many institutions would like to change the current paradigm in which they pay faculty to create scholarly content, which is then given to publishers and then sold back to the university through journal subscriptions. Experimentation with the concept of an 'institutional repository' attempts to address this issue.

It is also important to understand the difference between an 'institutional repository' and a digital library. An institutional repository seeks to exploit the intellectual capital produced by the institution and therefore 'owned' by it. A digital library, on the other hand, is a broader collection of not just these materials, but materials published elsewhere and licensed and distributed to users of the library. It is an aggregated and accumulated system, allowing access to interconnecting information created at many different locations and in many different media types. This information is subject to different interpretations, classifications and purposes (the core elements of the 'scholarly primitives' outlined above), which should be supported by the underlying infrastructure of the digital library. One approach to developing such an infrastructure is the Open Archival Information System (OAIS; http://ssdoo.gsfc.nasa.gov/nost/isoas/), a conceptual framework for an archival system that can be adapted and expanded to preserve and maintain access to digital information over the long term. Many library standards organizations (including RLG and OCLC) are looking at ways in which the OAIS model might be adapted for a digital library environment, and the relevance of the OAIS model is discussed extensively in Deegan and Tanner (2002).

There are a number of ongoing initiatives developing tools and architectures for institutional repositories and digital libraries, notably MIT's DSpace (www.dspace.org/) and the FEDORA (Flexible Extensible Digital Object Repository System) Project (www.fedora.org), a collaboration between the Universities of Virginia and Cornell. DSpace is a digital repository, created to capture, distribute and preserve the intellectual output of MIT (and organizations that are involved in the DSpace partnership) by providing stable long-term storage for digital content in a secure preservation environment and repository which is accessed via an easy-to-use interface for faculty depositing the materials. The FEDORA Project is creating a repository management system with an extensible architecture for managing the digital content so that in can be re-used and re-purposed for many interpretations.

Such initiatives raise a number of important questions. If libraries and other institutions are digitizing content and making it available to mass audiences, are they becoming more like publishers? What are the economic implications of this, and how does this affect research and culture? And who should pay for these initiatives? DSpace is presently supported by MIT's core library budget, as well as by charges to users of 'premium' services offered by the repository (such as metadata creation) besides external grant support and in-kind support from members of the DSpace federation who are participating in the development. This raises the question of what an institution can charge for this sort of repository service. There is little information available on what the market will actually bear in terms of paying for such services. These kinds of models require strong institutional support, leadership, and business and operational planning operated in parallel with the research and development process to build the system, not after it has been created, when it might be too late (Barton and Walker, 2003).

New economic models

New economic models are emerging as digitization initiatives develop at various organizations. What are the economics of having services on the desktop that, until very recently, could only be obtained by physically going into a library? What is the cost to the library of offering this sort of service online at no charge to the user? And is there a saving to the institution now that they no longer have to provide the traditional services (Lesk, 2003)? Such questions are beginning to affect some of the ways we think about digitization, as we try to resolve the question of how we can pay for digital collections. Presently there are several possible sources of funding and revenue for digital projects, including:

- institutional subscriptions
- individual sales
- outside grant support

- institutional support from the host institution
- revenue generation, for example by the provision of digitization services.

These models are based on the development of business practices from the print environment. In addition, most models are based on the considerations of particular collections, and the funding structures of individual institutions – there is no one size, or model, that will fit all conditions (Wittenberg, 2003).

Cost savings: indirect costs

However, the more significant question is how to actually realize the dividend from our investment in digitization. In examining this question, it is necessary to look at the indirect costs of digitization, and to examine ways in which cost savings might be turned into revenue. This involves examining some of the institutional practices and logistics associated with acquiring, storing and delivering electronic information, and looking at potential savings created by electronic storage, access and circulation (Lesk, 1996). In both the digital library and the institutional repository many cost models and potential sources of revenue, including advertising and direct taxes, have been investigated. Some of these are discussed by Michael Lesk in his essay 'How to Pay for Digital Libraries' (Lesk, 2002). Lesk concludes that no one model of funding dominates. We see a mix of models: free distribution; institutional funding; and some sales and subscriptions.

Electronic journals are an example of the shifting paradigms in delivery of resources. Libraries now 'rent', rather than purchase, serials. The costs of renting versus buying journals are very different. Costs related to buying serials include the cost of storing, shelving, retrieving and cataloguing the materials, as well as costs related to the physical storage of the content: the costs of building libraries, the cost of power for heat, light and air conditioning, which are a direct cost to the library. The shift to renting electronic content has reduced the costs of maintaining the physical materials, but has increased the cost of preserving the content. Who is paying or is willing to pay to preserve this digitized information (Guthrie, 2001)? It may take less space to store collections electronically, but how can these kinds of savings be captured? For example, buying JSTOR and other electronic journals will save library shelf space, but will this saving on space be so large that it will only be necessary to build a new library in 12 years, not ten? Furthermore, many institutions continue to maintain the paper publications as well as subscribing to the electronic serials, and indeed publishers will often require that an institution purchases a paper version of the journal in order to qualify for a discounted rate on the electronic journal. Buying the electronic journal alone is often a more expensive option.

Costs such as storage come out of different parts of the overall budget, and are 'indirect'. They are monitored at the most senior administrative level (such as the vice-chancellor in the UK or the provost in the USA). As such, these costs are rarely seen, let alone able to be truly accessed by libraries. Universities, for instance, often fail to recognize or directly charge departments for all indirect costs (e.g. most university libraries don't pay rent for their building) and so a library may not realize, in deciding whether or not to buy an electronic publication in place of a paper one, the extent of shelving and cataloguing costs that are saved by going electronic. These issues are tied up with complex questions on the 'value' of information, making it almost impossible to put a numerical value on delivering information to the desktop instead of the library reading room (Lesk, 2003). There is a lack of real figures on which to base these assumptions, as we don't have enough experience with these resources and funding models to develop properly predictive figures. An additional complication is that technology and network costs have decreased dramatically in the last 20 years, making comparative calculations relating to the cost of digitization over a long period of time almost impossible. The savings that we see at present are also aggregate, that is, they are shared by a large number of institutions. Collectively, this could add up to a significant figure – but individually, the sums involved probably do not yet offset the cost of digitization. This is one reason why the Library of Congress digitization initiatives do not focus on the large-scale conversion of books. It is better to focus on the conversion of unique materials that would otherwise have limited use.

If these savings could be captured, they could provide a significant fund for further digitization. But in order to evaluate what these savings might be, it is necessary to take account of all elements of the financial equation, including the long-term implications for building plans, capital costs and maintenance. Few institutions think in such terms, preferring to see digitization as merely another competitor for inclusion in an already strained acquisitions budget. But this is not the way decisions of this kind should be made. In the digital world, a broader institutional perspective needs to be applied to resource allocation decisions, and to evaluate how this revenue can be quantified. The larger academic community needs to work together to realize the economies of scale that are possible. It is also necessary to look at added value benefits (such as user satisfaction or the advancement of scholarship) and work out a methodology for putting a value on them at some level, in order to gain an understanding of the true benefits, both financial and scholarly, of digitization (Waters, 2003).

Cost savings: widening the evaluation

We now suspect that digital resources *should* be creating cost savings for institutions (especially libraries) at some part of the digital life cycle. Proving this is another matter. In order to quantify this sort of revenue, more research is needed on the economics of hidden costs. For example, the trend towards using public domain materials for digitized courseware saves payment of copyright fees to authors and publishers for 'course packs'. Other costs that could be re-allocated to digitization might include resources such as travel grants awarded to scholars and PhD students to visit large research collections and archives. For example, if the series of medieval judicial materials at the National Archive in London (including Common Pleas, King's Bench, Ancient Indictments and Gaol Delivery Rolls) could be digitized, how many scholars would not have to seek research travel grants to work on these materials? (See Byrd et al., 2001, for a quantification of savings to the organization by the use of online patron access.) Similarly, there will be an overall saving to the institution if digitization eliminates or reduces curatorial and librarianship costs (W. Arms, 2000), and such cost savings could be explored to develop digitization funding. Again, it is extremely difficult to quantify the sums involved in this type of saving, to unravel from whose budget it is coming, or to fully understand how such savings can be exploited.

Developing a critical mass of digital content may enable savings elsewhere in the institution by, for example, reducing the hours that a reserve or short-loan collection needs to be open, reducing the time spent re-shelving bound journals, but taken to its logical conclusion, this line of argument about savings of library staff time and reducing salary lines could be at the cost of redundancies for librarians (W. Arms, 2000). This isn't practical at any level, especially as we know from experience that even if librarians' time is saved, it is just moved to other tasks – such as developing training programmes on how to use electronic resources.

It is also important to realize that the costs of digitization are just beginning at the time of starting digitization projects:

> The programmatic capacity to distribute and maintain electronic resources, and to migrate them to new forms as original digital platforms fail and formats and software are superseded, is fundamental to long-term efforts . . . rising user expectations may require that existing digital files be reprocessed in new ways. When OCR software is perfected, for example, unsearchable bitmap images of texts could be thought unsatisfactory. Projects that do not plan for change may become obsolete, and therefore irrelevant.
>
> (Hazen, Horrell and Merrill-Oldham, 1998)

Nonetheless, some institutions are looking to cost recovery models based on potential savings as digitization replaces and improves some existing services. Especially when they are feeling the strain of having to support both analogue and digital resources with the same number of staff and with the same budgets as in previous years (literally in many cases – during the present US economic crisis, many institutions have had budgets frozen). Consequently, some digitization funds are being diverted away from other collections-based activities, and may even be taken from budgets dedicated to acquisitions. This is a strategy that will not pay off for the institution, unless funds are diverted from existing activities based upon a strategic approach and an assessment of where technology is actually saving money. Using this approach, we can examine several activities and services, including the following:

- Transitioning from analogue to digital photography has seen real savings at many institutions as photographic order backlogs are cleared.
- As buildings and spaces within the institution are refurbished to include 'wired' classrooms and meeting spaces, it is no longer necessary to pay for 'Campus Media' service organizations – projector rentals, staff to set up equipment on an event-by-event basis, etc.

In addition, emerging initiatives and ways in which institutions are going digital may, in the long run, realize some savings in terms of library staff and space:

- As informational websites become the norm for most institutions, and online access becomes the preferred delivery method for certain collections, there may be some savings to staff time as they find themselves having to deal with fewer face-to-face queries. However, library staff invariably report that any anticipated time savings are instead spent addressing questions regarding electronic resources. Also, as noted elsewhere, digital initiatives are a wonderful advertisement for the institution, and may increase requests from users to see the analogue resources.
- The development of electronic reserve, or short-loan, collections will certainly be a great service to library users, as will electronic access to past examination papers. Such services may realize cost savings at some institutions as the library hours, or staff time, needed to administer such popular and labour-intensive collections are reduced.
- Some institutions may realize savings from other forms of publication or distribution. In some library contexts (as in many business contexts), some simple substitutions may provide new revenue sources. For example many non-profit organizations offer certification programmes as a major source of income (for example, many library schools in the United States offer certification for public librarians). Such operations can replace the post-

ing of print documentation and print test materials with web-based documents and tests, and the savings in postage and administration can pay for the whole online operation.

The models outlined above, and the qualifications associated with each, illustrate that it is still premature to anticipate digital 'cost recovery' in existing service areas; because many real costs are hidden, it can be difficult to see such opportunities for what they are – so it is not economically advisable to invest in such initiatives with the expectation of cost saving, although this may be an agreeable outcome. Above all, resources should not be diverted from some service or acquisitions area to start a digitization programme, unless the decision can be defended in the terms set out above.

Another approach is to consider if there are hitherto untapped funds that can be used for digitization, such as developing approaches to leverage college tuition fees for digitization. One area of exploration is providing continuing access to digitized content provided by a university as an ongoing benefit for its alumni as part of their tuition fees. This would scale especially well for professional education, such as medicine and the sciences, by giving alumni access to new research. Other ideas come from organizations like Digital Promise (www.digital-promise.org/), a US lobbying agency trying to have funds from the sale of unused, publicly owned telecommunications activities (mandated by Congress) allocated to a national Digital Opportunity Investment Trust. Whatever the future sources for digitization, whether tuition or government grants for technology development funds, digitization will be far easier to sustain if there is a guaranteed revenue for the long-term preservation of and continuing access to these programmes.

Conclusion

Digitization of cultural heritage materials is changing the ways in which collections are used and accessed. Many materials are amenable to digitization, including scarce, fragile and ephemeral materials, as well as the whole spectrum of moving image and audio materials. All can be safely used by a wider audience in digital form. Research and interrogative tools for digitized source materials can also make digital surrogates more amenable to certain types of interpretation, such as full-text searching and indexing, as well as comparison of materials for multiple sources. Nonetheless, there will always be times in which no digital surrogate will be adequate for scholarship, and it will be important to be able to evaluate whether or not digitization is truly worthwhile before undertaking a digitization initiative (Nichols and Smith, 2001). Many factors will come into play when evaluating the 'value' of digital resources, but these factors may help in assessing when digitizing collections can be cost effective. Valuable digital resources, which will bring prestige to the institutions that create and maintain them, will be those that can support scholarship without any loss of the benefits of working with the originals.

With no definitive evidence base to give concrete numbers about the economic value of digitization to an institution, assessing the value of digital resources is a question of also assessing whether digitization is also causing information to 'lose' some of its value: for example, what is the loss to scholarship if electronic resources cannot be browsed in the same way as conventional library stacks? In a recent presentation, Michael Lesk gave a compelling example of the value of information, and of the 'serendipity of the stacks', which should be preserved in the digital library, in telling the story of Sir Alexander Fleming and the lucky discovery in the library (by a browsing scholar) that led to the discovery of penicillin:

> Fleming (a doctor) first discovered that some substance from the mould Penicillium killed bacteria in 1928, and wrote a paper about the substance, hoping for help from a biochemist. But little happened for over a decade. Prompted by the Second World War to look for antibacterial agents, Sir Ernst Chain, a researcher at Oxford, found Fleming's 10-year-old paper in the British Journal of Experimental Pathology. This discovery in the stacks led Chain and Lord Howard Florey to test and then exploit the first modern antibiotic, to the great benefit of medicine and humanity; Chain, Florey, and Fleming shared the 1945 Nobel Prize.
>
> (Lesk, 2003).

This describes the type of research and discovery that should be replicated in the digital collection, and which will ensure that digital collections have value to all users in a digital future.

2

Selecting materials for digitization

Introduction

This chapter looks at the development of selection criteria from the following viewpoints:

- collection building
- strategy
- preservation.

It also introduces the importance to the decision-making process of the copyright status of the original materials (a topic that will be developed further in Chapter 3) and of the institutional framework to sustain any digitization projects (developed in Chapter 4).

Libraries, archives and museums hold disparate collections in a variety of media, representing a vast body of knowledge accumulated over the institution's history. These collections have been acquired by judicious selection policies, which have evolved from the practices and decisions made by curators, subject specialists and archivists as they built and shaped the collections by acquiring, preserving and discarding materials based on the demands and requirements of a particular institution and its patrons. Such well established policies are composed of the following elements: appraising materials for acquisition, evaluating priorities for long-term preservation and conservation, and selection of materials for exhibitions and publications. In developing collections policies institutions must take into account many factors, including the suitability of materials to an institution's mission or collections focus, as well as any broader institutional mandates, such as those influencing collections development in organizations like national libraries or museums: the value of the materials in comparison to other materials in the collection, the demand of visitors or researchers for such materials, restrictions resulting from the legal status of parts of the collections, and accessibility and availability of collections; for example, are materials stored remotely, oversized or otherwise inaccessible to patrons (Vogt-O'Connor, 2000)?

Similar considerations will inform the selection of collections for digitization. It will not be possible or practical to digitize everything in a collection, and, generally, there will only be one opportunity to digitize a collection, as such projects are expensive and require a significant capital investment to start up. Policies for selection of materials should be developed prior to digitization. They will be influenced by a focus on the nature and intellectual content of the collections, their condition, and usage; and also by an examination of the strategic motives for initiating digitization projects, and the institutional framework that will support them. These concepts are introduced in this chapter, and expanded in Chapter 4. Developing digital collections can be an important opportunity to strengthen and articulate institutional policies and information goals. Digitization policies will make it possible to identify collections – or parts of collections – that can add value to these goals. Digitization can give new life to valuable resources, and enable access to a broader user community. As such, a decision to digitize should be based upon an understanding of what is compelling and unique about the information in the collections, and a desire to share that content with a wider audience. Digitization initiatives may also focus on rarely seen or special format materials such as maps or recordings that might not otherwise be easily usable. Selection policies will be a core component of any institutional digitization policy. It will be necessary to consider whether or not the institution is ready to do such projects – whether the right investments in staff, equipment and support have been made (although the paradox is that it may be that only by starting digitization projects can the institution be persuaded of the necessity of making such investments).

One of the most important selection criteria for digitization will be the copyright status of the original materials. Are the materials in the public domain, and if not, will it be possible to obtain permission to digitize? After digitization, will the institution be able to protect the digital assets by managing the rights to their use? Issues related to copyright and licensing are so crucial that they have been addressed in greater detail in Chapter 3. If the institution does not have the right to digitize, or the means to manage the use of digital assets, then digital projects should not proceed.

Another broad category to consider is the way that digitization can augment and complement existing preservation and conservation activities. Digitization is not a replacement for microfilming, or other preservation activities, as the digital format is too unstable to be recommended as an appropriate medium for preservation. Durable acid-free paper or preservation microfilm are still the preferred, proven preservation media (Gertz, 2000b). Properly processed and stored, we can expect film to be available more than 100 years from now, whereas digital media have a relatively short lifespan. Further, microfilm reading is not dependent on unique, proprietary or rare playback devices. In order to read microfilm, all that is required is a variation on a light source and a magnifying lens. Nonetheless, digital files are suitable for improving access and usability, and for reducing handling of originals, and so many organizations, including Harvard, now use digital files for access, while continuing to rely on analogue media for long-term storage (Gertz, 1998). Such hybrid approaches are currently recommended. Consequently, it is extremely rare for a digitization project to be undertaken with the goal of replacing original materials with a digital surrogate and then de-accessioning the original. The only exceptions would be 'just in time' digitization initiatives to document fragile or brittle materials before they become unusable or dangerous. An example of this is the Memoriav project (www.memoriav.ch/), a collection dedicated to preserving the audiovisual culture of Switzerland, which involves making digital copies of unstable nitrate film stock, subsequently discarded. For a discussion of the role of microfilming in digitization initiatives, see the section 'To film or to scan?' in Chapter 7, and see also the discussion of preservation in Chapter 9.

Developing institutional policies on selection for digitization

Existing digitization policies

In some cases, digitization policies may already exist. Many national and consortial initiatives already have guidelines for the digitization of materials in their holdings. See, for example, the guidelines for digitization produced by the National Library of Canada (www.nlc-bnc.ca/8/3/r3-409-e.html) which urges federally funded cultural heritage institutions in Canada to digitize collections with a view to supporting lifelong learning, reinforcing a 'shared national consciousness and informed citizenship', and supporting 'economic growth and job creation'. Similar initiatives and national policies can be found in the national archives and libraries of many other countries.

Many institutions have developed internal digitization policies to facilitate the decision-making process. Columbia University Library, Oxford University, Harvard and the Library of California are all examples of institutions that have developed and implemented such policies, which vary greatly in detail and complexity. Some contain information about specific collections that should be targeted, others focus on the need to protect fragile source materials from over-zealous digitization that may damage the originals. Brown University Library's policy also includes a list of technical feasibility criteria, which state that:

> Potential projects should be evaluated as to whether it is technically possible with current equipment and software to capture, present, and store images in ways that meet user needs. Collection type may dictate some parameters, depending on level of ambition, size, imaging requirements, cataloging requirements, conservation requirements . . . beyond support for equipment, operating budget, technical support and staffing, considerations include:
>
> - condition of materials allows for them to be digitized safely
> - condition of materials requires conservation/rehousing for safe digitization.
>
> (Brown University Library, 2001)

Some institutions have also found it useful to express their policies as decision trees or matrices to help work through the various factors and choices attendant upon a digitization project. For an excellent example, see the decision matrix developed by Harvard, available at: www.clir.org/ pubs/reports/hazen/matrix.html. Based on the conditions which exist at Harvard, it asks 12 key questions: if the answer to any of these questions is 'no', an alternative approach should be considered:

- Does the material have sufficient intrinsic value to ensure interest in digitization?
- Will digitization significantly enhance access or increase use by an identifiable constituency?
- What goals will be met by digitization?
- Does a product exist that meets identified needs?
- Are rights and permissions for electronic distribution securable?
- Does current technology yield images of sufficient quality to meet stated goals?
- Does technology allow digital capture from a photo intermediate?
- Are costs supportable?
- Does an institution have sufficient expertise in project management?
- Is the local organisational and technical infrastructure adequate?
- Can the project be re-defined to recast objectives?
- Can infrastructure needs be addressed? (Hazen, Horrell and Merrill-Oldham, 1998)

An institutional decision matrix can help the selection process, but will be dependent upon the local conditions, and be weighted towards internal concerns and priorities. Furthermore, technology (and its potential) is changing so rapidly that such policies are effectively 'guidelines' that will require constant updating (Ayris, 1999). The concept of the decision matrix, like risk assessment and usability testing, has developed from business processes (particularly business process re-engineering). Such tools are used to create documents that can help to develop workflow and ideas about what to do or buy, but ultimately the decision tree will reflect institutional priorities and conditions. While it is instructive to look at examples such as those referenced above, given the awareness that there will be many more significant issues at every institution that will inform such policies, some institutions have found it helpful to hire a consultant with expertise in this area to help develop such documents.

Developing selection criteria for digitization

> The process of deciding what to digitize anticipates all the major stages of project implementation. Digital resources depend on the nature and importance of the original source materials, but also on the nature and quality of the digitizing process itself – on how well relevant information is captured from the original, and then on how the digital data are organized, indexed, delivered to users, and maintained over time.
>
> (Hazen, Horrell and Merrill-Oldham, 1998)

Selection policies will be a core component of any institutional digitization policy. The process of selecting specific items to be digitized will employ such standard library selection criteria as value, significance to the overall collections, patron demand and interest in the materials. The availability and fragility of the original are also factors, as is the appropriateness of digital reproductions for use and access. Institutions developing policies should take a consultative and consensus-driven approach, involving many stakeholders. The process of identifying project stakeholders should be inclusive and wide-ranging, both within and outside the institution. Interested parties may include:

- discipline specialists and faculty with expertise on the themes of the project
- educational specialists appropriate to the intended audience
- digitization specialists
- librarians, archivists and curators
- research teams with experience in working with online resources
- conservators and preservation specialists
- Information Technology departments
- legal advisers (Vogt-O'Connor, 2000).

The UNESCO, IFLA and ICA *Guidelines for Digitization Projects* (2002) suggest that digitization projects should be:

- user driven, based on a high demand for (enhanced) access to content
- opportunity driven, when money is available for a particular initiative
- preservation driven, when there is a need to protect fragile materials from handling
- revenue driven, where there is an opportunity to generate income from digital resources.

These considerations will influence the development of the selection process of nomination, evaluation and prioritization based on these factors and the strengths of the collection. Any institutional collections policies should be the foundation of deciding what to digitize.

In summary, the main criteria for digitization should be:

- The informational content of the original materials – what is the intellectual value of the collection?
- Demand for the materials – how are they used, and with what frequency, by which users?
- Condition of the originals – are they fragile or damaged, and is digitization viable?

One of the most useful guides to the factors to be considered when embarking on a digitization project is the Northeast Document Conservation Center's (NEDCC) *Handbook for Digital Projects* (Sitts, 2000), which the reader is encouraged to consult. Another useful guide is the *Selection Criteria for Preservation Digital Reformatting* developed by the Preservation Reformatting Division at the Library of Congress (2002). Both guides develop a methodology for selection for digitization, by assessing the value, use, and risk factors of collections. *Value* can be identified as: informational, administrative, artifactual, associational, evidential or monetary. Priority should be given to high-value, at-risk materials of particular interest. Digital reproduction is highly advantageous for materials of this nature. It can reduce handling of the originals, as well as protect them from theft. *Usage* can be assessed using library use statistics. Original materials that have high frequency of demand or high retrieval costs are strong candidates for digital reformatting. *Risk* types can be classified as legal, social and preservation. Other factors influencing the decision will include the condition and characteristics of originals. Often, collections can't be used because of damage or fragility, or because they are stored on unstable media, are oversized, stored remotely or otherwise difficult to deliver to users.

It will also be crucial to anticipate the end use of the digital materials. S. Chapman (2000) has suggested that project planners should always be able to 'state functional requirements that can only be fulfilled by digital reproduction', and if this is not possible, reformatting should be to a conventional medium such as microfilm, particularly where preservation conversion is required. Funders are increasingly stringent about such requirements, and will seek ample evidence that digitization projects intend to create resources that will not only enable broadest access, but also actively allow new types of use, and advanced research. Decisions should also be based upon the current state of technology, and should anticipate how technology changes will influence future uses of a digital resource (Hazen, Horrell and Merrill-Oldham, 1998). However, there are always going to be new and unanticipated uses of materials, so projects should be very flexible.

Decisions about what to digitize should be, at every level, collections driven. The strengths and intellectual value of collections, and the factors that make these collections appealing to scholars and/or members of the public, should be the primary motivation for digitization. Digitization should be undertaken to enhance the collection, to provide enhanced scholarly access, or to accomplish any of the benefits of digitization for scholarship outlined in Chapter 1. Decisions should then be taken about whether the collection *should* be digitized, as well as whether it *can* be digitized – does the institution have the legal right to do so? Will digitization cause damage to the originals? Will the creation of digital surrogates add sufficient value to the materials to justify the cost of digitization?

The National Digital Library at the Library of Congress has developed a project planning checklist. They suggest that the following aspects of collections analysis will assist in selecting collections for digitization:

- Determine the scope or extent of digitization – is the whole of a collection to be digitized, or a subset?
- Assess the status of the custodial division processing and housing
- Assess the status of access aids (their degree of completion, readiness and format)
- Assess the physical status of the materials, and their readiness for digitization
- Assess access restrictions or copyright and licensing considerations.

(Library of Congress, 1997)

Assessing collections

Before starting a project, a careful assessment of the intellectual content of the material in the collection is necessary. What is the informational content and intellectual value of the materials that make them worth digitizing? What is the subject content of the collection? Is the collection coherent? Is the collection related to other collections materials that have been, or should be, digitized?

Similarly, an assessment of the potential impact of the physical attributes of the collection must be conducted to determine whether the digitization process will compromise the original materials. What is the size of the collection and where is it housed? Is preservation or conservation treatment required? Is it uniform or diverse in terms of format and size? Can it be easily handled? Does it have intrusive mounting or bindings? Does it lend itself well to digitization (Ostrow, 1998)? Fragile materials can be damaged or compromised during digitization, so it is important to initiate needs analysis before undertaking digitization. These factors will also be useful in subsequently developing risk assessment strategies, feasibility studies, pilot projects and detailed project plans. Four steps can facilitate the development of an institutional digitization plan:

1 A collections survey
2 A user needs analysis or survey of users
3 A cost/benefit analysis of digitization
4 A consideration of strategic, institutional issues.

A collections survey

A collection assessment can inform decisions about what to digitize, by revealing what is compelling and valuable about the collection material itself, and whether it is worth going to the trouble and expense of digitizing. The following exemplify the questions to ask in such a survey, based on the Association of Research Libraries' *Survey of Special Collections* (www.arl.org/collect/spcoll/).

1   What are the materials in the collection that are most valuable for teaching and scholarship? What is the intellectual value of such materials, and their informational content? How much demand is there for them? How accessible are they to users? Do they reflect the institutional mission and collections policies?

2   Is adequate intellectual access being provided for all collections materials, including materials held remotely, in special storage facilities (e.g. cold storage) or in special collections? Can materials be accessed if they are in a rare or unusual form (such as oversized maps, or textiles) or require unique playback devices (e.g. 8 mm film, 78 r.p.m. records). Are the materials catalogued adequately? What finding aids are in use?

3   Are staff levels and available skills appropriate to support the growing size and scope of the collections, and access to these materials by users? Is there adequate space at the institution for storage of, and access to, these materials?

4   Is a sufficient investment being made in the preservation of special collections materials? Are there concerns about the condition and conservation of materials? Is the physical condition or fragility of original materials limiting their use?

5   What are the intellectual property rights issues of these materials? Does the institution own the copyright? Are access restrictions in place for materials for which the institution is not the copyright owner?

6   Are these materials suitable for digitization? Will the digital image be adequate as a research or reference surrogate?

Initiating a collection survey prior to undertaking digitization projects can also inform the development of an institutional plan to control conditions of the original collection in the future, for example by providing better storage facilities or enclosure materials. Preparing a collection for scanning often includes an improvement of the physical conditions of the collection. When Nebraska State Historical Society started an imaging project of the entire Solomon D. Butcher glass plate negative collection of 19th-century plains communities, many of the 3000 negatives had not been touched since 1915. Part of the workflow of this project was for every single negative to be cleaned, scanned, re-sleeved and stored in new boxes. Cleaning and re-housing the collection was an important added benefit of the digitization project, but such handling of every item in the collection is a highly unusual occurrence (Koelling, 2000).

Conservation measures completed prior to digitization will ensure safer handling of the original, but this approach will increase costs associated with the project. For an understanding of the amount of work this may involve see www.loc.gov/loc/lcib/0105/conservation_corner.html, an example of conservation procedures undertaken by the Library of Congress prior to the digitization of a collection of early Russian photographs.

Even more crucial is the issue of cataloguing the materials. Special collections have often been catalogued merely as a whole. For example, New York University is undertaking a digitization project with a selection of late 19th-century Afghan materials, which have been selected for digitization from a number of private collections. Because the materials come from a variety of sources, they have never been comprehensively catalogued. Before digitization can take place, each paper, letter, document or item from the collection needs to be given RLIN cataloguing information for identification purposes. Although a level of formal cataloguing is necessary before digitization takes place, this can be minimal in detail, as richer cataloguing can be added incrementally, and at a later date – metadata is extensible, and can always be incrementally improved. A key advantage of online catalogues is the open-ended character of databases, which facilitate easy and dynamic updating, provided that there is someone behind the scene to refresh the data on a regular basis. A report describing the Duke Papyrus Archive explains that when a catalogue of pictures with descriptions is given in print, whether on paper, in microform or on

CD-ROM, it almost has to be final. 'An online database, however, does not have to be perfect right away and can therefore be made accessible at an early stage. This allows extensive screening of preliminary work by colleagues worldwide, who will all bring their expertise to bear on problematic pieces' (Minnen, 1995).

User needs analysis

It is important to think about who will actually use digitized materials. Users of analogue materials are a good place to start. The chances are, if people are interested in the analogue materials, they will be interested in digitized versions of these materials. Whether digitizing materials automatically makes them attractive and useful is not so clear cut, despite the often infectious enthusiasm of subject specialists and researchers who are filled with certainty that the digitization of infrequently used materials will suddenly make them vitally interesting to a huge community of users. There is no point in selecting materials for digitization if there is no support for using the resource among target user groups, just as a conventional collection development policy would advise against the purchase of paper material by a library if potential use could not be identified among patrons (Ayris, 1999).

Issues to consider include, who uses these collections, and how do they use them? Are the collections being used to their fullest potential for teaching and research? Are there restrictions to accessing collections – through library opening hours, fragile conditions of the materials, or other concerns prohibitive to their use?

Looking at usage patterns will help the selection process for digitization, and some institutions actively seek suggestions from the user community about what should be digitized. Oklahoma State University Library Electronic Publishing Center has an online 'suggestion form' inviting the library's patrons to nominate materials or collections for digitization (http://digital.library.okstate.edu/suggest.html), and about 12.5% of digitization at the Library of Congress Geography and Map Division is 'on-demand' (NINCH, 2002).

Is it possible to perform front-end evaluation on potential users of digital resources, or even to evaluate how users work with any existing digital collections offered by the institution? Is this part of a dig-itization project plan?

Most crucially, it will be necessary to address how digitization will help core groups of users. Will users have reliable and easy access to electronic resources? Is the technology infrastructure in place to sup-port broadest access? Is ongoing support and training available for anticipated users of electronic resources? For example, users of pub-licly funded museums and libraries will be the general public, who will have very specific expectations of access to collections. In terms of access, anyone can walk into a public museum or library and look at the materials. It will be necessary to ensure the broadest access to collections to replicate this level of service, and to meet and manage user expectations. Will this be possible? Can the technical infrastruc-ture support mass access, especially in such enormously popular fields as genealogy? In January 2002, the UK government published the 1901 Census (on its website www.familyrecords.gov.uk) with a great fanfare. The site promptly, and very publicly, collapsed under the weight of 50 million hits – and then faced questions about the quality and accuracy of the transcribed records (Rayner, 2002).

There are many contradictions to the question of usage. For exam-ple, certain collections may be under-utilized because they are inac-cessible, or fragile. A digital copy would increase access to such materials, but the process of digitization might damage the originals. Similarly, intensive use of resources does not automatically mean a collection should be digitized. Frequent users of local history archives will often live within a close proximity to the archive, and existing access (for example, by microfilm) may well be sufficient to their needs. Photocopies and interlibrary loan services may serve infre-quent users of the collection more cost effectively than digitization. Online access that restricts access to the originals will be undesirable for patrons that do not own a computer or have Internet access. How-ever, high-use materials, such as the type of journals made accessible to JSTOR subscribers, will often be a prime candidate for digitization. Similar materials include slide libraries and image collections, which cannot be browsed or searched in analogue format (Hazen, Horrell and Merrill-Oldham, 1998). Another issue is that the availability of electronic resources sometimes increases demands for the original materials – projects that have digitized small samples of special collections materials may discover increased interest in the whole collection, as digitizing and putting collections online can be a very effective form of drawing attention to the collections. If users do not have access to high-quality surrogates (for example, if low resolution, cropped or incomplete materials are delivered), they may need to go back and consult the original (Stefano, 2000), in which case institutions will have to support the delivery of both digital *and* analogue versions of the same item.

Defining the potential audiences for electronic resources will also facilitate the planning and selection process. One project which has asked the question 'who are the users of electronic resources?' is the Colorado Digitization Program. In January 1999, the CDP Advisory Council held a meeting to address this question. The meeting broadly identified five user groups: casual users or browsers, students/school-children/lifelong learners, information seekers and hobbyists, scholars and academic researchers, and the business community. Each group will have different information needs, be interested in different types of content, and have a variety of needs related to an interface, display capabilities, system design, and method of delivering digital resources, although audiences cannot always be anticipated prior to the project (CDP Advisory Council, 1999).

Assessing the risks: a cost/benefit analysis

> Cost-benefit analysis assesses the relationship between functionality, demand, and expense. Limited resources and competing demands on organizational time and energy mean that the analysis must be rigorous and complete.
>
> (Hazen, Horrell and Merrill-Oldham, 1998)

Assessing the cost effectiveness of digitization is crucial, but notoriously subjective. There are few guidelines on this question, and a need for more research into it. There are few detailed, evaluative assessments of digital resources to which the project manager may turn, and it is therefore difficult to do truly informed cost/benefit analysis. There is some emerging research, notably from the UK's Higher Education Digitisation Service (HEDS), on some of these issues. HEDS examined the question of charging mechanisms for digital photography versus analogue photographic services at museums and art galleries. Their survey asked some of the questions that can contribute to developing an understanding of the 'real costs' of delivering a digital service, but ultimately showed that none of the institutions interviewed for this survey 'were fully recovering all the costs of creation, management, storage and providing the service solely from the sale of the digital item itself' (see Tanner and Deegan, 2002).

Although the factors affecting 'costs' and 'benefits' will vary enormously across institutions, there are some concrete facts that should be considered. We know that there can be numerous benefits to developing digital collections, as discussed in Chapter 1. These can include enhancing access, either to rare or damaged materials or collections in high demand; facilitating advanced or new types of scholarship; and unifying disparate collections. Such benefits will be intrinsic to the content in question, and will be the driving force behind most digitization initiatives. Digitization can increase the scholarly 'value' of source materials: by undertaking collaborative digitization projects to combine collections electronically (virtual re-unification), the individual objects in disparate collections will be more useful to scholars. Similarly, a resource such as the Canterbury Tales Project, which enables the comparison and collation of manuscripts, facilitates research that would not be possible without a unified approach. Further, investing in the digitization of materials in the 'public domain' will add value to materials that have ceased to be of economic value to their authors or publishers.

Offset against these benefits will be the 'costs', or risks that can be anticipated. There will be the cost of actually doing the digitization project – paying for staff, equipment and the technical infrastructure to support such projects, as well as ensuring long-term management and preservation of the digital materials. These costs are discussed in greater detail in Chapter 6. Furthermore, there is a cost associated with the risk of loss of the digital information – technology is changing rapidly, and it is not unheard-of for digital resources created as recently as five years ago to be either inaccessible, or incompatible with the computer systems of today. For example, in 1986 the British

Broadcasting Company spent £2.5 million to develop the Domesday Project, a compilation of digital materials related to all aspects of British life in 1986 to celebrate the 900th anniversary of the 1086 Anglo-Saxon *Domesday Book*. The project developed special BBC computers to play 12 in. video discs of text, photographs, maps and archive footage. Within 15 years, the materials were obsolete and unreadable, whereas anyone with the right credentials could see the original 11th-century *Domesday Book* in the Public Record Office (McKie and Thorpe, 2002). In this high-profile case, successful efforts have been made by researchers working as part of the CAMILEON project, based at Leeds University and the University of Michigan, to recover the data by developing software which emulates the obsolete BBC system (CAMILEON, 2003). However, there are plenty of other examples of unresolved cases where investments have been made in developing digital data in now obsolete formats. The History Data Service, part of the UK's Arts and Humanities Data Service (AHDS), maintains over 500 data collections of historical source materials, including statistical materials, manuscript census records, state finance data, demographic data, mortality data, community histories, electoral history and economic indicators (http://hds.essex. ac.uk/access.asp). Some of the data (including census data) is on punch cards, and the archive must maintain the equipment – and expertise – to use this format.

Another serious consideration is the potential risk to the collections of the digitization process. Digitization can be an extremely invasive process – it involves handling original materials, removing them from storage, and exposing them to some degree of light and heat, which can damage or even destroy brittle materials. Management of these factors is discussed in Chapter 8.

A collections survey should establish which materials are most in demand, most at risk by handling, and most valuable for scholarship. The institution will then have to make an assessment as to whether the benefits of digitization for access and scholarship outweigh the risks and costs. Additional expenses may include cataloguing, metadata creation, cleaning and re-housing, and the time of preservation and conservation staff. Rigid institutional policies may exist regarding moving and handling materials. Insurers may prohibit certain types of work, or the moving of certain materials – in which case, digitization equipment may have to relocate to a special collections area. However, there may be cost savings: reducing or even eliminating the handling of certain original materials may even reduce insurance premiums as well as the cost of security staff or measures.

Developing a framework to assess whether the benefits of digitization will justify the costs is, therefore, a highly subjective exercise, which will involve many of the key institutional and strategic considerations that are explored in greater detail elsewhere in this book. For such analysis to be effective, all costs should be taken into account and compared to the costs and benefits of acquiring and storing print-on-paper (Ayris, 1999), or preserving collections on microfilm.

Strategic issues

Institutional priorities and standards should always be at the forefront of digitization priorities and strategies. What are the collections for which the institution is best known? Are there policy goals and objectives which inform digitization – is it necessary for the institution to get on board 'the digitization bandwagon' for political reasons? Are there particular disciplines or departments that should be showcased? For example, if an institution is one of the few remaining places where the teaching of Old English is still a core part of the curriculum, then digitization initiatives may focus on Old English materials from the library's special collections that might be used for teaching and instruction. If the institution is known for contemporary performance studies, then materials related to the study of film and performance will be a top priority for digitization. This has been the case at New York University, where there is a strong focus on digitizing moving image performance materials.

However, some digitization projects are also undertaken for reasons of expediency, based on the accessibility of grants and funding for digitization (a circumstance that can lead to a perception that sometimes funds are earmarked for digitization that might previously have been allocated to microfilming or conservation). This illustrates another example of the need for institutions to have a carefully established strategic plan for digital activities, against which funding opportunities can always be assessed. If the needs of a benefactor are in opposition to the needs of the institution, some serious assessment of the benefits to both sides must be done. The strategic issues of donor-driven funding and the potential dangers of adopting this approach are discussed in the section on funding in Chapter 6.

Existing projects

Having selected materials in the collection that could be represented in digital format, it will be necessary to ascertain whether or not digital copies already exist that might be used. In the case of unique holdings this will not be an issue – it's safe to assume that the British Library will not find another copy of the Magna Carta online. However, before investing resources to develop projects to digitize collections of printed works, for example, it is important to investigate whether or not such materials have already been digitized, or whether there is another product which meets the educational or research goals of the project.

There is general agreement that duplication of effort is undesirable. This concept is found in conventional collection development policies, which try to avoid the purchase of duplicated material (Ayris, 1999). However, the issue is rather more complex in the digital realm as there are some practical concerns which may make duplication impossible to avoid. Primarily, there are few fully comprehensive international registries of digitization projects on the scale of the scholarly 'registries of active research' that exist for many academic disciplines. Some services providing limited registries are emerging, such as MINERVA, which is developing an overview of EU digitization initiatives (www.minervaeurope.org/publications/globalreport.htm). OCLC is also developing a Digital Registry project via its WorldCat service for OCLC subscribers. The HUMBUL Humanities Hub, based at the University of Oxford, maintains an online catalogue of online humanities resources (www.humbul.ac.uk/). See Chapter 5 for a discussion of some initiatives in this area. Unfortunately, none of these resources are fully comprehensive in terms of either academic or international scope. Digitization initiatives take place in a context broader than any particular 'institution, discipline or country' (Hazen, Horrell and Merrill-Oldham, 1998). One solution is to support initiatives that provide more information about resources created elsewhere. The Canadian National Library digitization strategy addresses this issue, stating that: 'The government should generally not digitize information that is available digitally elsewhere, but may provide a valuable service in cataloguing, publicizing or in some cases validating material disseminated by others' (National Library of Canada, 2001). The use of standardized descriptive metadata schemas can ultimately provide users with standard tools to access digital collections. However, initiatives to develop such comprehensive and standardized metadata schemas are rarely retrospective.

A further reason why re-digitization may be necessary is the likelihood that electronic resources created in previous years using older technologies may not be accessible, or compatible with new technologies (Hazen, Horrell and Merrill-Oldham, 1998). Materials that were created using proprietary or non-standard formats may become obsolete: Chapter 7 outlines the role of standards and good practice in digitization.

A third reason for duplicating effort is that of copyright – permission to digitize a resource that is not in the public domain may be granted only to a specific institution, and access may then be restricted to only registered students or patrons of that institution. This is especially problematic for digitization of art historical slides for teaching. Many institutions hold extensive slide collections of similar materials, and because of copyright restriction, each is digitizing very similar content for distribution for teaching. One of the goals driving the establishment of ARTStor (www.artstor.org/) is to develop a collaborative model that will overcome this problem.

Doing extensive research on existing projects is always advisable, as it may be possible to create resources that complement, enhance or add value to digital resources created elsewhere.

When is it advisable *not* to digitize?

There is, undeniably, a cachet and an appeal to developing digital collections. In an attempt to be able to say they are creating digital collections, some institutions are undertaking conversion projects without understanding the resources required and without careful analysis of their choice of collections. Developing internal expertise by carrying out exploratory conversion projects can bring definite benefits to a library, but if this is done without fairly broad-based institutional consideration and buy-in on the decision of what collections to digitize, the drain of money and professional time in such projects could easily derail other important programmes.

Webb (2000) suggests that three rules or principles apply:

1. Digitisation projects are complex, and the bigger they are, the more collaborative, the more ambitious, the more experimental they are, the greater the complexity.
2. Almost anything is achievable, at a cost – sometimes the cost is financial, sometimes it is in tying up expertise that might be needed elsewhere, sometimes it is in accepting compromises on other objectives.
3. The cost is always more than you expect.

Despite an institution's best efforts to create digitization programmes, there may be some roadblocks that are insurmountable – at least in the short term. It is important to be able to recognize the situation as soon as possible and not waste resources trying to effect large-scale change. Conditions may alter in the future, allowing ideas to be revisited. It is always wise to use scarce resources in such a way as to achieve maximum benefit from them.

Some particular issues that may bring a halt to, or seriously derail, digitization projects include the following:

- *Copyright status.* If permission cannot be gained to digitize materials, digitization should not proceed. (See Chapter 3 for more information on this topic.)
- *Funding.* It is important to calculate the costs of a digitization project accurately, and to ensure that adequate funding is available. If it is not available, the project should be scaled down or postponed. It is also important to consider right from the beginning whether the project and the resultant resource is sustainable, and whether that matters.
- *Institutional buy-in.* The question of institutional resources is addressed in Chapter 4, but in general, while money, technology staff and space are important to the success of digitization, what

is most crucial is institutional support. Resources will not be allocated to projects that lack the blessing of senior management.

- *Technical drawbacks.* Committing to digital format requires a commitment to maintaining a technical infrastructure that will continue to enable access to resources created. Good planning at the outset is essential, but it will be necessary to contemplate future strategies and costs for migration and storage of digital content.
- *Conservation of originals.* If the digitization process will damage or compromise the original materials, then the project will have to be abandoned unless the institution has already decided to discard the materials after digitizing (as is sometimes the case with newspapers and journals).

The wrong motives for digitization:

- *Preservation.* As discussed elsewhere, digital formats are not suitable for preservation at this time, and this should not influence selection for digitization. Digitizing is not a substitute for microfilming, and a digital master copy is not a 'preservation master'. A digital master contributes to preservation only in that it reduces handling and the physical 'wear and tear' of the original.
- *To save space.* It may take less physical space to store collections electronically, but this probably does not yet offset the cost involved (despite the success of JSTOR, which has saved libraries a great deal in terms of both costs and space, on aggregate). This is one reason why the Library of Congress digitization initiatives do not focus on the large-scale conversion of books. It is better to focus on the conversion of unique materials that would otherwise have limited use.
- *To save money.* This is a motive often used when justifying the digitization of resources that will be used for teaching – the argument will go that a certain number of online courses will save staff time, and deliver savings to the institution. Such arguments rarely bear up under scrutiny, as their costs plans do not factor in all foreseeable costs, e.g. start-up costs of projects, and running costs of supporting the technical and intellectual aspects of the resource. At this time, no individual institution has managed to

make digitization projects completely cost effective. It is extremely difficult to entirely recoup the costs of digital imaging through user fees or subscriptions. Furthermore, there will be costs associated with maintaining the digital files as long as they need to be available, and these costs can be unanticipated (Puglia, 1999).

• *'Because we can'*. Not every collection is worth digitizing. Successful digital projects are the result of careful planning and collection evaluation. Digitization should focus only on those items that will provide the greatest benefit to the users of these collections, and should be based on an understanding that the true benefits of digitization will be allowing users to do searches, collations, analysis and interpretations that would be difficult or impossible with analogue materials. Having firm, quantifiable project goals and objectives will establish if this is the case.

• *Collection management*. Digitization is not a substitute for collection management. Although the development of detailed catalogue entries about source materials is often a by-product of digitization, this should not be the primary motive for digitization. Similarly, digitization should not be used as a reason to consider discarding materials for which there is no longer space: digital surrogates should never replace the original analogue item, even when trying to save shelf space. For example, if an institution decides to de-accession brittle newspapers, it should first obtain microfilm copies to serve its patrons (A. Smith, 1999).

Conclusion

When evaluating materials for digitization, and evaluating whether or not the time is right for an institution to embark on such an initiative, it is important to consider the experimental nature of digital projects. Much work that will be undertaken in the completion of digitization programmes will be at the 'bleeding edge' of new technologies. This concept is relative: for institutions that have never worked with electronic resources before, all aspects of technology implementation can be traumatic. It will be necessary to ascertain the willingness and preparedness of institutions to embrace a certain degree of risk and experimentation, and to understand whether or not such experimentation is acceptable or indeed necessary. Sometimes, it may even be necessary to experience failure in order to fully understand all dimensions of a particular project. Many projects will experience an unsatisfactory conclusion, through various unforeseen complications: collaborations that do not work, technology that will not work, or institutional frameworks that simply cannot support digitization activities. John Unsworth, in a 1997 article on 'the importance of failure', discusses 'the importance of reporting and analyzing failure in any research activity, humanistic or scientific', yet points out that in many cases, 'the patterns of funding . . . discouraged such reporting and analysis'. Often there are disincentives to provide this information: such large sums of money are invested in digitization that few people will be completely frank about the drawbacks, or about lessons learned from projects that didn't work out. A leap of faith is necessary – not least on the part of funders – before such information can be openly shared. Chapter 4 will provide an overview of some of the factors that can contribute to project failure, and areas where there may be risk. By understanding such issues, it will be possible to decide whether the risk is worth taking, and to assess whether the potential benefits of digitization outweigh the risks.

3

Intellectual property, copyright and other legal issues

The digital library will not come about unless the legal issues are addressed.

(Oppenheim, 2002)

Introduction

This chapter looks at the legal issues involved in creating digital collections and making them publicly available, including:

- copyright
- public domain materials
- library and preservation copying
- getting permissions to use copyrighted materials
- legal issues of defamation, pornography, data protection, etc., and ethical questions of privacy, publicity and public dissemination of potentially sensitive materials
- caretaking online content
- managing copyright of digital materials
- managing or restricting access
- risk management.

Different rules, conventions and assumptions will apply to publishers, museums and libraries, but essentially, digitization of any material constitutes re-publishing, with all the responsibilities this entails.

Project managers should have access to training, up-to-date information, and expert advice on legal issues, and should always keep accurate and comprehensive documentation about all legal matters relating to a project, e.g. copies of correspondence regarding licences. They should ideally be able to refer to internal guidelines and practices: as a matter of institutional strategy, the institution should establish a copyright/intellectual property framework, or set of guidelines, in collaboration with legal counsel (for examples of such policies, see www.copyright.iupui.edu/). If this is unworkable, it may be advisable to establish an interdisciplinary working group devoted to these questions, which could act as a clearing house or 'help desk' to answer frequently asked questions. It may be possible to draw on the in-house expertise of librarians, instructional technology experts, computer lab staff, archivists, faculty and administrators who may be called upon to develop some level of expertise on legal issues associated with digitization, and may have skills and knowledge to share. Smaller institutions, which do not have an office of legal counsel or access to a great deal of expertise in house, may decide to group together to collaborate on such issues, or even to retain a legal advisor. Information managers should have access to training in legal issues and to the most up-to-date legal information.

The material in this section is not intended to be a substitute for legal advice. Rather, it is an overview of the key issues and questions which may arise. There are many sources of further information on the internet, including useful listservs, such as Lis-copyseek in the UK, and Liblicense in the USA.

The Library of Congress maintains a very useful copyright website: www.loc.gov/copyright/. *Copyright Guide for Museums and Other Cultural Organizations* is a similar guide to copyright law in Canada: www.chin.gc.ca/English/Intellectual_Property/Copyright_Guide/index.html. The National Library of Australia hosts the Preservation Access to Digital Information (PADI) website, which has an extremely comprehensive section on copyright: www.nla.gov.au/padi/topics/28.html. The UK's Technical Advisory Service on Images also maintains web pages devoted to legal questions: www.tasi.ac.uk/. For definitions, and further clarifications of many of these issues, see the World Intellectual Property Organization at www.WIPO.int.

Articles, updates and references to new sources of information on these topics can be found in online publications such as *RLG DigiNews* www.rlg.org/preserv/diginews/ and *ARIADNE* www.ariadne.ac.uk.

Another excellent resource to bookmark and check often is IP @ The National Academies, an important new website and newsletter which serve as guide to the US National Academies' extensive work on intellectual property and as a forum to discuss ongoing work: http://ip.nationalacademies.org/.

It is especially important to stay abreast of current developments – the law as it relates to technology and digitization is subject to regular changes and amendments to existing legislation. This is partly because of a need for the law to catch up with technology, and partly in recognition of the need to address discrepancies in international laws. For example, in the USA, the Digital Millennium Copyright Act of 1998 significantly modified the US Copyright Law to accommodate digital formats and copying. In Europe, a development that will have a great impact is the EU Copyright Directive. This is an attempt to level out the differences in copyright law throughout Europe, and is in the final stage of transposition into the national copyright legislation of EU member states and central and eastern European candidate countries as this book goes to press. This will be a major development – for more information, see http://europa.eu.int, and www.WIPO.int for an international analysis and perspectives. It is also important to follow key decisions; a number of law firms worldwide offer free updating commentaries on cases relevant to IT law. In any digitization project that involves materials that are not in the public domain and so are subject to some aspect of copyright, permissions, intellectual property rights, or moral rights, building in fees for legal counsel and copyright advice is advisable. Institutions may themselves have in-house legal counsel, but they may be generalists who are not well-versed in the ever-changing issues in this area.

Copyright

The unfortunate truth is that copyright is a confused and confusing body of rules.

(Patterson and Lindberg, 1991)

A strategy for dealing with copyright and other legal issues must be planned at the outset of the project, and these activities co-ordinated with the institution's office of legal counsel. It is necessary to document all decisions and findings on copyright and other legal issues extensively, including form letters seeking permissions and the responses received. Copyright metadata must be developed as part of project administration procedure for every item that is digitized.

It is important to understand that copyright law applies to both the owner and the user of copyrighted materials, and different legal perspectives, guidelines and community practices apply to both situations. The project manager must identify at the outset what is to be done, and why, and how it will be accomplished:

- If you are the *owner* of copyrighted materials, it is necessary to be aware of how your institution should protect such materials from unlicensed copying and use. You should also plan for managing the rights to the digital surrogate materials.
- As a *user* of material to which your institution does not hold the copyright, it will be necessary to identify the copyright status of any materials you plan to digitize, and, where appropriate, obtain permission from the copyright holder to digitize the materials.

It is imperative to be aware of the copyright status of all materials at the outset of a project. We have all heard 'urban legends' of digitization initiatives being shut down by copyright holders who were chagrined to discover digital copies of their works on the internet, or being distributed on CD-ROM. Such cases are rare – funding agencies will generally not support projects which have a cavalier attitude to intellectual property – but digital copyright law is an organic, developing entity that is shaped by case law. This means that infringements may well have to be defended in court. The penalties for infringement may be harsh.

Copyright is an intellectual property right (as are trademarks, patents for inventions, and industrial designs). It is a limited monopoly given to creators of original material, including literary works, musical works, dramatic works, choreographic works, pictorial, graphic and sculpture works, motion pictures and other audiovisual works, sound recordings and architectural works. Ownership of copyrighted material allows the control of copying, adaptation, issuance of copies to the public, performance and broadcasting. The copyright holder may be the creator, the creator's family or estate, or an authorized representative (unless the material was produced as 'work for hire', in which case the employing or contacting organization will own the copyright). Copyright protects creators from unauthorized copying of their work for a fixed period of time, and enables them to benefit and profit from their work. It is their 'pension', and their insurance. As such, it is not merely illegal to use copyrighted materials without getting permissions, but it may be depriving an artist, writer or composer of income.

However, copyright does not last indefinitely. It has a limited term, so that the public can eventually use these works freely, with the hope that such fluid use will inspire new creativity and invention, benefiting society at large (Levine, 2000).

Copyright term limits vary, depending on when and where the work was created. Under the Berne Convention, which is followed in most of the world, copyright is usually protected for the life of the author plus a minimum of 50 years. In the European Union, the usual term of copyright is life plus 70 years. However, there has been a trend among copyright owners (particularly large commercial entities such as film companies, broadcasters and publishers) to push for copyright extensions in order to protect products that are still commercially viable. In the US, under the Sonny Bono Copyright Term Extension Act of 1998, this protection now lasts for the life of the author plus 70 years, and items are protected whether they have been published or not.

Several websites exist advising on copyright terms and their national variants. The British Library maintains a copyright website containing this information at: www.bl.uk/services/information/copyright.html. Laura N. Gassaway, Director of the Law Library and Professor of Law, University of North Carolina, Chapel Hill, has developed a helpful website with a (regularly updated) chart demonstrating when works pass into the public domain under US law, which is available at: www.unc.edu/~unclng/public-d.htm.

Many institutions will seek to avoid having to negotiate copyright rules by focusing on materials within their own collections, and developing digitization selection policies based upon the copyright status of materials in the collection. Copyright ownership is not merely a convenience – such materials are often the most significant and compelling components of a collection, and the works for which an organization is famous. The Art Institute of Chicago, the NYPL with its Digital Library programme and the Metropolitan Museum of Art are among many institutions who own the copyright of most of the materials they have digitized and made available on their websites.

Possession or ownership of a physical item, however, does not automatically confer copyright ownership, especially in the case of gifts or bequests (Levine, 2000). Even if an institution has been granted copyright to the analogue material, it will still need to check whether these rights extend to the digitization and distribution of electronic copies.

There are particular concerns to note when working with collections of letters and photographs. With photography, it is necessary to ensure any photographer's contract takes into account the digital environment and that rights have been cleared for digitization and distribution of digital copies (NINCH, 2002). If the photographs are of people, it will be necessary to check that the subjects in the photograph have given permission for the distribution of their image.

When checking the copyright status of correspondence collections, it is necessary to ensure that permission for reproduction has been granted by the author of each letter in the collection.

Some countries, including the UK, France and Canada, also give the creator of a work 'moral rights', which cannot be transferred, and which usually last as long as the duration of copyright. Moral rights protect the attribution and integrity of the creator. The right of attribution requires that the creator be known or identified, preventing others from taking credit for the work. The right of integrity prevents the work from being distorted, mutilated or misrepresented (Levine, 2000). In practical terms, this means that care must be taken to represent this information in the metadata relating to the digital object, and not to deface, severely crop or otherwise digitally 'alter' works. In the USA, moral rights are limited to the 1990 Visual Artists Rights Act, which recognizes only visual art authors' right of attribution and of integrity – works are not protected from destruction. For a useful summary of this issue, see www.nea.gov/artforms/manage/vara.html.

If the institution does not own the copyright on the materials, a decision must be taken about whether or not digitization should proceed. If the decision is taken to go ahead – and many projects will not – there are three available options: identify if the works are in the public domain, or change the project's focus to works that are in the public domain; invoke an exception to copyright, such as preservation copying or fair use; or obtain permission from the copyright holder.

Works in the public domain

If works are in the public domain, they are not protected by copyright law, and can be used freely without paying royalties or other fees, or asking permission. The most common way for works to fall into the public domain is that their copyright term has expired, but works can also enter the public domain by other means, for example work produced by employees of the US federal government as part of their job is in the public domain. Mary Minow of LibraryLaw.com has suggested a useful mnemonic to indicate a public domain realm through which we can forage: FRIDGE, meaning that Facts, Recipes, Ideas, Dedicated works, Government works and Expired works all fall within the public domain (see Minow, 2002; Fishman, 2001).

Projects like the Library of Congress 'Making of America', which have put their materials into the public domain for educational use, may also be helpful. It may be possible to find usable images, texts and materials in collections like this. These materials can augment collections, or provide the basis for instructional tools.

If appropriate for the topic in question, it may be expedient to attempt to find materials that are in the public domain before paying to use copyrighted materials – this may mean using earlier editions of certain works. Sometimes, making a compromise on the materials to be used can save a lot of time researching the copyright status.

One other way is to look for items where the copyright owner has chosen to explicitly waive copyright. Assuming the source is reliable, this type of material can be regarded as being in the public domain. It is worth remembering that just because material happens to be on the web does *not* mean the owner has waived copyright.

Exemptions to copyright: library and preservation copying and fair use

Some exceptions to copyright exist which may allow the digitization and distribution of materials that are not in the public domain. Under allowances for **library and preservations copying**, libraries have always been allowed to make copies of materials in any format (including music, images and audiovisual materials) to use in house for replacement, preservation and security. Amendments to the copyright laws of many countries have extended this privilege to allow digital copying and limited distribution. For example, the Canadian Copyright Act was amended in 1997 to allow copying to 'an alternative format if the original is currently in an obsolete format or the technology required to use the original is unavailable'. The Australian Copyright Act of 1968 was amended in 1999 to allow digital copying of material held in libraries and archives for preservation or internal management purposes, the creation of digital preservation reproductions, and reproductions of artistic works which can be displayed to the public on electronic kiosks provided that the original is unstable or has deteriorated. This preservation copying exception is not yet harmonized in the EU. The UK does allow a very limited exception for preservation copying, but France, the Netherlands and Germany do not allow any such copying.

Note that preservation copying of digital materials (which may become necessary if, for example, a format or playback device becomes obsolete) is another area where the law has still to catch up with the technology. At this time, it is necessary to have a licence or permission to copy electronic materials. For more information on this topic, see the Cedars final report (2002) at www.leeds.ac.uk/cedars/guideto/ipr.

Section 108 of the United States Copyright Law, as modified by the Digital Millennium Copyright Act (DCMA) of 1998, is a provision which allows libraries and archives to copy, digitize and make accessible published documents in their collections under certain conditions, even if the work in question is in copyright. This ruling applies only to libraries and archives which are open to the public or 'available not only to researchers affiliated with the library or archives or with the institution of which it is a part, but also to other persons doing research in a specialized field', and the purpose of digitization/copying must be preservation, scholarship or research. For more information, see the relevant section of the US copyright code: www4.law.cornell.edu/uscode/17/108.html.

There are many conditions attached to this rule. Most importantly, it applies only to published documents. Music, audiovisual materials, pictorial, graphic or sculptural works cannot be copied under this exception. The work in question must be within 20 years of its copyright term expiring (and so this ruling may mitigate some of the limitations of the Bono act). Institutions wishing to invoke this rule must also be able to demonstrate that 'the reproduction or distribution is made without any purpose of direct or indirect commercial advantage'. Copies made under this exception must include a notice of the copyright status of the materials. The exemption also requires that a reasonable amount of investigation has demonstrated that (*a*) the work in question is not subject to normal commercial exploitation (e.g., is not a bestselling novel), (*b*) the work cannot be obtained at a reasonable price, and (*c*) the copyright owner has not provided a note on file to the copyright office demonstrating *a* or *b*. These conditions ensure that this exception does not undermine the Bono term extension (www.llrx.com/features/digitization3.htm#108).

In the USA, the DMCA permits the making of up to three preservation copies (three copies for unpublished and 'damaged' works, and one copy for everything else) of material for library patrons, and for interlibrary loan, but these copies may not be put on the internet, or made publicly accessible. For more details of this aspect of the DMCA, see www.copyright.iupui.edu/ sec108.html. The relevant sections of the DMCA are Section 108(b) for unpublished works and 108(c) for published works where the existing copy is damaged, deteriorating, lost or stolen, or in an obsolete format.

Fair use is a much misused, and much misunderstood, term. It is a provision outlined in Section 107 of the US copyright law of 1976 (and it is unique to US law – other countries have a similar, though more restrictive, concept known as *fair dealing*; for more information from a UK perspective, see the report on the JISC/Publishers' Association code of practice on fair dealing in the electronic environment at www.jisc.ac.uk/index.cfm?name=wg_fairdealing_summary). Fair use allows people and organizations to reproduce copyrighted materials under certain circumstances without receiving permission from the author or owner of the copyright. Under Section 107 of the 1976 US Copyright Act, copying

> for purposes such as criticism, comment, news reporting, teaching (including multiple copies for classroom use), scholarship, or research, is not an infringement of copyright. In determining whether the use made of a work in any particular case is a fair use the factors to be considered shall include:
>
> (1) the *purpose* and character of the use, including whether such use is of a commercial nature or is for nonprofit educational purposes;
> (2) the *nature* of the copyrighted work;
> (3) the *amount* and substantiality of the portion used in relation to the copyrighted work as a whole; and
> (4) the effect of the use upon the potential *market* for or value of the copyrighted work.
>
> (www.loc.gov/copyright/title17/92chap1.html#107)

All four of the above criteria have to be balanced to assess whether or not usage is, indeed, fair, and all are ultimately value judgements. For example, a student on the Museums and Interactive Technologies course at NYU recently asked the estate of a 20th-century artist if she might reproduce one of the artist's images on a website devoted to her final project. The request was denied on the grounds that hers was a 'for profit' enterprise – the profit to be gained being her final grade.

While fair use as a concept has enabled some flexibility in the creation of digital resources, it is a flimsy concept to hide behind. The fair use exemption has been legally challenged only for analogue materials, and contrary to some popular belief, there is no legal definition of fair use as a defence for copying and distributing materials electronically. In fact developments such as the No Electronic Theft Act would imply that digital reproduction would be weighted on the infringement side of the fair use balancing act. For more information on this topic, see www.gseis.ucla.edu/iclp/hp.html/hr2265.html.

The lack of a fair use provision in the Digital Millennium Copyright Act was a noticeable oversight, and one on which much discussion has taken place (see, for example, www.arl.org/info/frn/copy/primer.html). There was an attempt to formally establish and ratify fair use guidelines: from September 1994 to May 1997, representatives in more than 60 commercial, public and educational interests participated in the Conference on Fair Use (CONFU), which sought to establish mutually acceptable fair use guidelines on a variety of subjects, including digital images. Ultimately, the CONFU guidelines were not endorsed. For more information on CONFU, see Hall and Albrecht, 1997. Its failure is instructive: analysis of the discussions illustrate that what seemed to be a laudable goal, on which it would be easy to agree, turned out to be a concept that is very hard to pin down into a workable framework. There have been no subsequent organized approaches to develop a fair use framework for digitization.

Whole books and many years of work have been devoted to making the case that fair use laws should be applicable to digital materials. There have been calls for 'openness' and understanding of the need for academic work to flourish, copyright constraints notwithstanding. This is a laudable case, but nonetheless this is still a grey area, and one that is still evolving. Unfortunately, laws evolve through case law, which means that challenges are determined in court on a case-by-case basis. The penalties for losing a case can be severe, and no library or archive wishes to be the institution that finds out how a court would apply the fair use factors to their use of copyrighted materials.

This is an area where it is necessary to be extremely risk-averse. It would be extremely unwise to proceed with a large-scale digitization project of copyrighted materials shielded only by the fair use exemption.

Getting permissions to use copyrighted materials

If you do not have the right to use materials that are in copyright, if they are not in the public domain, and if none of the exceptions outlined above apply, it will be necessary to obtain permission from the copyright holder before beginning digitization. A member of the project team should be made responsible for clearing copyright and maintaining records associated with the process. The New York Public Library Digital Library project, for example, is digitizing a large collection of materials related to the African Diaspora. Recent photographs (including materials from the Associated Press Photo archive), newspaper articles and writings, in particular those relating to the Haitian migrations of the 1980s, are still in copyright, and so the project has dedicated 50% of a full-time employee to managing the copyright clearance process.

In order to work with copyrighted materials, the first step is to identify the copyright holder(s), contact them, and negotiate an agreement to use the materials. A good start is to contact the creator of the materials, or his/her estate, executor or publisher. Rights holders may be hard to find – the issue is complicated if there have been transfers of the rights, if unclear licences of contracts were negotiated, or if the material was created as a 'work for hire'. However, even if the copyright holders cannot be identified, or they do not respond, it is essential to show 'best endeavour' by making an attempt to contact them before deciding to digitize the materials (although best endeavour is no legal defence against infringement, it would probably reduce the penalties imposed if an infringement occurred), and documenting all communications. This is a long process, and plenty of time – and money – should be allowed to accomplish it as part of the overall project management plan.

Once the copyright owner has been identified, they should be contacted by a letter of enquiry, which should outline the following:

- a description of the project
- a description of the potential audience for the project
- a description of what the materials will be used for (research, teaching, etc.)
- an emphasis on the non-profit nature of the project
- a precise description of how long the project will be available
- a precise description of the mode of distribution (CD-ROM creation, online course, part of a digital edition).

It may be appropriate to include a draft permission agreement with the letter, listing the specific uses that can be foreseen. This should be drafted in association with legal counsel and should state in detail the exact nature of the permissions that are being granted. This should ideally be in perpetuity. For example, sample documents from the University of Florida suggest requesting 'non-exclusive' 'Internet Distribution Rights' for an unlimited term. A grant of non-exclusive rights leaves the copyright holder the ability to grant distribution rights to others. 'Internet Distribution Rights' limits dissemination to the internet, and especially, of course, the world wide web.

If rights to other distribution formats are sought or anticipated, they should also be requested with specific mention of the distribution format, e.g. 'CD-ROM/DVD Distribution Rights', 'Print Distribution Rights', or more broadly, 'Electronic Distribution Rights'. Distribution rights transfer a privileged use of a copyrighted work rather than the copyright, which remains with the copyright holder. See http://palmm.fcla.edu/strucmeta/permit.html.

The copyright holder(s), if they respond, may well permit the use of the materials at no charge. This is often the case in academic projects, and is a satisfying solution for all concerned. However, they would be well within their rights to ask for a sum of money for use or licensing of their materials, which should be paid prior to publishing the digital materials. If the owner denies permission, digitization should not proceed.

As noted earlier, once a written agreement with the owner is secured, this needs to be kept for as long as the materials are to be used.

Costs associated with obtaining copyright permissions should be factored into the project budget, as should staff time allocated to this endeavour. Estimating the costs of copyright clearance is very difficult, and there are few guidelines available to suggest how much one should be prepared to pay. Copyright holders may also be inconsistent in how much they wish to charge per item, and fees may be charged on an arbitrary or ad-hoc basis. Guidelines on this question are urgently needed, for both the holders and users of copyrighted materials. One potential source of advice on how much one should expect to pay may be the museum community, as museum photography departments have a great deal of experience of charging a fee for reproduction and use of slides or photographic copies of materials in their collections, many of which are used in publications.

Some important considerations:

- Assume, unless told otherwise, that a payment will have to be made to use copyrighted materials.
- Set aside a sizeable amount for copyright clearance in grant applications, factoring in the exact number of materials to be digitized.
- Copy fees vary a great deal, and may appear to be completely arbitrary. It may be necessary to haggle over the rate suggested by the copyright holder if the fee they suggest seems unreasonable. Although public institutions have an arbitrary approach to charging for permissions, they will charge a scholar far less than they would a major commercial publisher.
- Strongly emphasize the academic, non-profit-making nature of the project.
- Target collections held by museums and other public collections, as it can be easier to get permissions to use these materials.
- Stress the ways in which copyright will be protected (watermarking, password protection of web pages, etc.)

Forced Migration Online, produced by the University of Oxford's Refugee Studies Centre, has developed a useful and adaptable workflow and methodology for getting permission to digitize materials for their digital library, and have written up the project in *RLG Diginews*. Their article includes sample letters of inquiry and a permission agreement (see Cave, Deegan, and Heinink, 2000).

The important aspect of this whole process is that risk is established at the outset of the project. If permission is not granted, or is contingent on the payment of an exorbitant fee, digitization cannot proceed. Copyright owners may not want their work reproduced. That is their prerogative, and their right.

On the other hand, this process can have some unforeseen benefits. Contacting a copyright holder directly in this way may engage or interest them in a project. Some copyright owners – authors, artists and their executors or descendents – may be flattered to discover that their work has been 're-discovered' through the marvels of technology. Recently, an NYU student working on an electronic edition of the poetry of a postmodern author of the 1950s contacted the author's estate to request permission to digitize some letters and poems. The executor turned out to be the author's brother, who was so delighted that this neglected work was to find a new audience that he engaged in a lengthy correspondence with the student. This epistolary friendship ultimately developed into a close working relationship – the pair are now collaborating on a new edition of the author's work, and the student has enviable access to primary source materials which have been unseen by any other scholars.

Potentially sensitive materials

There are other legal considerations and potential areas of concern, that may require more sensitivity, as they are not guided by a clearly defined set of laws or code of practice – different international laws (and in the USA, different state laws) may apply to the following categories. When working with materials that are sensitive, or which could prove embarrassing to their subjects, it is necessary to tread carefully.

There is a right of *publicity*, which is associated with public figures, and addresses potential commercial gain from using the likeness of a well known person (such as a user downloading an image from your website and subsequently using it in a beer advert). Generally, the right of publicity ends with the death of the subject. However, in the USA, certain states (including Tennessee, California and New York, not coincidentally the home states of much of the entertainment industry) enshrine the rigorous, and posthumous, protection of celebrity image in their legal codes. Exercise caution and obtain permission to use any images that may be protected.

The rights of *privacy* tend to be far more serious. These rights are non-commercial, and protect people for the duration of their lifetime from intrusion, from public disclosure of private affairs, and from being presented in a false light (Levine, 2000). Particularly sensitive materials will include oral histories, political documents and medical records or images. Particular concerns are raised if documenting the histories of political prisoners or holocaust survivors. A recent project to digitize performance arts materials from the 1970s had to request permission from all performers in the collections archive. One artist refused permission to digitize or make publicly available any recordings of her performance – she is now an upstanding member of the community, and no longer wished to be associated with what she now regards as the racy fringe world of performance art. Her right of privacy afforded this protection.

Any applicable legal guidelines on *data protection* must be observed. This is an area of law that is common throughout the European Union and many other countries (although not the USA) and regulates computerized (and manual) processing of any personal data, i.e. anything that relates to a living individual who can be identified from that information. This can include recognizable images of people, names of people in an object's descriptive metadata, and information about the creator of the digital object in the technical metadata.

In the UK, the project manager must register as a data controller, and follow the legal requirements of the Data Protection Act for the duration of the project. See www.dataprotection.gov.uk/ for more information on the UK law.

Other materials may be perceived as *defamatory*, if they facilitate libel or slander. Although this right does end with the death of the subject, their heirs or children may decide to complain or file a suit. Correspondence and administrative political history are particularly sensitive areas. The laws of defamation differ widely from country to country (with some countries, such as the UK, being particularly friendly towards litigants who claim they have been defamed) and readers are strongly urged to obtain advice regarding the law in countries where digitized material is likely to be viewed, and to take any necessary precautions.

Obscenity and pornography. It is not illegal in many countries to put materials online that feature nudity, but 'pornography' is a famously subjective concept, and norms vary greatly from country to country. It is not the only kind of controversial material that could break local laws. Controversial materials that may contravene certain religious, cultural and ethical standards can draw unwanted attention to an institution. Many libraries and museums have collections of artistic materials that have attracted angry complaint when displayed in analogue format – digitizing such materials may re-ignite such hostility.

This is an area where common sense should be the best guide. A warning notice may be appropriate, but it may be necessary to check the laws of the countries that are likely to have regular access to the digitized materials.

Sensitive content. It may be inadvisable to digitize some sensitive materials, or at the very least to make sure you have permissions from interested parties. Cultural sensitivities should always be observed: digital collections are by their very nature international and it is essential for developers to consider how their creations will affect different people. It is particularly important to proceed with caution when planning to digitize anthropological records, materials related to Native American communities or heritage, or any type of 'cultural property' (the ideas, practices, music and writings of a culture). For example, the concept of *tapu*, usually translated as 'sacred', has great significance in Polynesian cultures. Many objects have differing degrees of *tapu*, and it is considered offensive to refer to them inappropriately. Significantly, representations of people are considered *tapu*, and it is inappropriate for them to be publicly displayed (Witten and Bainbridge, 2003).

The Native American Graves Protection and Repatriation Act of 1990 is a US statute that requires the proper care and disposition of Native American remains and artifacts, and that requires museums worldwide to notify the proper entities about their collections. The spirit of the Act now informs museum conduct worldwide with regard to Native American collections. In 1999, the city of Glasgow repatriated a Lakota Ghost Dance Shirt after representations from the Lakota Sioux of South Dakota. The shirt had been in Glasgow's Kelvingrove Museum for more than a century – it had arrived in 1891 with Buffalo Bill Cody's Wild West travelling show, and was believed to have been taken from a fallen warrior at the 1890 Battle of Wounded Knee in South Dakota. Such sensitivity should also be observed in creating digital resources, and this is the case at the National Museum of the American Indian, in Washington DC. The Museum has a commitment to repatriate human remains and funerary objects, religious and ceremonial artefacts, communally owned tribal property, or any holdings acquired illegally, As part of the process of repatriation, the objects are digitized in consultation with

Native Americans, and the digital surrogates allowed to remain in the collection of the Museum.

In New Zealand, there have been developments underlining these concerns in the creation of an Indigenous Digital Library. Toi Iho, a registered trademark of authenticity and quality for Maori arts and crafts, has been developed. This is in response to a concern that 'indigenous communities themselves control the rights management of their cultural intellectual property. Local cultural protocols need to be documented and followed prior to the creation of digital content, and communities must be consulted with regard to the digitization of content already gathered by institutions of social memory' (Sullivan, 2002). See also the special edition of *D-Lib* on this topic: www.dlib.org/dlib/march02/03contents.html.

Caretaking online content

> With this expansion of a museum's constituency, the likelihood that the content it offers will be objectionable to someone increases accordingly.
> (Reilly in Jones, 2001)

All copyright and legal issues are exacerbated by the openness and ubiquity of the internet. The potential for unauthorized and unlimited use of materials on the internet means that access cannot be managed as carefully as in a traditional setting, where access restrictions allow sensitive materials to be presented with commentary, background materials and guidance. Materials on the internet may be taken out of context or otherwise misused – the Margaret Sanger Papers Project at NYU finds that materials from its online collection are frequently copied and misquoted to support spurious arguments on eugenics or birth control.

Another project which is digitizing material that will need curatorial oversight is The Survivors of the Shoah Visual History Foundation (www.vhf.org/static/organization.htm), which has developed an archive of 50,000 video testimonies from survivors and witnesses of the Holocaust. The goals of the project are to further academic research and also to preserve the oral testimonies of witnesses. The project has had to grapple with the dual concerns of wishing to disseminate and distribute the content while protecting the privacy of the subjects. To this end, the project retains the copyright on all testimonies and users must agree to the project's terms of use. Access is presently limited to five academic partner institutions. Ultimately, however, the project will have decide if they wish to release the materials to a broader audience, and when to do so. Waiting to solve all the ethical, proprietary and privacy issues associated with this material will result in the material never being released. At some point, the informational value of the content will be judged to outweigh the privacy concerns.

Furthermore, museums and archives usually have in their charter a provision that they must exhibit their collections to the public on a regular basis. The International Council of Museums (ICOM) defines a museum as: 'a non-profit making, permanent institution in the service of society and of its development, and open to the public which acquires, conserves, researches, communicates and exhibits, for purposes of study, education and enjoyment, material evidence of people and their environment'. Organizations must ensure that they are able to control and curate their digital collections to provide meaningful, educational access to them (Beamsley, 1999). Museums' collections management systems must allow the addition of detailed contextual and artefact information to obviate this concern and to assist in the interpretation of the image information. Subject catalogues are increasingly important in this regard.

Managing copyright of digital materials

> Loss of control over digital assets can be the result of failure or inability to establish and publicize copyright. Even if copyright is established and enforceable, failure to enforce rights has the same effect as having no rights at all.
>
> (Beamsley, 1999)

It will be necessary to develop a plan for managing the rights to the digital surrogate materials created by a project and for monitoring the use of these materials. Even when digitizing work that is in the public domain, or for which you own the copyright and wish to distribute freely, it will be necessary to manage and monitor usage of the materials. Accurate statistics on who is using your collections will inform decisions about what to digitize in future, and provide usage statistics, which may be required by funders.

At the very least, information should be included in the relevant metadata about the copyright status of the materials. A clear statement outlining the copyright status of the digital images should be visible to users. If you plan to recover costs of your project by selling or otherwise licensing the content, you will need to protect the content in such a way that it cannot be freely used, and develop a licensing scheme or charging mechanism of the content. The electronic profile of your organization can be an opportunity for a revenue stream, and many stakeholders will be involved in approving licensing practices – legal counsel, administrators, funders, etc. Licence agreements are also used to define the amount of access that may be provided to a digital publication. Organizations like the *New York Times*, which sell digital copies of images from their photography archive (www.nytimes.com/nytstore/photos/index.html), can provide templates for how such agreements might work. Another organization which has implemented such a system is the city of Vancouver archive (www.city.vancouver.bc.ca/ctyclerk/archives/photos/photrepr.htm) which has digitized the city's photographic archives and made them accessible online for a fee.

Deciding how much to charge is also problematic, and again, there are no clear guidelines on this issue. Institutionally, you should develop a charging threshold, a sum below which it is not worth doing, but which users will agree to pay. Working in a consortium with other organizations (such as the model developed by AMICO, the Arts Museum Imaging Consortium (www.AMICO.org)) is one way to manage licences.

There are two ways to prevent unauthorized access to the digital materials: by implementing technical measures that will prevent copyright abuse and/or by limiting access to licensed users or subscribers (Oppenheim, 2002).

Technical solutions can be very simple. Many organizations have decided that the images they make available to users must be of a low resolution, in order to prevent re-publishing (the oft-invoked fear that people may steal the digital images to produce coffee table books). Unfortunately, this also prevents users from carrying out advanced research on the digital images.

More advanced technological measures enable projects to take steps to protect their ownership of materials without compromising on image quality. One solution is to apply 'credit' information that is superimposed on to the image, usually around the border or edge, or appended to the file. See, for example, the Henry Ford Museum and Greenfield Village website (www.hfmgv.org/).

These tools are not ideal, and their use can threaten the integrity of the digital information. The addition of this information is at the expense of pixels from elsewhere in the image, cropping the image and potentially causing corruption to the original file (Beamsley, 1999).

The field of steganography (literally 'covered writing', from Greek) is influencing research into advanced technologies to encode visible and invisible 'signatures' and other information as a means of controlling and monitoring use, and limiting copying. The best known of these methods is watermarking, which inserts marks or labels into the digital content in a subtle, or transparent, way. This watermark is inseparable from the source data of the file, so in theory it cannot be removed or altered. There are two types of watermark – 'robust' and 'fragile' watermarks. Robust cannot be altered and will survive a variety of processes, including cropping, copying, compression and the application of image analysis tools. This watermark is used to determine ownership of an image. Fragile watermarks are designed to break if the image is altered in any way, and are used to establish the authenticity of images. For examples of watermarking, see the online (and for profit) image archives of the *New York Times* (www.nytimes.com/nytstore/photos/ index.html), and the Gaelic Village cultural heritage project (www. ambaile.org), partly funded by the New Opportunities Fund in the UK.

Unfortunately, watermarking and related emerging technologies (including encryption) are expensive and are not foolproof, as has been ably demonstrated by armies of computer enthusiasts keen to expose weaknesses in security mechanisms preventing access to images, music and films (for research purposes only, of course) and to develop software (such as StirMark and UnZig) to remove copyright information from files.

Managing or restricting access

Again, the simplest methods are often employed: access can be limited to registered users or users logging on from a university or library domain name or IP address. If a more advanced system is necessary, or if it is necessary to charge users for access, software tools have been developed to manage the use of electronic content. These are known by a variety of names, such as ECMS (electronic content management systems), ERMS (electronic rights management systems) or DRMS (digital rights management systems). Functionality offered by these tools includes the ability to limit the number of times a file is viewed, opened, copied or printed. They can control IDs and passwords, or manage payments for viewing materials (Oppenheim, 2002). These tools typically incorporate the end-to-end management of the rights, including setting access rules, encrypting, attaching metadata, securing distribution of content, providing access keys to paying consumers, enforcing permissions and transaction processing, as well as usage tracking, measuring and reporting. They allow huge variation in the type of payment method (e.g. pay-per-use, subscription), access rules (e.g. first chapter free, pay for the rest) and distribution method (e.g. download, peer-to-peer, streaming). Digital downloads can be limited by the number of plays, or restricted to one machine.

For more information on DRMS and tools, see the European Information & Communications Technology Industry Association of the European Union (www.eicta.org/copyrightlevies/index.html), and an EICTA position paper on DRMs: *Delivery of Digital Content by DRM Systems*, which can be downloaded at www.eicta.org/copyrightlevies/resources/additional_resources.html.

Some commercial tools available include the following:

- Adobe's Content Server is an all-in-one system that secures and sells Adobe PDF-based e-books (www.adobe.com).
- ContentGuard is a modular DRM platform, based on XrMl (eXtensible rights Markup Language). It can protect PDF and

Microsoft Reader formats (www. contentguard.com).

- IBM's Electronic Media Management System (EMMS) is an end-to-end DRM-based content distribution system, allowing the delivery of digital content over multiple systems and devices (www-3.ibm.com/software/is/emms/).
- Info2Clear's Get-a-view Publisher is a DRM solution designed for book publishers using Microsoft's Digital Assets Server or Adobe's Content Server. It has focused on the field of European copyright registry and clearance (www.info2clear.com).
- InterTrust's DigiBox container holds the encrypted files securely during transit, and the usage rules can only be amended by Inter-Rights Points. Rules can be set governing payment, playing, viewing, copying and printing (www.intertrust.com).
- Liquid Audio provides a range of music distribution software and services for publishing, hosting and distributing secure digital music content over the internet. Its DRM solution incorporates a number of technologies and features, including watermarks, encryption, permission sets, revenue distribution and data control (www.liquidaudio.com).

Many of these initiatives have a commitment to promoting open standards for DRM interoperability. In March 2003, the Association of American Publishers (AAP) and the American Library Association (ALA) jointly issued a 'White Paper' entitled *What Consumers Want in Digital Rights Management (DRM): making content as widely available as possible in ways that satisfy consumer preferences* as a snapshot of e-book users' experiences and preferences, with a view to identifying those features that vendors should take account of in implementing DRM software for e-books. While specifically focused on e-books, the report may well have relevance for the wider deployment of DRM software, especially as it relates to practitioners' behaviour and their requirements for the use and re-use of digital material. See www.publishers.org/press/pdf/DRMWhitePaper.pdf.

Conclusion

Protecting and managing copyright, and avoiding infringement, is ultimately more a question of risk management than it is of the law. When cultural institutions design digital collections, they may well select material in which they do not hold copyright. Unfortunately, many of the works most urgently in need of digitization for preservation and access – photography and film collections – are recent enough that they are still protected by copyright. Finding the copyright holders and getting permission to digitize these materials can be particularly difficult, especially if both the photographer and subjects have to be contacted. Fair use will not apply, and 'preservation copying' will have limitations depending on the national jurisdiction. Managers in charge of these projects will have to negotiate the path of copyright legislation and risk management with great care, and in close consultation with legal advisors. Risk management will require considering the benefits of digitizing (wider access, preservation, greater availability of the materials for research) against the potential risks of infringing copyright – and putting materials on the internet makes it that much more likely that the infringement will be discovered. It is essential to ensure that you can quickly and readily block access to a particular item, or that the offending item can be rapidly deleted. Risks may include negative publicity, costs of litigation, financial penalties that might be awarded, costs of lost human resources (e.g. administrative time) or financial loss incurred by having to withdraw the digital resource. In some cases, the staff might conclude that there are important considerations favouring limited use of the material that would counterbalance the risk of infringing the legal rights of the unidentified copyright owner (NINCH, 2002).

It is also helpful to frame questions regarding copyright in terms of the risk that various actions may pose to the institution. The following questions are suggested to help develop an understanding of the size and likelihood of the risk involved:

- What are the consequences of using the material without specific permission, pursuing a fair use or mitigation of damages argument?
- How will the institution address the risk if it does occur?
- Will the institution be able to afford legal expenses?

Employing some of the strategies for managing copyright and intellectual property outlined in this chapter can help to manage and anticipate these risk factors. These strategies may include being prepared to undertake a thorough search to identify the rights holders, regardless of the possible results, and being able to demonstrate through good documentation that the search was conducted in a comprehensive manner. It will also be important to anticipate the level of risk that an institution is willing to assume with regard to copyright. Where possible, discussing these factors with legal counsel at the outset of a project may help to develop an approach to copyright management that might mitigate any problems throughout the course of a project. Ultimately, certain decisions (such as negotiating with rights holders, or deciding whether or not fees can be paid) will often be made by an institution's legal counsel, who will have the final say in assessing the impact of risk, and deciding how risk averse a project – and the institution – can afford to be.

4

Project management and the institutional framework

Introduction

This chapter examines the following aspects of project management:

- identifying and quantifying costs
- knowing when to outsource
- knowing what staff to use and how to train them
- risk management.

Large-scale digitization initiatives can be found in many sectors of industry, commerce, and government. These include projects to digitize millions of tax or other government records, industrial training manuals, and mechanical and engineering blueprints, as well as the retrospective capture of scientific data. Such initiatives are often driven by the same imperatives underlying digitization for cultural heritage materials, such as a desire for greater access to resources, or to provide training or research materials, and similar technical solutions may be employed to facilitate such projects.

Some lessons learned from such large-scale initiatives can be instructive, as essentially the processes of digitization are the same regardless of the sector commissioning such work. However, there are unique considerations that come into play when such work is carried out on cultural heritage materials. Firstly, economies of scale will not be realized when smaller numbers of source materials are to be digitized. Secondly, cultural heritage materials and objects may be more fragile and unique, meaning that additional care and handling (and therefore additional costs) are required. If the loss of records is an unacceptable outcome, it will be impossible to employ large through-put options for scanning. The potential risk to the originals posed by the scanning or digital imaging process means that conservators and preservation teams will usually only agree to digitization as a 'once only' opportunity, so it will be essential to capture the best possible digital image the first time, and to ensure that it will continue to be usable over the long term. It will also be necessary to capture the total informational content of the original source materials, rather than just the core sense of the information. Most significantly, there is a lack of funding and staff that can be allocated to digitization projects. Even generously funded library digitization initiatives will spend a small fraction of the resources available to, for example, a digitization undertaking at a major corporation, or scientific agency such as NASA.

Consequently, in addition to careful project management, and the development of contingency plans for the management of risk at every stage in the project life cycle, it will be necessary for cultural heritage institutions to address the unique institutional and strategic considerations that will inform the decision to develop digitization initiatives, to ensure that resources are not wasted. Successful projects will necessitate buy-in from many parts of the institution, and will involve many active stakeholders, including curators, librarians, academics, legal experts and other categories of staff not directly involved with technical departments. This will ensure that any digitization initiatives are in keeping with existing policies relating to access, conservation and collections management.

It will be necessary to fully and comprehensively address the costs of undertaking such projects, and to assess where these costs will have an impact, at every level of the institution. Costs will include the initial predicted cost of doing the work (the project budget), cost as a function of time, and the rate of change of cost as a function of time (i.e. any deviation from the planned spending profile).

Assessing whether or not the institutional framework will support digitization will involve considering the available staff, budget and technology. Successful digital projects are a result of careful and comprehensive project planning, developing a clear vision of the goals of a project and also understanding how a project can fit in with the overall priorities of the institution. It will be necessary to understand the benefits of digitization in this context, and how these benefits will be assessed in terms of institutional prestige, staff development, improvement to scholarship and access, and enhancing the technology infrastructure of an institution.

When to digitize: cost considerations

The main factor in determining the right time to digitize is, ultimately, cost. Anyone who has ever hankered after the latest laptop or digital camera will identify with the feeling that there is always something better 'just around the corner', and that a purchase should be postponed. In terms of developing large-scale digitization projects, the problem is magnified: there is a sense, to quote Doug Greenberg, Director of the Shoah Archive, that 'what costs $10 million today may cost 35 cents in a couple of years'. This can seem especially pertinent when working with cutting-edge technologies for image enhancement, audio and moving image digitization, or machine translation, where the technology is subject to dramatic shifts. But waiting for market-led developments in technology can be counter-productive, as the demise of 'industry leaders' such as Quest, WorldCom and Global Crossing recently demonstrated (Greenberg, 2003). And waiting for the 'perfect' moment means that a project may never be started. At some point, a leap of faith is needed in order to stop planning and start working.

Developing costing models is a key strategy for empowering the information manager to take such a leap. Identifying realistic costs for developing the project and maintaining the resources over the long term is a way to take charge of the problem, and ensure that the investment is not wasted. Cost factors are not simply those of actually creating the digital surrogates, of course – they include the cost to the institution of creating resources that can be used in the future, and for purposes other than those originally intended. Costs and benefits will not be solely financial, but will include time, opportunity costs, institutional prestige, staff training and morale. Any calculation should include a need to evaluate the bigger picture at the institution, evaluating overall investments (and plans to develop such investments) in staff, equipment, technology architecture and support. It will also require examining the broader, long-term issues related to managing digital assets: is there a possibility of developing a business model which will allow cost recovery, or a means of recouping the cost over the life of the image?

In order to address such questions, the UNESCO, IFLA and ICA *Guidelines* (2002) recommend that budget development should involve the following steps:

- Investigate cost-recovery options of income-generating activities.
- Build business models to support income generation.
- Form partnerships to develop trusted digital repositories.
- Budget in terms of unit costs, i.e. costs per image.
- Form consortia for collaborative development and shared expenses.

In order to develop business models, however, it will be necessary to start investigating the true, institutional cost of developing digital resources. It is also important to be able to make the distinction between price and cost. Price is the amount paid by a customer for a good or service and is set by the marketplace. Price may be only tangentially related to cost, and the difference between price and cost defines profit (or loss). All projects will have to juggle three numbers: cost, price and value. Cost is spent to make a product, price is what it is sold for, and value is what it is worth to the customer. If cost is above price, the project will lose money. If the price is above value, there will be no sales (Waters, 2003).

Measuring the actual value of information has always been very difficult, and it is especially hard to measure that of digital resources. For example, a resource like the Blake archive has dramatically improved the ease of access to Blake's complete works. The three editors of the archive are the foremost scholars of this material, and they have all attested to the tremendous value to their scholarship of working with such an archive. In terms of volume, the Library of Congress receives over two million requests a day for digital files, compared to two million requests a year for analogue materials, delivered to readers in its rooms. Over 50 million historical documents are now posted by the United States National Archives on their website, Access to Archival Databases (AAD; www.archives.gov/aad/), which are extremely convenient for genealogists and family history research. Informal and anecdotal evidence of this sort indicates that there is value to be gained from the use of the digital materials, but there is no way to measure this in monetary terms. One of the problems is that new modes of dissemination promote new or extended uses, so more people are benefiting from the value of an information resource, but how many is a completely unknowable factor when deciding to digitize.

There is a need for institutions to be able to define and defend their choices related to digitization in terms of their institutional mission, be this exhibiting, public service, teaching or scholarship. Furthermore, within an institutional context, such clarity of mission will allow the costs of digitization to be offset by economies of scale.

One thing that should be emphasized is that expenditure on digitization initiatives is a unique and often unprecedented expense, often in response to a new funding opportunity. It should not be compared to, or substituted for, existing expenses and activities.

Estimating costs: areas of expenditure

There will be several categories of expenditure associated with every stage of the project's life cycle. These can broadly be broken down into the costs related to the digitization of source materials, and the costs related to activities in maintaining and managing the digital assets that have been created. Steven Puglia of NARA (National Archives and Records Administration) has estimated that expenses incurred by digitization initiatives can be broken down as approximately one-third of the cost on digitization, one-third on cataloguing, description and indexing, and one-third on administrative costs, quality control, institutional overhead and similar costs (Puglia, 1999). Many project managers have also found that digitization is the lowest cost factor to consider in the whole life cycle of a project.

Broadly speaking, the main areas of expenditure will be staff salaries, technology and workflow costs, intellectual property, and institutional or indirect costs.

Specifically, project costs will include:

- selection, preparation, handling and conservation of original source materials
- metadata creation, as well as cataloguing/description/indexing
- production of an intermediate copy of the source materials, if necessary, prior to digitization
- digital capture costs, including the purchase of hardware, software and peripheral equipment
- quality control of images and metadata
- the maintenance of the technical infrastructure, including hardware maintenance and network costs
- ongoing maintenance of images and metadata, including long-term storage costs
- rights clearance
- staff costs, including technical support, project management, web programming and interface design staff, and training
- user evaluation
- documentation
- travel.

How much will the project cost?

Projections of costs, derived from a reasonable timescale in conjunction with the breakdown of tasks and technical requirements, can only be made on the basis of sound experience. One way to obtain this is to perform a large-scale production benchmarking study. Since this would in most cases be impossible to do as a general preparation because of the sheer cost of such an endeavour and the bias it will inevitably have, it should be considered best practice to base cost estimates and projections on sound independent advice. Using the lessons of other benchmarking studies that can be adopted and adapted greatly enhances this best practice.

(Cultuurtechnologie, 2003)

Developing a better understanding of the digitization process, and its many components, will help inform an understanding of what it all costs. General guidance on the costs of digitization is available from organizations such as NOF-Digitise (2002b) and HEDS (2003). The reader is also encouraged to consult articles by Steven Puglia of NARA (Puglia, 1999) and Maria Bonn of the University of Michigan (Bonn, 2001) addressing these issues, and a report sponsored by the National Initiative for a Networked Cultural Heritage (NINCH, 2002) is also helpful.

Real costs and prices are bound to vary from those given in any guidance documents. As Abby Smith points out in her 2001 study, *Strategies for Building Digitized Collections*, the only way to really get at the issue of costs is to actually undertake projects, in the hope that documentation of expenditures will yield some meaningful data (A. Smith, 2001c). This also indicates the need to develop prototype projects and feasibility studies based on real costs, a theme that is discussed at greater length in Chapter 6. The experience of working with one's own collections is one of the best ways to forecast project costs, by working with a representative sample of the materials selected for conversion. In many cases, just a few items will be sufficient. The project budget should be finalized only after a sample has been put through an entire workflow – scanning, processing, metadata creation (including full text) and quality control – and the results have been inspected and approved by the appropriate stakeholders in the project. Some vendors are willing to provide this service as part of their response to the RFI (request for information) or RFP (request for proposal) in order to compete for a contract (C. Chapman, 2002), but are likely to only consider this for potentially large-scale projects. Practitioners who have done these kinds of projects in the past are also an excellent source of advice and expertise on all aspects of a process. The cost of a piece of equipment can be estimated, but expertise and experience will assist with anticipating unexpected or additional costs. A project budget will always be more than the sum of its parts.

Budgets should also include risk-related considerations, or contingency funds for expenditure related to overtime, inefficiencies or delays. The manpower requirements for projects will not stay constant with time and early delays may require catch-up, leading to the need to hire additional short-term, potentially more costly, staff to regain the project schedule. There are also cost factors that will vary throughout the course of a project. Just as there will be more financial costs at the beginning of a project, as initial hardware and technology purchases are made, there will also be ramp-up costs, costs associated with staff learning to use the equipment, developing workflows, and learning ways of handling the original materials. These costs are seldom reflected in a cost-per-image type of itemization, but can cause problems to the overall time allocated to the project (Bonn, 2001).

Developing costs per image

It will usually be necessary to create an estimate of the digitization cost per image prior to requesting or allocating funds to a project. This is the type of headline figure that funders will want to see (although as the following example will show, it is an extremely subjective figure). Many vendors and digitization services, such as HEDS as well as commercial vendors including Luna Imaging, Inc. and Systems Integration Group, Inc. (SIG), have developed methodologies for calculating such costs. RLG has also produced a helpful guide to calculating per-image costs, the (RLG, 2002).

Before developing detailed cost calculations, it will be necessary to have a good understanding of a number of issues, including the nature of the project, the goals of the project, including the uses of the digital objects, the location for digitization, and the timeframe. Most importantly, the characteristics of the materials need to be considered:

- What format are the originals – slides, manuscripts, colour images, text, black and white images?
- How many items have to be digitized?
- Are the items bound or unbound?
- What are the dimensions?
- Are the originals easily accessible or available?
- Are there special handling requirements?
- Are there insurance requirements?
- If they are within copyright, do permissions payments have to be made?

A large number of variables will quickly complicate the process. Dan Pence of SIG describes a worksheet demonstrating the number of choices and variables as a 'Chinese menu' (see Table 4.1).

Table 4.1 Digitization choices

Category	Number of choices
Bound/unbound	2
Page size (8.5x11, 11x17, 17x22)	3
Scanning resolution (300, 400, 600)	3
Scanning bit depth (1, 8, 24)	3
Handling (fragile/non-fragile)	2
Place of digitization (on/off-site)	2
Possible combinations:	216

(Source: Pence, 2003)

Considering the range of choices, it becomes apparent that a standard price schedule is only the starting point for a cost estimate. Every digitization project has a unique profile and must be priced individually.

Once decisions about all of the above factors have been made, it will be possible to calculate the cost per image for a particular project. This will be determined by such factors as:

- the number of pages/objects that can be scanned per day
- the cost of labour for scanning
- the cost of labour for post-capture processing and quality assessment
- the cost of equipment
- institutional overhead.

(Pence, 2003)

The number of pages that can be scanned per day is a function of the condition and size of the originals, page size and binding, handling specifications, digital image format specifications and the scanning technology available (for example, is equipment shared with other projects?). There will be a wide range of variability on costs, depending on quality required. The following example will demonstrate the cost implications of decisions that are made.

Example: decision processes in developing a cost per image

The cost-per-image calculation is not the amount of the available funding divided by the number of images. It is a complex, layered calculation, incorporating many more factors than the cost of equipment, more activities than digitization, and many more people than those engaged in scanning or digital imaging. Thinking holistically about the whole digitization life cycle, as illustrated in the example below, introduces this idea, and illustrates where these additional layers of expenditure come in to play.

In a hypothetical example: costing methodologies suggested by Bonn (2001), Puglia (1999) and RLG (2002), as well as the type of cost models used by some digitization vendors such as SIG (Pence, 2003), are adapted to develop an estimate of the cost of scanning, and creating digital images, of 20 volumes of a Victorian periodical, each containing 100 pages, which are approximately A4 in size. There are no copyright restrictions on digitizing this particular material, which is one of the reasons that digitizing this resource was appealing to the senior administration of the archive that holds the volumes. The project plan is to scan all 20 volumes. They are bound and on fragile paper. Most of the pages are just text, but each volume contains six full-page colour illustrations: a frontispiece, illustrations for articles, portraits of authors, etc. There are a total of 120 illustrations. One of the goals of the project is to do authorship analysis of the unsigned articles in the journal, since some are believed to have been written by well-known figures of the time. The journals must be preserved, so cannot be disbound. Digitization must take place within the special collections department, as the materials are determined to be valuable and may not leave this area. The library office of legal counsel has determined that additional insurance does not have to be paid because conservation staff will oversee all aspects of the digitization. The institution has decided to scan at the highest quality affordable because these are fragile, archival resources, vulnerable to excessive handling, and there is a concern that digitization should not have to be repeated at a later date.

Excluding the illustrations, the volumes consist of 1880 pages. However, there are several blank pages at the start and end of each volume. As the primary goal of the project is research use of the content, rather than an exact representation of the original artifact, it has been decided that it is not necessary to scan the blank pages (four per volume). Therefore, the amount of materials to be scanned is 1800 pages of text, which will be scanned at 8-bit greyscale and 400 dpi, and 120 pages of illustration, to be scanned at 24-bit colour at a resolution of 600 dpi (total number of pages 1920). Greyscale images were selected, despite being a more expensive option, because of the preservation concerns outlined above. Output for both will be uncompressed TIFF image files (archival quality master copies, which will not be used on a day-to-day basis). These will vary in size, but be approximately 44.4 Mb per image for the images of the colour illustrations and slightly less than 14.8 Mb for the greyscale image. A JPEG copy of each image, about 100 Kb in size, will be generated and published on the project website. For each page, administrative, structural and technical metadata will have to be created and entered into a database system (including the file name, project item, capture device, image type, etc.).

Because of the fragility of the originals, a digital camera must be used to capture the images. The volumes can only be opened 120°, using archival supports for the spine. The originals may not be disbound for copying. The digital camera workstation required will be a significant capital purchase, incorporating the following equipment, at the approximate cost outlined below:

PowerPhase FX 4x5 scan back	$35,000
4x5 view camera with 150 mm lens	$ 5,000
Heavy-duty TTI copy stand	$ 9,000
330 W hi-freq fluorescent lights/stand	$ 5,500
Mac G4, 512 Mb RAM, 100 Gb HD	$ 4,500
Diamond Pro 21" monitor	$ 500
Adobe PhotoShop and OCR software	$ 500
Total:	$60,000

(Pence, 2003)

The amortization of this equipment will depend on the number of images to be scanned, and the number of projects using it. At most institutions, equipment of this nature has a three-year lifespan, during which time it can be used for many other projects. Sharing use with other projects will bring the total cost down, as will digitizing a greater volume of materials. This is the point at which decisions will have to be made about the overall scope of the project, and its role in the institution. In our example, the equipment is to be used for four additional projects at the library. Therefore, the cost to our project is $15,000. Dividing the equipment cost by the number of images will come up with a capital cost of $7.81 per image.

In addition to the cost of the equipment, there will be expenditure on labour. This will depend on the salary of the staff who are doing the digitization, and the time available. In this case, a mid-level staff member has been assigned to the project, and their salary is $40,000 per year. If they are able to dedicate their time to working on this project alone, and to produce 40 images per day, the project will take about 50 days (ten weeks). Calculating that there are 50 working weeks in the year, ten weeks' work is one-fifth of the year. So total staff costs will be $8000. However, benefits paid by the institution (such as national insurance contributions, etc.) will need to be added to this salary – this will vary according to institution, but in this hypothetical example we shall say that this will add about a third to the salary cost. So the staff salary component will increase to $10,600, or $212 per day. This calculation produces a per image cost of $5.52.

A senior conservation expert, who will spend a total of two days on the entire project, must supervise this work. Their time must be factored into the project, and if we calculate that their salary is double that of a junior project member, their time will be worth $424 per day, adding $828 to the staff budget, which is now $11,428. Divide this by 1920 images, and we come up with a total staff cost of $5.95 per image. Were it possible to scan the pages, or to disbind the volumes, more images would be scanned per day, bringing costs down. We could also see a difference between the cost of digitizing the images and scanning the pages which only contain text. It would also be far less expensive to scan from microfilm rather than the originals (although then the calculation would have to add the cost of microfilming the originals). However, working around the particular constraints of the project, our total cost per image so far is $13.76.

There will be costs associated with creating metadata and cataloguing. This may be carried out by the project staff member as they digitize each image, which is a good way to avoid errors, or it may be the responsibility of another staff member, for example someone from the library's cataloguing department. The latter option will add additional costs; so we will assign that task to our designated project staff member and require that their salary will also cover this cost.

Above all, in our example, it will be necessary to put the output through an Optical Character Recognition (OCR) software application, in order to produce an accurate textual transcription of the text for subsequent authorship analysis. This may require different expertise, as it is essentially a quality assurance task, and will take some time. In this example, we shall allow 20 additional days (five minutes per digital image), on the same salary scale as before. This will be an additional $4240, or $2.20 per image.

It will also be necessary to decide who is going to carry out the quality assessment and assurance (Q&A) for the digital output, checking both images and metadata. This should not be the same person who does the image capture: most usually, the project manager will oversee this activity. Many projects consider that 10% of the time allocated to the project should be spent on this activity, and in this case, the project manager has decided that one hour per week is adequate for Q&A over the ten weeks spent digitizing. Putting the project manager on the same senior salary as our conservation expert, this will come to a total of $4240.

Workstations for Q&A and OCR will be necessary, although equipment for these activities can usually be shared with other projects and activities. It will also be necessary to purchase consumables such as CD-ROMs or additional hard drives for storage and ease of access. In this case, as we are dealing with a small collection, we will assume that this will only be in the region of $200. As stated above, our hypothetical collection has no copyright limitations, so we do not need to allocate a payment for permissions to use the images.

Therefore, adding up the total costs, we come up with the final total of $35,108 for the digitization, or $18.28 per image.

Of this budget of $35,108, the categories of expenditure breakdown are as follows:

Equipment and consumables:	$15,200	43.2%
Staff: digitization and metadata:	$10,600	30.1%
conservation:	$828	2.3%
OCR:	$4240	12%
Quality assessment:	$4240	12%

However, the most important component has yet to be added – institutional overhead. If this project is grant funded, it will be necessary to add in the region of 30 to 50% (depending on the rate at the institution in question) to this sum to pay for all the 'indirect' costs incurred by the institution, such as rent for buildings, electricity and power, and technology infrastructure costs, i.e. network and internet costs. Even if core institutional funding covers digitization projects, such internal costs will have to be paid for at some level. If these costs are 40% at our hypothetical institution, the total overhead will be $14,043. This will add as much as $7.31 to the cost per image, leading to a total cost per image of $25.59, or a project total of $49,151.

Looking at the categories of expenditure now, we see the breakdown is as follows:

Institutional overhead:	$14,043	28.5%
Equipment and consumables:	$15,200	30.9%
Staff: digitization and metadata:	$10,600	21.5%
conservation:	$828	1.6%
OCR:	$4,240	8.6%
Quality assessment:	$4,240	8.6%

As these examples show, adding categories of expenditure changes the overall layering of the price per image, and alters the percentage of costs allocated to the different categories of activity. This shows that the cost per image is a highly subjective figure.

Keeping costs down

In order to reduce the costs of the digitization component of the projects, it will be necessary to examine the digitization and scanning workflow, as well as all the other categories of spending (Lesk, 2003).

There are certain elements of the project design and workflow that can be automated or compromised in order to reduce costs, such as:

- *Understanding the technology*: technology development paths that result in lower costs have now been identified for various formats, including the capture and markup of text, and OCR. It is possible to make informed choices about the possible tradeoffs related to cost and quality, such as reducing image size or resolution, scanning from a surrogate or reducing page size.
- *Project management*: organizing materials, working with accurate data about the condition, location of materials. Developing metadata to track workflow and for quality control, clear communications channels between project participants (including vendors) and working within clearly defined project goals can all really help.
- *Economies of scale*: working with a large volume of consistent materials can result in cost savings overall.

Working with a digitization vendor to save costs

Given the high cost of equipment purchase, there can be advantages to outsourcing this type of work. Vendors can bring their experience of working on many similar projects, and the benefits of their mistakes. Some of the questions to assess whether or not digitization should be outsourced will include:

- *Staff*. Will the project be based in house with current resources, or with a new team? Are trained staff already in place, or is it possible to bring in new staff to start up the project?
- *Timeline*. Are there critical deadlines? Are there internal risk factors that may compromise such deadlines, e.g. sharing staff with other projects?
- *Workspace*. Is appropriate physical space available for these tasks or is the space best used for other activities?
- *Equipment*. Is the right combination of equipment available? Can other projects share equipment to reduce internal capital costs (Harm, 2003)?

Selecting a digitization vendor

There are some key considerations that will influence the outsourcing decision, and a vendor's willingness to accommodate the client's requirements on these issues should be evident.

Firstly, can they conform to the standard output formats that are required by the project? The vendor should be prepared to provide substantial benchmark samples so that the client is able to assess the quality of the work that will be produced before signing a contract. It is appropriate to take third-party advice from independent experts on whether the proposed quality of the digital image is acceptable.

If digitization is to take place off-site, a vendor should be able to demonstrate that they are able to protect fragile original materials. Ascertain that they have safe storage facilities for the originals away from the production area, in a temperature-controlled area if required. Essentially, the vendor must be able to account for the protection of the original materials at every stage of the process, including any times when they are in transit.

Some vendors may sub-contract digitization to a third party. If this is the case, ensure that any third-party organization can also conform to these requirements.

Ensure that any contract sets out what you expect from the vendor, including technical procedures, output formats, quality assurance procedures, handling requirements and timescales. Insist that they will rework any data that fails quality assurance procedures stated in the contract without further cost.

Ensure that you work with a vendor that has experience with the type of materials that are to be digitized – for example, is their experience primarily with high-quality images, or with high-volume paper materials?

Although vendors will always be willing to provide cost estimates for digitization, it can be difficult for institutions to effectively compare output and services from a range of vendors. It is difficult to compare results without generalized points of comparison such as bit-depth, resulting file size and associated vendor services. When assessing quotes, remember that the cheapest quote may not be from the vendor most suitable to do the work. Experience, longevity of the company (have they been around for long enough to have a proven track record with cultural heritage materials?) and the quality of the work they are able to produce based on samples will be more important considerations than price alone. (For some useful sample vendor agreements see those developed by Janet Gertz, in the NEDCC handbook: Gertz, 2000b.

Digitizing images in house vs contracting work to a vendor

There are advantages and disadvantages to both conducting a digitization project in house or contracting the project out to a vendor.

The advantages of conducting the project in house involve control of the project and value added to the department or institution conducting the project. In-house production allows the institution to control all aspects of imaging, to be flexible in the requirements of the project and to maintain the security of the source material. It also allows staff to learn by doing and therefore develop in-house expertise, not to mention the production capability that is built.

The disadvantages of in-house digitization involve cost and ability. In-house production entails a huge investment of time and money. Equipment must be purchased and the institution incurs the cost of technological obsolescence when this equipment becomes outdated. In addition, staff must be trained. This investment of time and staff, of course, impacts on other institutional activities if the money and staff hours are being diverted from other projects.

The advantages of contracting the digitization project out to a vendor involve the expertise of the vendor and cost control. A qualified vendor will have readily available the expertise, equipment and staff to carry out the digitization project. And since there will be no start up-costs associated with equipment or training, the only costs incurred will be the negotiated cost per image. As described above, there may be cost savings that can be realized by outsourcing digitization.

The disadvantages of contracting out involve quality control, security, flexibility and subject matter expertise. The contracting institution will be one step removed from the imaging functions, and so there can be a reliance on the vendor to produce a quality product with limited supervision and oversight. If the source materials have to be sent to the vendor, there can be a risk to the security and preservation of the materials (especially fragile or three-dimensional materials). Though most vendors will be flexible as the project develops, typically the contracting institution is bound to the terms set in an original contract, and a new contract will have to be negotiated if the project changes its scope. There may be copyright considerations, as vendors do not have the same copyright and fair-use protections as non-profit organizations. Lastly, a vendor typically will not have the subject matter expertise of museum, library or archival staff, and therefore may not be sensitive to the needs of cultural heritage institutions. These are all ways in which outsourcing can expose the institution to additional risk.

These are all issues that will have to be negotiated at the outset of a project. Needs have to be clearly defined in all contractual materials, to obviate any problems. The vendors should also be evaluated as to their experience and understanding of cultural heritage materials, and the overall stability of the company in question (Kenney and Rieger, 2000).

Staffing and human resources factors

All aspects of human resources management must be considered at the planning stage of digitization initiatives, in order for directors and senior managers to develop an understanding of the impact of digitization on the organization and its human resources. This will include the following considerations:

- Who will oversee digitization initiatives?
- What kind of staff are needed and what sort of jobs will they do?
- What institutional support and leadership can they expect?
- Who will be responsible for the ongoing administration, outreach and preservation activities related to ongoing digital programme development?
- How will digitization affect changing staff roles and new service paradigms at the institution?

Unleashing the long-term potential of digital collections will require careful planning and attention to detail in the short term (W. Arms,

2000), and careful management of the human resources related to all aspects of the digitization life cycle will enable successful project development. It will also facilitate the subsequent transition to digital programmes. Thinking about the broader human resource issues will illustrate ways that developing digital collections can affect the entire institution by offering important opportunities for staff development, capacity building, and change management.

There are two areas that will have to be addressed. Firstly, who will be involved in the digitizing initiatives – who will scan the pages, collect the metadata, develop catalogue entries, design websites, etc.? The chances are that the majority of staff involved in this phase of digitization projects will be short-contract project staff, and the work may even be outsourced to a vendor. There will be a need to find appropriate staff to work on projects, and also to find staff to manage and evaluate their activities and progress.

Secondly, after the projects are complete, who will continue to manage the digital information that has been created as a result of digitization projects? Who will maintain access to the materials through updates to the organization's catalogues and websites? Who will train patrons and visitors to access the digital resources? Who will develop outreach programmes and educational tools which will continue to add value to the digital information many years after the original project has completed its objectives? If we are to anticipate that digital resources will become institutional assets, then it is necessary to consider the long-term human resource aspects (at all levels of the organization) of providing access to, and preserving, these assets. Librarians, archivists and curators, and their directors, will find themselves increasingly responsible for managing digital information.

The implementation of technological programmes throws into a sharp focus the fact that the information professions have changed dramatically in recent years. Digital information has augmented and sometimes replaced conventional forms at many institutions (W. Arms, 2000). The digital age is moving memory institutions into new paradigms of delivering both services and content, and library, archive and museum staff now have to advise patrons and visitors on the use of electronic catalogues, databases and electronic collections. The perceived value of information is no longer vested in its ownership, but in the trusted, value-added services of skilled information professionals to guide and direct the user in turning the overwhelming volume of electronic information into knowledge (UNESCO, 2002).

Technology has been introduced at all levels of administration and content delivery in 'Memory Institutions', who are faced with some users who demand the latest technologies immediately and other users who resist change and insist that traditional services (like the card catalogue) be maintained (W. Arms, 2000). It goes without saying that salaries for cultural heritage staff are still extremely low, despite the demands of new service models. Furthermore, museums have had to operate in a far more competitive environment than ever before, as pressure increases to develop 'headline' exhibits and to compete for paying visitors. Archives and libraries have increasingly had to cope with 'performance-based' reviews of their services – having to itemize and provide detailed accounts for all aspects of their services, and to increase opening hours and client numbers.

This process of transformation brings with it additional demands, and a need for staff development and training for both staff and managers in the use of new technologies and information management. Recognizing the training needs of staff who are faced with new roles and responsibilities, and providing training opportunities to support those involved in the creation and management of digital information, can be a crucial component of staff development and empowerment, and an opportunity to transform the challenges of changing roles and responsibilities into an opportunity (S. Smith, 1998). Digitization projects are complex, and it will be necessary to find staff to fulfil a complex rage of tasks, requiring an exceptional blend of skills and knowledge (TASI, 2002b). It will be important for the project manager to identify all tasks at the outset and to decide how best to allocate staff to carry them out. This will require assessing whether the work can be done by using existing staff at the institution, outsourcing to vendors or by hiring new staff.

Developing teams to work on digitization projects is another area where collaborative and consortia-based projects with other institutions can be advantageous, especially when forming partnerships with 'early adopters' for capacity building (UNESCO, IFLA and ICA, 2002).

The following list outlines all of the functions related to the creation, and subsequent long-term management, of digital collections. It will be necessary to find staff to undertake some or all of these activities throughout the development of digitization initiatives:

1   Project management. The responsibilities associated with this include:
    —   managing digitization projects and staff
    —   fundraising and grant writing
    —   managing budgets
    —   writing job descriptions, hiring staff
    —   setting goals and targets
    —   writing documentation and reports.
2   Selection, evaluation and preparation of original materials, including:
    —   selecting materials, in association with subject specialists, e.g. curators or faculty
    —   conservation assessment of originals
    —   preservation handling or treatment where necessary
    —   preparing objects for digitization, including encapsulation or de-encapsulation, packing in acid-free containers where necessary
    —   transport to the digitization centre
    —   creating basic catalogue records or tracking lists where necessary
    —   evaluating the copyright status of originals.
3   Digitization activities:
    —   digital capture – scanning or digital photography
    —   technical operation of digitization hardware and software
    —   applying file formats, and naming conventions
    —   metadata creation and management
    —   cataloguing and indexing digital objects
    —   monitoring of digitization procedures and performing of quality assessment
    —   documenting digitization guidelines for other project staff or volunteers.

4 Technical support:
- creation or implementation of technical systems for creating, managing or delivering the digital material
- systems and network support
- hardware support and maintenance
- software installations, upgrades and licensing.

5 Post-digitization activities:
- developing delivery mechanisms and finding aids
- graphic design and authoring
- manipulating the images post-scanning
- webserver and administrative technical expertise
- implementation of online marketing strategies, digital rights management and e-commerce where appropriate
- evaluation, dissemination and learning resource creation.

6 Long-term management of digital resources:
- preservation and archiving of digital objects
- instruction and end-user support
- migration of digital assets where necessary.

This broad scope of activities implies the involvement of people from many different backgrounds – academic faculty, IT experts, librarians, curators, cataloguers and preservation experts. Interrelated skills may also be necessary: for example scholars investigating advanced imaging will have to understand image analysis software and related hardware; evaluation experts will need experience in online assessment and evaluation of computer interfaces. Boundaries between the various tasks can also be blurred by local factors, including where digitization takes place (for example, will fragile materials be allowed to leave the special collections room?) and the time, staff and resources available to the project.

Finding and retaining specialist project staff

Developing digital collections and getting projects off the ground is contingent upon finding staff with an ever-expanding array of special skills, prepared to work for the lower salaries offered in the cultural heritage sector. There is an increasing expectation that people who will work on these projects have to be 'chameleons', able to adapt their skills to new technologies and work environments. Often, project budgets will cover only one or two dedicated staff, so institutions will try to combine as many roles for that person as possible (as evidenced by the inevitable job adverts seeking 'Applicants for the post of web designer/XML programmer/English professor. . . '). This is especially the case in smaller museums and archives, where one designated 'technology person' can find themselves responsible for every aspect of technology in the institution: fixing hardware, writing grant applications, digitizing artifacts, developing websites and even administering databases associated with staff salaries and ticketing. This workload is not merely frustrating for the staff in question, but short sighted from the institutional perspective, as even if one person can be found who is capable of doing a large number of these tasks, it is not always advisable to rely too much on one person. What will happen to these services if this polymath leaves, or is promoted to a new position?

The skills and talents that are required for digitization projects, including familiarity with technology, web design and managing systems, are also much in demand in the lucrative commercial sector. In times of economic plenty, it is difficult for non-profit cultural heritage institutions to hire and retain technical staff, who are often lured away by the siren call of higher salaries (for example, a systems analyst working on Wall Street can earn a salary well in excess of $100k per annum). During the dot.com boom, it was extremely hard to appoint and retain staff on university, library and museum salaries. In times of economic hardship, however, the relative job security and professional development opportunities afforded by working in the heritage sector make it more likely that staff will stay. The downside is that, in times of extreme fiscal uncertainty, staff on 'soft money' are especially vulnerable, as programmes may come to an end when fixed-term contracts expire. As this book is being written, a US recession has led to dramatic budget cuts for state institutions. Libraries and universities have been especially hard hit, with hiring freezes imposed on many institutions and redundancies threatened at others. Situating digitization activities as a core component of the institutional mission, with clearly stated imperatives and goals, will not eradicate this sense of instability completely, but will make such initiatives less of a 'fringe' or 'boutique' activity. Involving collections directors, senior curatorial and preservation staff as key stakeholders will all contribute to this sense of institutional buy-in. Creating long-term digital 'programmes' rather than short-term 'projects' will make it easier to attract staff, and make it less likely that highly trained, experienced staff will be lost to the institution at the end of a short-term contract.

Developing digitization skills in existing staff

While there will be a need to find some new specialized staff for digitization projects given the concerns outlined above – as well as practical issues such as hiring freezes and layoffs at some institutions – an alternative to trying to find an unrealistic array of skills in one person is to augment the skills of the core project staff by combining or splitting posts with other projects (or even institutions), or using the skills of additional categories of staff from elsewhere in the institution. Digitization initiatives can present valuable opportunities for staff development and it is important not to overlook existing staff:

> Digital projects require new skills. Project planning should allow time to teach current staff new technologies. Even if an outside vendor completes a project, or new staff are hired specifically to work on a digital project, permanent staff should at least learn the basic theories and practices of digitization. Institutions often hire short-term staff for digitization projects which can result in the loss of digital expertise when the project ends.
>
> (Jones, 2001)

Presently, existing library and curatorial staff are rarely involved in digitization to any significant degree, except in digital photography and metadata creation (NINCH, 2002), but developing digitization skills in existing inquisitive and highly motivated staff is an opportunity to invest in, empower and develop the skills of existing staff, and thus build the human resource capacity of the organization. Training permanent staff in all aspects of digitization will also make it easier to establish integrated, digital programme development – if, for example, preservation staff can move seamlessly from advising one digital project to advising another within the same institution.

Some library digitization policies now actively encourage this strategy. For example, the National Library of Australia digitization policy states that 'digitization will be integrated with routine, mainstream and ongoing activities in the library', and that scanning should either be outsourced or undertaken by library staff, who will be supported and trained in all such activities (National Library of Australia, 2003). The training of personnel to perform these functions requires a coordinated approach within an institution, and potentially across many institutions (S. Smith, 1998). The European Union's DigiCULT recommendations state that:

> Cultural institutions should put human resources development high on their priorities list: set measures to speed up the transfer, integration of knowledge into professional training and develop special courses for key areas such as digital management and preservation.
>
> (Mulrenin and Geser, 2001)

Fortunately, it is now possible to find excellent educational opportunities specifically aimed at cultural heritage staff who are new to digitization. A few examples of some short, inexpensive (certainly compared to commercial training rates) courses available include the following:

* The Northeastern Document Conservation Center (NEDCC) offers the School for Scanning series (www.nedcc.org/).
* Cornell University Library's Department of Preservation and Conservation, home of the popular Moving Theory into Practice series, is to offer a course on digital preservation starting in Autumn 2003 (www.library.cornell.edu/preservation/workshop/).
* The EU-funded project SEPIA (Safeguarding European Photographic Images for Access) has provided a central point for resources about digital imaging. Although this project will officially end in Autumn 2003, many of their training materials will still be available (www.knaw.nl/ecpa/sepia/events.html).
* At the University of Glasgow, the Humanities Advanced Technology and Information Institute (HATII) offers a summer school on digitization for cultural heritage professionals (www.hatii.arts.gla.ac.uk/SumProg/).

- The Technical Advisory Service on Images (www.tasi.ac.uk/) also offers short courses at various locations in the UK.

With regard to basic qualifications, initiatives such as the European Computer Driving Licence (www.ecdl.com/) can play a role in continuing professional development. This is an information technology qualification that verifies a person's competence, declares their computer skills and improves employability within business and across the European Union. European employers and job seekers all agree on the need for this standard definition of practical competence in IT.

However, it must be established that other programmes will not suffer if staff are engaged in digitization activities – time allocation is very important (hence the need for senior managers to establish priorities).

It is tempting – and may even appear easier – to invest in technology rather than people (Deegan and Tanner, 2002), and to focus on finding new, external staff who come pre-packaged with all the available skills. However, fostering such internal staff development and creating new professional opportunities is simply a matter of investing in the most valuable resource an institution can have – its staff, who will have developed a unique and exhaustive understanding of the organization's collections, users and mission through years of service.

Moreover, the task of managing long-term access to the digital resources will probably fall on core staff of an institution long after digitization projects are completed. It is, therefore, best that they become familiar with electronic resources: 'In the digital Information Age, librarians will have to foreground their information management roles in relation to their physical custodial role' (Deegan and Tanner, 2002).

Other sources of expertise

It may be possible to look to other sources of staffing and expertise for digitization projects.

Faculty and subject specialists: in a university or academic setting, every opportunity should be taken to foreground faculty involvement in the selection, editing and digitization of materials for digital libraries or archives. An example of a successful collaboration between academic faculty and library staff in developing digitization projects can be seen at the University of Virginia, where both the Institute for Advanced Technology in the Humanities (IATH) and the Electronic Text Center became a focus for a model of collaboration that models a different type of relationship between content-builders and collection-users (Unsworth, 2000).

Students with temporary placements at archives and museums are often deployed for all aspects of technology integration. At universities, it can sometimes be possible to arrange academic credit rewards for students engaged in high-profile digitization projects; for example the University of Virginia Library's Electronic Text Centre has a very competitive Graduate Associate initiative for postgraduate students assisting the project. The University of Florida's Caribbean Newspaper Imaging used student assistants to perform the bulk of tasks.

Many libraries and museums have a formal *volunteer* programme in place, and this can be another potential pool of staff for various aspects of digitization projects, with careful management and a sensitivity to the fact that volunteers are giving their labour for no financial reward. The Virginia Historical Inventory programme at the Library of Virginia successfully relied on volunteer labour to help with many aspects of their project until permanent staff were allocated to the project.

Members of the *project's steering* or *advisory group* may also be asked to provide specialized expert advice and guidance in some specialized areas: as a matter of course, as many stakeholders as possible should be included in the project's steering committee. As a pragmatic approach, consider including subject experts and assessment experts on the project's steering committee, as well as senior IT staff in order to broker IT support. Steering groups are at their most effective when they are international, or multidisciplinary, such as the Forced Migration Online project team, which has brought together a collaborative team of partners representing all aspects of the project, both technical and subject based (see the project partners' web page at www.forcedmigration.org/partners/).

Staff and management of internal *information technology services* and computing centres can also provide assistance for some aspects of the project, such as network and systems support, maintaining servers, back-up systems, long-term digital access and maintenance, etc. Even if such an organization has a fee-for-service arrangement, this is worth investigating to see if it can make a human resources saving for the project. It is a good idea to cultivate and develop relationships with IT professionals as a matter of course: as we shall see below, boundaries between content specialists and IT professionals are becoming increasingly artificial and counter-productive at many institutions (NINCH, 2002).

The changing professions

Training existing staff and management to work on digitization projects is a key component of change management within the institution. The digital age is moving memory institutions into new paradigms of delivering both services and content, and this process of transformation brings with it a need for development and training for both staff and managers to gain knowledge and experience in managing information resources in the mixed environment of digital and traditional resources. Similarly, there will need to be a focus on re-developing academic preparation for those entering cultural heritage professions to reflect this shift (Marcum, 1998).

Digitization of collections and the provision of public access to electronic resources has had a significant impact on all aspects of memory institutions. As digital information augments and sometimes replaces conventional forms, priorities and roles for both staff and managers in the information professions are changing (W. Arms, 2000). The changes that technology has brought to cultural heritage organizations have been so profound that we literally cannot envision what museums, libraries and archives will look like in 50 years' time. This was not the case 50 years ago, when people entering these professions had a reasonable expectation that their jobs would be fairly unchanged throughout their working lives. But in spite of uncertainty about the details, we can be fairly sure that it will prove necessary for staff and management at every level of the institution to develop an understanding of, and familiarity with, the skills required to support digital programmes and digital collections. Digitization initiatives provide an important opportunity for institutions to develop institutional capacities that will enable them to manage this change. A key component of this will be visible leadership that encourages staff development and acknowledges that bold steps must be taken by senior managers to empower their staff:

> It may also be necessary to analyze interactions within the organizational culture for obstacles related to territoriality, a lack of informed managerial support, and fear of change within the line of management, including technophobic barriers to technological innovation. These issues are often underestimated. The functional units of organization within the institution may need to be deconstructed to enable change by focusing less on procedures and more on common goals of providing an information service. It is inevitable that existing lines of authority and responsibility will be relaxed.
>
> (UNESCO, IFLA, ICA, 2002)

For example, at many organizations, there are rigidly enforced and maintained physical and cultural barriers between library and curatorial staff and IT professionals. This is despite the fact that memory organizations are increasingly dependent upon reliable technological infrastructures to support online catalogues, records management and circulation records. Increasingly, 'IT managers bear a significant responsibility for the stewardship of heritage assets' (Price and Smith, 2000). The objectives of IT managers and collections managers are increasingly similar and interdependent, and compartmentalization of these roles is increasingly undesirable for both sides. There is also a need for common vocabularies to enable better communication: collections managers must be adept at translating technical information and implementing the recommendations of computing professionals, and IT staff will have to make some of their work methods and procedures less opaque. In terms of acquiring another perspective on the changes brought by technology, computing professionals have always experienced dramatic changes in their jobs: in the last 20 years, mainframes have been replaced with distributed systems, new programming languages have emerged, and new methodologies for almost all aspects of computing have appeared. Even the most senior staff have always had to re-tool and re-train where necessary. This is an area where the 'two cultures' can benefit from each other's experiences.

Changing academic preparation for cultural heritage staff

Although helpful, five-day workshops and assiduous reading of *D-Lib Magazine* alone will not redevelop the core competencies of cultural heritage professionals. It is necessary to give serious thought to how the professional training available to archivists, curators and librarians can be significantly altered in order to reflect the changes in their professions. This is increasingly essential for small organizations, which will have only a few staff. These institutions are being left behind in the digital revolution, since they have neither the resources nor the staff capacity to re-train staff:

> As a curator in a small institution, I feel the lack of employee expertise in technological areas is one of the most pressing problems for adoption of new technologies.
>
> (An interview in Mulrenin and Geser, 2002)

In 'Developing digitization skills in existing staff' above, we looked at short courses specific to digitization. In addition, a growing number of institutions offering training in librarianship, archival and museum studies are recognizing this technological shortfall in their staff and re-organizing professional training for librarians, archivists and curators to address the need for courses and programmes in creating and administering digital resources. Notable among these institutions are the library schools at the University of Michigan and the University of Illinois at Champaign Urbana, and the School of Library, Archive and Information Studies at University College London. Museums studies programmes at New York University, Harvard and Berkeley now offer training in creating and administering digital resources. The School of Information Management and Systems at Berkeley has gone even further, offering PhD and Masters programmes in the 'emerging discipline' of information management. The School hopes that its graduates will take up diverse leadership roles, as information architects, database managers, security engineers, web designers, project managers, usability specialists, knowledge managers and librarians.

Such programmes represent a fairly recent development, and furthermore, technology changes so rapidly that skills learned in college will soon become obsolete. What is more important than acquiring a particular skill set is having an enthusiasm for learning, curiosity about new technologies and interest in keeping up with new developments (Deegan and Tanner, 2002).

Management of change and change management

Senior managers and directors of museums, national libraries and archives, like managers of most similarly sized commercial organizations, were mostly educated before computing technologies became ubiquitous, and certainly before the advent of the world wide web. Their professional training pre-dated the information age, and the speed and all-embracing uptake of technology has challenged managers to anticipate the changes and to adapt themselves and their organizations appropriately. The successful transition to the online world and to new business models, enterprises and collaborations imposed by technology will depend to a large extent on the degree to which managers are able to re-tool and acquire new skill sets where necessary in order to incorporate technology into their organizational vision. Management issues affected by technology will include the redeployment of human and physical resources, budgeting for digitization, staff training, acquisition and maintenance of new equipment, systems implementation, the preservation of digital objects, prioritizing what to digitize, and maintaining current projects (S. Smith, 1998).

CLIR has partially addressed the question of how to educate information professionals and potential leaders of digital libraries and provide training in new disciplines and techniques related to managing information resources by developing the Frye Leadership Institute, an advanced, interdisciplinary workshop based on the assumption that the emerging framework within which cultural heritage institutions are creating digital resources is an environment where librarians, information technologists, university press directors and database creators will have to work collaboratively. The Institute addresses all aspects of information management, including academic, technological, economic, public-policy, student and constituent-relations dynamics. One of its goals is 'the blurring of the formerly distinct boundaries among teaching, research, information management, and scholarly communication; and the extension of information resources, and services beyond the walls of traditional organizations (such as libraries, computer centers, and museums) to permeate the educational enterprise'. (For more information, see the Frye Institute website: www.fryeinstitute.org/).

These new responsibilities to inspire and drive digital initiatives, coupled with the existing responsibilities of managers, have given senior managers at many institutions cause to contemplate any generous early retirement packages which may be on offer (W. Arms, 2000). However, there are many organizations and fora for collaborative development and exchange of ideas. The Coalition for Networked Information has regular workshops aimed at senior managers, as does the Digital Library Federation. Many EU initiatives also provide access to training and professional development in appropriate areas that will minimize the burden of change and maximize the efficiency of the transition, such as registries of projects, workshops on risk management and copyright, national and international best practice case studies, and registries of ongoing projects.

The Association for Research Libraries also offers training sessions as part of its Library Leadership for New Managers programme (www.arl.org/training/institutes/managers.html).

Risk management and project planning

Any digitization initiative will necessitate a significant institutional investment. All projects that involve new activities and methods will have elements of risk associated with them, and anticipating and managing areas of risk and uncertainty will be necessary at every stage of the project: pre-project planning, selection of materials, digitization and long-term stewardship of digital assets. Developing strategies to manage risks at the outset of a project will empower the information manager and provide tools to make the decision process easier at each stage.

A key component of project planning and management is identifying and analysing areas of potential risk (risk assessment) and using this information to develop and implement plans to respond to and minimize risk (risk management). Risk is defined as 'an implication of the existence of significant uncertainty about the level of project performance achievable' which may be 'upside (welcome) or downside (unwelcome)'. Risk involves both threats and opportunities: a threat is a source of downside risk, with synonyms like hazard or outage. An opportunity is a source of upside risk (Chapman and Ward, 1997). One of the goals of risk management is to maximize the results of positive events and minimize the consequences of adverse ones.

It will also be necessary to examine the risks of not doing something – what are the informational losses if decaying materials are not digitized? What is the loss to institutional prestige if there are no online collections available? What are the costs to staff development of not developing digital collections? Once a digitization path is undertaken, what are the cultural changes to the institution and its mission that may be effected? Is digitization reversible? Are the effects of the digitization process reversible? Is this a treasure chest or Pandora's box?

There is a growing body of literature concerning risk management, mostly from the perspective of managing business processes and audits, as well as computer science where this is a key concept informing software development workflows and processes. A very helpful general guide is Chapman and Ward, *Project Risk Management: processes, techniques and insights*, 1997, a qualitative and quantitative guide for managers working with a changing portfolio of projects. There are few specific guidelines for risk management in cultural heritage. However, two excellent publications from the Council on Library and Information Resources (CLIR) have examined this issue:

- *Risk Management of Digital Information: a file format investigation* by Gregory W. Lawrence et al. (2000) is a risk assessment model which also deals with the preservation of digital formats.
- *Managing Cultural Assets from a Business Perspective*, by Laura Price and Abby Smith (2000) is a risk assessment model for evaluating and managing the collections of the Library of Congress within a

business framework, making explicit for financial decision makers the relationship between the library's assets and its mission.

Risk management plans can be developed locally by examining the available literature and developing models such as the one suggested below to fit local conditions. Processes for developing risk management plans are discussed below. It is also possible to purchase software tools which can provide a detailed analysis of the likelihood of identified risks occurring, such as OPERA (part of the Open Plan Professional system). There are also many consulting firms and agencies who can be contracted to develop such plans, and this may well be advisable if the project stakes are particularly high.

> Planning is an unnatural process; it is much more fun to do something. The nicest thing about not planning is that failure comes as a complete surprise, rather than being preceded by a period of worry and depression.
> (Sir John Harvey-Jones, quoted in Tanner, 2001b)

There can be a reluctance in the cultural heritage community to develop risk management tools and embrace this type of planning. The whole process may seem overly business oriented, or it may even be perceived as an unduly negative activity. This is ironic considering that risk is simply an extension of resource management, an area in which library, archive and museum managers have had to develop a great deal of expertise – especially the management of sparse resources to squeeze the maximum activities and resources out of dwindling budgets. If risk management is seen as a core component of resource management, it can be defined as an important and positive part of the conventional planning process. Not addressing the likelihood of unexpected or negative events at the outset means that when such events occur, they will require crisis management. It is also important not just to focus on the downside risk, or threats. An aim of improving performance implies a wide perspective and the potential to identify and exploit favourable possibilities, which might be considered upside risks, or opportunities. Planning and risk management should be proactive, not just reactive. Re-phrasing project objectives to identify potential areas of weakness or problems, and setting clear objectives and performance criteria, will enrich the whole process of managing project objectives. Effective risk management will influence planning and design and may influence the motives for key decisions.

There are four phases of risk management:

- defining and identifying risk factors, and their probability and impact
- assessing and measuring the likelihood and consequence of risks
- identifying controls and contingency plans to manage risks and opportunities
- monitoring risk factors as an ongoing process (Price and Smith, 2000).

These phases are outlined in detail below.

Defining and identifying risk factors

A general analysis of the risks associated with a digitization project should be performed at an early stage to identify them and scope their potential impact. Managers will require support and direction in identifying risks associated with their institution's digitization process that require application of risk management procedures (S. Smith, 1998). They will also benefit from expert advice if it is appropriate or possible to bring in a consultant with experience in identifying and managing risks. Most importantly, project managers will benefit from the collective experience of colleagues elsewhere in the cultural heritage community who have addressed such issues with regard to earlier projects: anecdotal evidence of both successes and failures are invaluable (Unsworth, 1997).

Risk management plans should be developed based on the unique nature of the institution's collections and the nature of the audience using them. Few institutions can afford to do everything perfectly: it is important to be aware of potential risks and the impact they may have, now and in the future, and to have mechanisms in place to reduce risk where possible.

Types of risk factor to watch out for will include:

- material risk factors
- project completion and workflow risk factors
- institutional risk factors.

Who can identify and influence risk factors?

The wise project manager will bring together as many people as possible who will be able to identify project risk factors. This group should do a brainstorming exercise about all aspects of the project that might be compromised by internal or external factors. The group should include department managers, project managers and staff, as all will have valuable input. While curators and collections librarians will be able to advise on risks related to the collections, it will be equally important to talk to administrative staff about potential delays or problems with the institutional purchasing systems. For example, many organizations will have accounting and purchasing systems that are slow to approve 'big-ticket' items. When purchasing computer equipment, a delay of a few weeks might mean losing a negotiated discount (which would be an unwelcome risk), or the opportunity to purchase an upgraded or enhanced system at a lower cost (which would be a welcome risk). Regardless of whether the outcome is positive or negative, the most important thing is that either option should be anticipated and managed. Doing a pre-digitization risk assessment may have wider implications, as it can uncover other areas where the collection or institution is exposed to risk, by uncovering issues such as inadequate cataloguing of collections, inappropriate storage of originals or poor IT support. This consultative process should take place at the beginning of a project, and at regular intervals as things change and the project matures.

Material risk factors

There will be potential risk factors associated with the objects to be digitized. These include the following:

- *Copyright status* of the originals and licensing of digital objects – can this be managed?

- *Fragility* of original objects – will they be damaged or compromised by digitization? Is conservation treatment required?
- *Accessibility* of objects to be digitized – where are they located? Do they have to be disbound, removed from storage or transported to the digitization site?

Project completion and workflow risk factors

Assessing the project plan, it will be possible to address the following areas of risk:

- *Staff*: do they have the requisite knowledge, skills and training for all aspects of the project? Are the right mix of people and skills employed on the project? What is the perception of key staff of the importance of digitization to the institution? Will this affect the balance of staff, or the priorities of the institution?
- *Time*: how much time is available? Is it sufficient? Does it allow for any delays?
- *Budget*: is the funding allocated appropriate?
- *Workflow*: are there any additional steps that might have to be added, such as scanning from microfilm rather than originals?
- *Space and equipment*: are they appropriate for the project? Is there over- or under-capacity in either area?
- Long-term management: what is the provision for storage medium, migration of digital objects and permanent access to digital objects? Are data standards employed?
- *External factors*: does the project rely on external factors or stakeholders, such as steering committees, suppliers or members of project consortia?
- *Innovation or novelty*: does the project involve new and innovative work or systems and equipment?

Institutional risk factors

- *Support*: does this project fit within an institutional digitization policy? Are such initiatives supported or encouraged by senior management? Is centralized IT support available?

- *Networks*: what is the institutional network and systems capacity?
- *Preservation*: is there a long-term commitment to preserve and maintain digital projects?
- *Reputation*: will this project significantly raise the profile of the organization? Is there tolerance for failure?

Assessing and measuring the likelihood and consequence of risks

Having identified project risk factors, measuring risk is a two-step process. First, develop a risk probability scale for various threats and opportunities. The scale should grade risks as high, medium or low, as indicated by Lawrence et al. (2000):

Very low	probability estimated below 1%
Low	probability estimated between 1 and 5%
Moderate	probability of between 6 and 10%
High	probability estimated between 11 and 25%
Very high	probability estimated between 26 and 99%.

Then, develop a risk impact scale adapted to the possible outcomes and impact or risk. The following is modified from Lawrence et al.'s risk impact scale for preservation and migration of data, but the impact will very much vary according to the nature of the project and the level of exposure or impact for each risk:

Catastrophic	irreversible negative impact
Very serious	partially irreversible impact
Serious	significant impact, with possibility of reconstructing parts of project
Significant	partial impact, with certainty of reconstructing parts of project
Minor	partial impact, with certainty of recovery.

This information can be represented in a table showing the probability and impact of risk (see Figure 4.1). The values of a risk impact scale will be subjective, and dependent on local assumptions and priorities. For example, a risk that glass slides may break may be con-

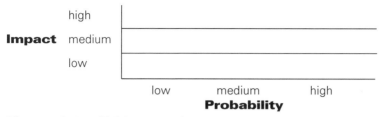

Figure 4.1   Risk impact scale

sidered an acceptable risk, as this is not a new problem for working with this format. However, a risk that strong lighting required for scanning might damage a watercolour may be slight, but considered to have such a high impact that it would be unacceptable. It will also be essential to ensure that all participants in a project (including outside vendors) have the same understanding of the significance of various risk factors.

Within this scale, managers will have to decide the level of risk that is tolerable or intolerable for their institution and project. For example, there may be a very low possibility that exposure to light will damage a rare or fragile object, but because of the value of the object, this risk is considered catastrophic. Similarly, there may be a high risk that disbinding a brittle volume will cause pages to be damaged, but because the institution has decided to discard volumes post digitization, or has many additional copies, this may be considered a minor risk.

Within the scope of the risk management process, things that are considered to be opportunities or benefits should also be included. For example, these may include situations like coming in under budget, and having to decide what to do with unexpected additional funds. Staff may be very efficient and finish a section of the project ahead of time – should they continue with the next phase, or diversify, say by doing additional research, or spending more time on another aspect, e.g. web design? Similarly, if there is equipment downtime, can computers, scanners or other systems be used by other projects? If these results are unanticipated, they may have negative consequences. Slack time might mean that staff seek alternative employment.

Identifying controls and contingency plans to manage risks and opportunities

A risk management policy should have two elements:

- *policies* and *work methods* that will reduce risk where possible or desirable
- *control mechanisms* and *risk management policies* for intervention when necessary.

Decisions taken at the outset of a project can reduce risk; for example, selecting materials that are in the public domain to avoid copyright concerns, working with microfilm rather than original materials to avoid damage to originals, not purchasing proprietary software systems or cutting-edge, untested equipment, and following community-wide best/good practice for image capture and dissemination. It may also be possible to limit exposure to risks by sharing risks with other institutions or partners, or even to transfer risks. Working within a consortium with multiple partners to develop projects can be effective in this regard – areas in which one organization is particularly strong (e.g. conservation, digital photography) can be shared accordingly. On all projects, internal workflow systems can also be developed to minimize risk, such as approaching digitization as a series of smaller, controllable sub-projects. Good quality-control procedures at each stage of digitization will also avoid replication of errors and detect any need for training for staff or equipment modification.

For risks that occur as part of the ongoing digitization process, management will have to introduce mitigating control activities and contingency plans. Good project management will incorporate risk management automatically into the workflow and prioritize risk management efforts based on the potential impact of the risk. Good practice in planning will include management input and collaboration, such as setting milestones and implementing change control processes. This involves general responses to pervasive sources of risk such as human error, omissions, communications failures and so on (Chapman and Ward, 1997). Some risks can be overcome by changes in policies or procedures, whereas others may require additional financial or personnel resources (Price and Smith, 2000). For example, digitizing fragile materials may require that all activities are supervised by conservation staff, which will add an additional personnel cost to a project. Delays resulting from clearing copyright permissions or equipment breakdown will require that staff are re-deployed on other activities in order to avoid downtime. New equipment may have to be purchased for such activities.

Some controls will have benefits that outweigh the costs – delays on one aspect of a project can be an opportunity to spend more time on other aspects, and equipment failure can enable creativity and new solutions: for example, an equipment failure may present an opportunity to purchase newer, more suitable systems, or to develop improved methodologies for backing up data.

Monitoring risk factors as an ongoing process

Risk management is the sum of all activities directed towards acceptably accommodating the possibility of failure in a project, and this will have to be monitored for the entire life cycle of the project, including the creation of the digital content and the subsequent stewardship of the digital assets which have been created (Beamsley, 1999).

Quality assurance mechanisms for all stages of the project will help to monitor progress and control risks, but controls are only effective if they are implemented and tested from time to time to ensure that they are still effective. This monitoring process will also involve checking the control mechanisms and contingency plans themselves. Are they still effective? Have institutional considerations or changes in technology made them redundant? Managers may have to decide to override controls. The focus of monitoring activities will also change as the project matures, and ultimately they will be concerned with preservation and long-term maintenance of digital resources, an area where most digital assets are at risk. Controls will include strategies to address issues such as server names changing leading to URLs that provide embedded links to the collection no longer working. Copyright controls of the digital objects will also have to be monitored, as will the ability to assign or withhold assignment of use rights to others. Continual vigilance is required to manage and monitor 'meaningful and useful mediated access to the collections' (Beamsley, 1999).

Conclusion

Evaluating the institutional framework will ensure that digitization initiatives bring benefits to the institution as a whole: by enhancing collections, training staff and increasing the profile of the institution. Implementing a digitization strategy based on the considerations outlined in this chapter will make this process easier, and introduces the idea of project management as a function of overall resource management. Investing in digitization requires a commitment to maintaining a technical and institutional infrastructure that will continue to enable access to resources created. Digital projects require a large investment of time and money, and at this point we can look to very few cost-effective examples of digitization initiatives.

Good planning at the outset is essential, but it will be necessary to contemplate future strategies and costs for migration and long-term storage and management of digital content. Approaching digitization with caution, or investigating potential, does not make one a Luddite. Far from it – it is only by investigating all aspects of new technology, both negative and positive, and rigorously assessing their uses, that one can thoroughly define what these technologies can bring to the advancement of scholarship and research. Only by educating ourselves about what can go wrong, and anticipating certain disappointments that may occur, can we truly take advantage of new technologies (Webb, 2000). Developing detailed project plans, feasibility studies and prototype projects, as described in Chapter 6 on project planning and funding, will also illustrate the implications of the digitization process in a more concrete way.

5

The importance of collaboration

Introduction

As the scope and potential of digitization around the world expands, the importance of collaboration is becoming clearer. Partnerships between individuals and organizations to co-ordinate activities, programmes, and products can be beneficial to all involved. Collaboration is increasingly regarded by funders as a desirable goal, and may even be a requirement for obtaining some types of grant support. This chapter will examine:

- opportunities for collaboration
- some frameworks and initiatives that support collaboration, including national policies, national and international partnerships
- the development of shared support organizations.

Libraries, archives and museums have a long tradition of working together. There are areas in which no organization, regardless of its size, can be entirely self-sufficient. Consequently, shared working practices have emerged, including interlibrary loan arrangements, and programmes to lend collection items to other institutions for exhibitions. Similarly, strategies and paradigms for digital partnerships are emerging. Collaborative arrangements with partner institutions for the acquisition and management of electronic information resources or software can often result in lower prices and savings in terms of time and staff. Resources have emerged to support such initiatives, including Liblicense, which presents guidelines and suggestions on developing licences for electronic contract (www.library.yale. edu/~llicense/index.shtml). Similarly, the Canadian National Site Licensing Project (www.cnslp.ca/) has developed guidelines and model licence agreements to facilitate the procurement of electronic resources.

Advantages

As organizations become 'hybrid institutions', delivering analogue as well as digital resources, internal collaborations are becoming necessary at all levels of the institution. Boundaries are disappearing, as the delivery of electronic resources involves stakeholders from many departments: faculty, librarians, information technologists, academic administrators and others (Lippincott, 1996). Similarly, strategic collaborations can be a key to the success of digitization initiatives. Such collaborations can be internal and external: with other cultural heritage institutions, with private corporations or imaging vendors, or with other external agencies such as technical support organizations or shared repositories, such as the Technical Advisory Service for Images or the Arts and Humanities Data Service; they can be local, regional, national or international. These partnerships are driven by the collections and economic aspects of resource building, and a need to leverage individual investments in digital infrastructure and staff (Renoult, 2000). Further, as we see a move away from isolated, experimental digital 'projects' to integrated digital library 'programmes', there is a perception that collaborative approaches to digitization are advantageous for all concerned. Such collaborations can avoid risk and increase the chances of project success. Some of the reasons for this are outlined below:

- Partnerships favour the definition and adoption of interoperable technical standards.
- Institutions can avoid duplication of effort. Sharing technical standards and best practices, and reducing the 'learning curve'

and ramp-up times can be the results of partnering with more experienced practitioners.

- Integrating collections and resources can build 'virtual' and re-unified collections. Consortial projects, with a variety of content, have the potential to reach larger and more disparate audiences, and can therefore achieve a greater breadth of educational goals. Shared metadata and delivery mechanisms mean improved resource discovery for users.
- Sharing the expertise of a larger number of experts, with greater and more comprehensive areas of expertise than a single institution can usually provide, increases the chances of success. There are opportunities for staff development, by partnering with 'early adopters' who can share their skills (UNESCO, IFLA, ICA, 2002).
- There can be cost savings from sharing costs on conversion by volume, as larger projects are more cost effective on a per-image basis.
- Collaboration can facilitate technology transfer, by developing opportunities for resource building and development for smaller and less financially stable institutions which do not have a great deal of technology infrastructure or expertise.
- Collaborative initiatives will increase opportunities for funding, as many granting agencies and foundations encourage collaborative initiatives, especially those that provide a basis for developing a shared information infrastructure, or 'global information network'. These are the sorts of benefits that are often invoked to justify public funding for digital initiatives (Renoult, 2000).

Particular areas of research that will lend themselves well to collaborative research and development projects were identified at a meeting held in 2001, the International Seminar on National Digital Cultural Content Creation Strategies. At this meeting, representatives of national and international cultural heritage digitization initiatives reviewed common issues and existing collaborative opportunities, and explored a number of areas for research, which can better be examined in a collaborative model. These include:

- technical standards and architectures

- usage surveys, market analysis, impact research and identification of user demand
- economic and business factors that inform the development of sustainability models
- assessment of the objectives, criteria and results of major content creation programmes
- assessment of the objectives, criteria and results of relevant major technical research programmes
- The establishment of national content creation policies to identify common, and pan-national, issues (Miller, Dawson and Perkins, 2001).

Frameworks for collaboration

Frameworks are emerging to support collaborative research and development, including the emergence of national strategies on the digitization of cultural heritage in the EU, Australia and New Zealand. Such strategies are, of course, easier to implement in smaller countries such as Denmark (for an overview of Danish Digital Library initiatives, see www.deflink.dk/), or countries such as Australia and New Zealand where the enormous geographic distances between some communities have created long traditions of distance education. National digitization strategies have many benefits. They allow funders to encourage consistency among digital resources, and to support standard frameworks for development and community-wide practice (Ross and Economou, 1998). The development of National Digital Libraries also provides an opportunity to involve traditionally excluded communities in the development of a shared national heritage, including indigenous populations and linguistic minorities (such as Gaelic-speaking communities in the UK).

The EU's DigiCULT report recommends that:

- National governments and regional authorities should formulate clear digitization programmes enabling cultural heritage institutions to formulate their own organizational digitization policies.
- Instead of funding individual digitization projects in separate Cultural Heritage institutions, governments should invest in comprehensive digitization programmes.

- National governments and regional authorities should build ongoing coordination initiatives for digitization programmes. They should strive to establish an information exchange infrastructure or interface connecting top-down initiatives vertically with regional initiatives, as well as horizontally with other member states.

(Mulrenin and Geser, 2001).

By recognizing that cultural heritage organizations should actively seek co-operation and partnership with other institutions in digitizing and managing cultural heritage resources, and building the infrastructures to support such initiatives, the DigiCULT Report (Mulrenin and Geser, 2001) echoes the Europe 2002 Action Plan (European Commission, 2000), which invites Member States and the Commission to 'create a co-ordination mechanism for digitization programmes across member states'. A European Commission report *Co-ordinating digitization in Europe* is now available (European Commission, 2003). This presents an overview of digitization funding, collaborations and strategic initiatives in all EU countries.

Although there are fewer national initiatives supporting digitization in the USA, and there is less of a trend for centralized initiatives than in Europe, there are encouraging signs. The US government has, for instance, funded the Institute of Museum and Library Studies (IMLS). In a recent report, this organization expressed its commitment to 'encourage collaboration among museums and libraries to develop digitized virtual collections of cultural heritage collections . . . IMLS will encourage partnerships and collaborative efforts through its grant programs' (IMLS, 2002).

Also in the USA, organizations such as Research Libraries Group (RLG), the Institute of Museum and Library Services (IMLS), and the Online Computer Library Center (OCLC) have all developed collaborative community building programmes. Lobbying groups such as the Council for Library and Information Resources (CLIR) and the Coalition for Networked Information (CNI) actively support the development of digital collaboration initiatives at a national level. CNI was particularly successful at facilitating collaborations between the Internet 2 initiative (www.internet2.org) and library and academic digital projects.

Making partnerships work

Though, as outlined above, collaborations can be hugely beneficial, there is a need to think strategically about them.

- What sort of partnerships will be advantageous: internal, external, with vendors or with other cultural heritage institutions?
- What sort of partnerships will assist in acquiring funding, building capacity, or building collections?
- What sort of support is necessary to make such collaborations work in practice?
- Are regular meetings required?
- If relying on electronic communication, what is the method most appropriate for all members of the partnership: e-mail, listservs, websites or instructional management systems like Blackboard or Web CT? Are these tools suitable for all parties – does every partner have web access, or easily accessible video conferencing suites, or the inclination to use such tools?
- Is it possible to identify when a partnership isn't working?
- What are the danger signs?
- Can difficulties be resolved?

Some of these concerns can be avoided by having agreements in place, carefully outlining defined objectives, as well as having an understanding of what each party is going to get out of the partnership.

Working in a consortium, or being part of a partnership, may mean little more in practice than having a shared funding agency, as project goals may be developed and concluded by each partner individually, giving them a great deal of autonomy. But it will often require developing close working relationships and delivering disparate parts of a project – to the same deadlines – across great divides of geography, language or discipline focus. Often, the technical development team will be in one location, and the content providers (and the actual digitization) may be elsewhere. In such cases, successful partnerships will require a great deal of communication, clearly defined roles and objectives, as well as shared goals. Technological tools can facilitate communication; more essential will be regular partnership meetings, including meetings with any advisory boards on an agreed schedule. It will be imperative that all sides talk to each other for the duration of the project – content developers and technical developers, or indeed any project partners, should not be estranged, and a good project manager will be key to bridging the 'knowledge gaps' and keeping the partnership functional without resorting to extreme measures like mediation. In a frank review of the collaboration that led to the development of the Blake Archive (when developers were based in California, North Carolina and New York as well as at IATH, The Institute for Advanced Technology in the Humanities, in Virginia), Morris Eaves describes collaboration as being about 'lots of things besides the division of labour, like reassurance in the face of technical panic' (Eaves, 1997). In order to assure success, it will be essential to agree the following points at the outset:

- the scope of the project, including selection of materials and degree of indexing and metadata to be accomplished, and when the project can be defined as 'finished'
- the legal framework within which the partnership will work – for example, who will have ownership of the various products produced as a result of this work?
- the roles and areas of responsibility for each institution – who will be responsible for managing databases, doing imaging, ensuring long-term preservation?
- the measurable objectives at key stages to ensure the partnership is progressing, and to evaluate success on completion
- common project goals including long-term preservation, maintenance and delivery of digital objects and their metadata (S. Smith, 2000).

Collaborative models

There are several paradigms for working collaboratively, often facilitated by granting opportunities, and the following outlines some examples of these approaches. They include consortia, national initiatives, international collaborations, registries and gateways. In addition the next section will look at support organizations and agencies that are available to certain constituencies and communities.

There are examples available too of hybrid projects, a good one of which is the Colorado Digitization Program (http://coloradodigital.coalliance.org/), which is both a gateway to digitization projects in Colorado and a support organization providing access to materials on all aspects of digitization.

In examining some case studies illustrating these models, we will see that some projects are collaborative at the outset, others become collaborations or partnerships throughout the life cycle of the project, while other projects have collaboration thrust upon them by outside agencies or by pragmatic considerations.

Consortia

Consortial projects are united by some common goal – they may have similar funding sources, or be digitizing similar content. Projects within consortia tend to work closely together – they will have common deadlines and objectives, may work to identical project management plans, and may even share staff. The most common objective for working within this sort of collaboration is to leverage strengths, collections and resources at disparate institutions. Collection materials will often complement and enhance each other.

The first Making of America project was conceived as a collaborative endeavour from the outset, bringing together the University of Michigan (http://moa.umdl.umich.edu/) and Cornell University (http://moa.cit.cornell.edu/moa/index.html) in a collaboration funded by the Andrew W. Mellon Foundation. The two organizations both held in their archives similar collections of 19th-century journals and monographs in brittle or fragile condition and wished to digitize these collections for both preservation and access. The project developed a thematically related digital library documenting American social history from the antebellum period through reconstruction (c. 1850–70). The two sites digitized different parts of the collection: Michigan focused on monographs in the subject areas of education, psychology, American history, sociology, science and technology and religion, while Cornell focused on the major serials of the period, ranging from general interest publications to those with more targeted audiences (such as agriculture serials). There was a strong mutual interest in digital as a format, and Cornell's experience with benchmarking and standards for digital imaging complemented Michigan's experience with online access provision based on their successes with putting page image collections – e.g. TULIP and JSTOR – online. The sites shared common workflows and standards, and developed a number of handbooks and publications on digitization for the benefit of other organizations.

Disparate projects related to the history and culture of Glasgow are accessible under the auspices of the Glasgow Digital Library consortium (http://gdl.cdlr.strath.ac.uk/). This is a 'virtual co-library' of the majority of publicly funded cultural heritage institutions in Glasgow that support teaching, learning and research at all levels in the city, bringing together material currently separated by ownership and physical location. It is building an archive of historical and cultural materials related to the history of Glasgow, centrally accessed through a shared website. Funding sources are varied, and the project is consolidating several existing resources.

In the UK, many collaborative projects have been funded under the UK's New Opportunities Fund Digitisation of Learning Materials programme (NOF-Digitise), a government-funded initiative to disburse money from the National Lottery's 'good causes' fund for the digitization of cultural heritage resources. An example of a collaboration funded under the NOF-Digitise initiative is the Am Baile (Gaelic Village) project (www.ambaile.org.uk/en/index.jsp). This is a collection of material, in both English and Gaelic, illustrating aspects of the language, culture and history of the Scottish Highlands and islands, and promoting an understanding of the *Gaidhealtachd* (Gaelic community). The project has developed content in a variety of media and from differing locations in the area. It has several partners:

- The Highland Council, the local authority for the area, co-ordinates the project's activities and develops content from archival materials and museum collections.
- The Taigh Chearsabhagh Trust, a local history and community arts trust, has responsibility for, among other things, the digitiza-

tion of the photographic archive and developing interactive and documentary materials.

- West Highland Animation, a Gaelic animation company, is developing animated films based on stories drawn from the whole range of Highland myths and legends, which are presented interactively on the Am Baile website. The films are aimed at children and Gaelic learners as well as the more serious user who can access, in Gaelic and English and text and audio form, the original materials from oral history records, on which the animations and interactive games and stories are based.

- Interactive Bureau Limited, a strategic partner, was contracted to design and build the bilingual website.

Under the NOF-Digitise programme, some projects had consortial arrangements thrust upon them. In certain cases, partnerships were imposed during the 'early assessment' phase for project proposals. Reviewers, with the benefit of a 'bird's eye view' of all the proposals, noticed that there were a number of related strands and ideas emerging across project proposals, which would lend themselves well to further collaboration. Projects were grouped into themed consortia, where groupings were intended to bring together bids addressing broadly similar themes or reflecting the character of a particular geographic area. The funders saw that good value for money could be achieved by eliminating duplication of effort, using economies of scale, and sharing experience and expertise. Such partnerships could deliver a managed body of content consistent with other major national initiatives, with greater potential for sustainability (www.nof-digitise.org/). These partnerships have turned out, in many cases, to be very beneficial.

National initiatives

Digitization initiatives are often set against the need to develop National Digital Libraries and digital records of a nation's heritage. These initiatives also manage and maintain records and provide information about what projects have been done in the past, as well as hosting papers on technical development and standards-based work. Such initiatives are often able to attract central government funds that have been earmarked for digitization. In the UK, such opportunities come from initiatives such as the UK Heritage Lottery Fund (www.hlf.org.uk), or, as we have seen above, from the New Opportunities Fund Digitisation of Learning Materials programme (http:/www.nof-digitise.org). Elsewhere, National Libraries are often funded to develop such resources (as has been the case at the US Library of Congress, or the National Archives and Records Association). A comprehensive overview of European initiatives can be found in Raitt (2000), and also in Cultivate Interactive, a publication that documents EU digitization projects: www.cultivate-int.org/. The recently published European Commission report (2003), inspired by the Lund principles calling for such a document, provides a detailed inventory of digitization funding, collaborations and strategic initiatives in all EU countries. This publication will be an important resource for understanding all aspects of EU-wide digitization and national priorities for the digitization of cultural heritage (www.minervaeurope.org/publications/globalreport.htm).

In the USA, the National Archives and Records Administration – Archival Research Center (www.archives.gov/) has developed a comprehensive digital collection of archival materials. It can be searched by means of the Archival Research Catalog (ARC), an online catalogue of NARA's nationwide holdings in the Washington DC area, regional archives and presidential libraries. The Archives include resources used for genealogical research, making this one of the most popular cultural heritage websites in the USA. NARA reports an average of 6.7 million hits per month, with 2.3 million hits per month, or one-third of the total, on the Exhibit Hall (where the digital collections have been organized into exhibits). Statistics show 46,000 search sessions per month, averaging 12 searches per session. This is compared to 6400 onsite researchers, 35,000 oral enquiries and 31,000 written enquiries per month for over 20 facilities nationwide.

The USA also hosts the National Science Digital Library (http://nsdl.org/). NSDL is a digital library of resource collections and services, organized in support of science education at all levels. Starting with a partnership of NSDL-funded projects, NSDL is emerging as a centre of innovation in digital libraries as applied to education, and a community centre for groups focused on digital-library-enabled science education. The National Science Foundation funds the project.

The National Library of Australia (www.nla.gov.au/) provides information on government policy regarding the information society, and maintains the Australia Libraries Gateway. This service aims to record and make accessible information about digitization projects undertaken by Australian cultural organizations. It also hosts Picture Australia (www.pictureaustralia.org/). This is a source of images in the collections of libraries, museums, galleries, archives, universities and other cultural agencies, in Australia and abroad. Interestingly, the front page of Picture Australia includes an advisory to indigenous Australians that the site may include images or names of people now deceased.

The National Library of New Zealand has an extensive collection of its holdings online as part of a digital library (www.natlib.govt.nz/en/digital/index.html). (This is not to be confused with the New Zealand Digital Library, at www.nzdl.org. This is a research programme at the University of Waikato aimed at developing the underlying technology for digital libraries, which is developing a publicly available set of digital library tools.)

International collaborations

The digital environment also supports international collaborations, which can be especially attractive to funders, and the following examples illustrate some of the benefits that make them so.

The African Online Digital Library (AODL; www.africandl.org/) is an American/African partnership to develop digital libraries and the technical infrastructure to support them. The project partners include several important research institutions in Africa, including L'Institut Fondemental d'Afrique Noire (IFAN), the largest repository of Francophone West African culture and civilization in Africa; the West African Research Centre/Centre de Recherche Ouest Africain (WARC/CROA); and the MATRIX project and African Studies Center at Michigan State University.

The goal of this digital repository is to adopt the emerging best practices of the digital library community and apply them to the

African projects. The goal of the project, which includes a large number of scholars and institutions, is to produce multilingual, multimedia materials for both scholarly research and public viewing audiences. AODL serves scholars and students conducting research into and teaching about West and South Africa as well as teachers and students of African languages in both the USA and Africa. It also provides a valuable model for creating and distributing a diverse array of materials in a region with limited electronic connectivity, and has engendered the creation of several spin-off collaborative projects, including the West African Digital Library Network (WADiLiN, to be found at www.warc-croa.org/main.htm, a comprehensive programme of digital library development in collaboration with Senegalese researchers, archivists and librarians. This programme is intended to serve as a model for the expansion of digital preservation activity to other countries in the region and assists in the creation of a network of mutually supportive cultural institutions engaged in the digitization of important documents from their collections, by providing West African cultural institutions with training and technical assistance to digitize collections and make them available online (Brandt and Ndoye, 2002).

Another international collaboration is UNESCO's Memory of the World project (http://portal.unesco.org/). This programme features a number of regional and inter-regional projects, which have been launched to showcase common themes and projects. These include Memoria de Iberoamerica, which displays materials relating to the 19th-century press. It includes collections from the national libraries of 12 countries: Brazil, Chile, Colombia, Costa Rica, Cuba, El Salvador, Mexico, Nicaragua, Puerto Rico, Peru, Portugal and Venezuela.

In 1998, the UK's Joint Information Systems Committee (JISC) collaborated with the US-based National Science Foundation (NSF) on an international partnership to create opportunities for research under the auspices of the International Digital Libraries Initiative (DLI). Six projects were funded for the period 1999–2002, with a total of £500,000 being allocated per annum to the UK project teams and the NSF giving the equivalent to the US projects. The goal of the programme was to enable users to easily access digital collections within a global information environment. Projects funded by the Initiative include:

- Cross-Domain Resource Discovery: Integrated Discovery and use of Textual, Numeric and Spatial Data, at the University of Liverpool and the University of California, Berkeley (http://cheshire.lib.berkeley.edu/index.html)
- HARMONY: metadata for the resource discovery of multimedia digital objects, at the ILRT at the University of Bristol and Cornell University (www.ilrt.bris.ac.uk/discovery/harmony)
- The Open Citation Project: Reference Linking for Open Archives: collaboration between Southampton University, Los Alamos National Laboratory and Cornell University (http://opcit.eprints.org/)
- Online Music Recognition and Searching (OMRAS) at King's College London and the University of Massachusetts (www.omras.org)
- CAMILEON: Creative Archiving at Michigan and Leeds: Emulating the Old on the New: technology emulation as a method for long-term access and preservation of digital resources, based at the University of Leeds and the University of Michigan (www.leeds.ac.uk/camileon)
- the IMesh Toolkit: an architecture and toolkit for distributed subject gateways, a partnership between UKOLN at the University of Bath, ILRT at the University of Bristol, and the University of Wisconsin-Madison (www.ukoln.ac.uk/metadata/imesh-toolkit/).

JISC is now commissioning a study that will undertake an analysis of the six funded projects and their achievements.

Registries, gateways and portals

In any project, documentation of the project process is very important, but because this is a meta-activity rather than an actual project activity, this information isn't always available. Researchers, scholars and project managers all need to be able to locate the work that has been done in the past so that we can develop an understanding of what constitutes a 'good' project, and what can be learned from it. One often-expressed concern is that it is difficult to get information about what digitization projects have been carried out elsewhere. Where they exist, registries and gateways to projects that have been created in the past provide a valuable tool for working scholars and funders to track the work done in a given area and to find existing, reusable resources. Such resources also play a key role in the development of shared technological frameworks or standards documents, although to be really useful in this regard they should include metadata with references to research goals, methodology used, and hardware and software employed, in addition to describing the product or project. Although no global, all-inclusive registry yet exists, one could argue that tools like Google serve an important purpose here. As search engines for the internet are refined, users can be more and more specific in their search terminology. However, search engines can only find whatever descriptive materials are in the project's metadata.

UNESCO and IFLA recently commissioned a Survey on Preservation and Digitization (www.ifla.org/VI/2/p1/miscel.htm) and published a report of their findings. The survey addresses the lack of a comprehensive worldwide listing of important digitized collections in libraries and other major cultural institutions, an issue that has been recognized by UNESCO as a major gap in our knowledge and awareness of accessible cultural heritage collections. The report provides a snapshot of the state of digitization activity worldwide, and gives an indication of the rapid growth in this area in recent years.

Some initiatives have been established to capture this information in a more formal way. Granting agencies are often our best source of information about projects that have been developed in the past, and a great strength of many national and international initiatives is that they manage and maintain records about projects that they have funded, and may even specify metadata standards so that such resources can easily be found by search engines. See, for example, the UK's New Opportunities Fund EnrichUK website that has just been launched as a showcase for NOF projects (www.enrichuk.net/), and is 'a searchable portal linking 150 websites that have been supported with Lottery good causes money distributed by the New Opportunities Fund. The project sites are working towards achieving compliance with the Fund's technical standards and guidelines'.

Other useful gateways to nationally funded projects include Culturenet Norway (www.culturenet.no), and the UK's 24 Hour Museum (www.24hourmuseum.org.uk), a thematic gateway to the websites of all UK museums. Similar resources can be found for Canada (www.culturenet.ca), and Austria (www.austrianmuseums.net).

Also in the UK, the Resource Discovery Network (www.rdn.ac.uk/) integrates subject-based hubs, which provide access to peer-reviewed internet resources for higher and continuing education learners and teachers. These include BIOME (Health and Life Sciences), EEVL (Engineering, Mathematics and Computing), Humbul (Humanities), PSIgate (Physical Sciences) and SOSIG (Social Sciences, Business and Law).

SCRAN (www.scran.ac.uk/) is a centrally co-ordinated network of digitized cultural artifacts relating to Scottish history and culture, collated from a number of participating organizations and all directly accessible. This resource also provides a degree of resource management and authentication for managing intellectual property by providing 'deep linkage' and e-learning facilities.

The New Zealand Register of Digitisation Initiatives (RoDI) contains basic information about digitization initiatives that are based in New Zealand or that relate to New Zealand topics (www.natlib.govt.nz/rodi/rodi.html).

The Association of Research Libraries Digital Initiatives Database (www.arl.org/did/) has been developed by a team at the University of Illinois, Chicago.

Some registries address the needs of users of particular types of digital materials. DIEPER (http://gdz.sub.uni-goettingen.de/dieper/) provides a central access point to digitized periodicals. The project is devised as a register on the model of the European Register of Microform Masters. Records of the register will be linked to reliable and comprehensive archives of periodical literature working at different sites throughout Europe.

UNESCO's Clearing House on Electronic Theses and Dissertations (ETD) enables the exchange of information on ETD, in close collaboration with the Networked Digital Library of Theses and Dissertations (NDLTD). It also provides a database of institutions (universities, libraries, computing centres, publishing houses, etc.) with ETD projects, experts in the field of ETD, and technical and educational materials available on the web to support and disseminate ETD (www.eduserver.de/unesco/).

Support organizations

A number of important organizations have been established to support and promote digitization initiatives around the world. Some of these groups provide free consultation to groups within a certain constituency or community, others may have a 'fee for service' arrangement. By developing partnerships with organizations of this sort, it may be possible for individual digitization initiatives to become greater than the 'sum of their parts'. Projects may also partner with such initiatives to accomplish specific goals, such as long-term archiving (with a repository service such as the OCLC digital repository), obtaining training on an aspect of digitization (by taking a course or workshop provided by the Technical Advisory Service on Images, or the SEPIA project), or developing DTDs for text encoding or markup (in collaboration with the TEI). The following organizations have all been endorsed at some level, either by the breadth of their experience and the received quality of their advice, or through recognition by funding agencies that allow projects to include in their budget proposals an allocation of some of their funds to services they provide. Funders may even suggest or require collaboration with such organizations.

This list is by no means exhaustive, but often staff of the organizations listed below will be able to direct queries to other resources. Many of these organizations also maintain useful publications on their websites, as well as listservs or discussion boards, which provide a means of communication with larger communities.

International initiatives

CLIR, the Council on Library and Information Resources (www. clir.org), provides a national information system for the USA on all matters related to digitization for cultural heritage resources. They publish a broad range of publications on issues such as preservation, archiving, metadata and the economic issues related to digitization, and sponsor many reports identifying key practices in the field.

The Digital Library Federation (DLF; www.diglib.org/) is a consortium of libraries and related agencies that are pioneering in their use of technology to extend their collections and services. Although a members-only institution, they have developed a number of initiatives that are useful to the entire digital libraries community, such as sponsorship of the METS initiative, which is a collaborative initiative to develop an XML framework for metadata capture.

I3A, The International Imaging Industry Association (www.i3a.org/), represents nearly all leading and emerging imaging companies, and is the largest imaging industry group worldwide. The organization provides an open forum for the discussion and development of global imaging infrastructure standards. Their website contains technical information on a range of emerging imaging standards as well as a comprehensive links page to many aspects of digital imaging.

The International Federation of Library Associations (IFLA; www.ifla.org/) is the leading international body representing the interests of library and information services and their users. Its programmes focus on seven themes: Advancement of Librarianship; Copyright and other Legal Matters; Free Access to Information and Freedom of Expression; Preservation and Conservation; Universal Availability of Publications; Universal Bibliographic Control and International MARC; Universal Dataflow and Tele-communications.

The Museum Computer Network (MCN; www.mcn.edu/) is a non-profit organization which supports museum professionals who work with technology. It maintains many useful resources and publications on its website and holds annual conferences and workshops. It publishes a journal, *SPECTRA*, which is available to all members.

OCLC, the Online Computer Library Center, inc. (www.oclc.org/home/), is an international non-profit, membership, library computer service and research organization dedicated to the public purposes of furthering access to the world's information and reducing information costs. It maintains many useful resources, and has organized several important collaborative projects, including the OCLC preservation co-op (www.oclc.org/digitalpreservation/), dedicated to developing resources for digital preservation.

PADI, the National Library of Australia's Preserving Access to Digital Information initiative (www.nla.gov.au/padi/), provides information to facilitate and develop strategies for the preservation and access of digital materials. It maintains a website for information and promotion purposes, containing many useful publications and links to external resources.

RLG (www.rlg.org/), formerly known as the Research Libraries Group, is an international member alliance of universities and colleges, national libraries, archives, historical societies, museums and independent research collections, and public libraries. RLG develops, co-ordinates, and operates many joint initiatives, and has a long, successful track record in managing and supporting interactions among its members. Key areas of focus include digital image archiving and the standardization of globally catalogued resources. It produces many free online publications, including the important journal *RLG Diginews* (www.rlg.org/preserv/diginews/).

SEPIA, Safeguarding European Photographic Images for Access (www.knaw.nl/ecpa/sepia/), is an EU-funded project focusing on the preservation of photographic materials. Their website contains many resources supporting digital imaging, including research on scanning equipment and handling procedures, preservation aspects of digitization, ethics of digitization, and descriptive models for photographic materials.

TEI, the Text Encoding Initiative (www.tei-c.org/), is a membership organization aimed at promoting the use of the TEI standard for document markup and exchange. Their website contains links to many useful materials, including standards documents and an extremely active listserv.

VRA, the Visual Resources Association (http://vraweb.org/), is a multidisciplinary non-profit organization. The organization serves a broad community of image management professionals working in educational and cultural heritage environments. It is committed to providing leadership in the field, developing and advocating standards, including metadata standards for imaging, and publications and training opportunities for its members, while promoting co-operation initiatives. Membership is open to anyone with an interest in the group's work.

UK academic service providers

The following organizations are usually funded to provide support for UK higher education institutions. Other organizations may be able to work with them on a negotiated basis. However, all maintain useful websites, with freely available information and links to other sources of advice. The UK organizations are listed to give a sense of the breadth of national services that can be centrally supported to answer questions and provide training on all aspects of cultural heritage computing, and also the breadth of services that can be needed to support digitization enterprises.

AHDS, the Arts and Humanities Data Service (www.ahds.ac.uk), is a national service which helps the academic community create, deposit, preserve, discover and use digital collections in the arts and humanities. The AHDS service providers maintain reference materials and guides to good practice in the specialist areas of the five separate subject service centres: archaeology, history, texts, performing arts, and visual arts.

The BUFVC, British Universities Film and Video Council (www.bufvc.ac.uk/), supports and promotes the use of moving images in UK higher and further education, and the use of moving images in research generally. It also maintains a number of projects related to moving image digitization and metadata for moving images.

HEDS, the Higher Education Digitisation Service (http://heds.herts.ac.uk/), provides advice, consultancy and a complete production service for digitization and digital library development. Its site provides many resources including reports of previous projects, planning advice and feasibility studies.

NPO, the National Preservation Office (www.bl.uk/services/preservation/national.html), provides an independent focus on issues related to the preservation and continued accessibility of library and archive material held in the UK and Ireland. Its website contains many useful reports and other materials on all aspects of this topic.

TASI, the Technical Advisory Service on Images (www.tasi.ac.uk/), provides advice, consultation and training on all aspects of digital imaging for the UK higher education community. It maintains useful documents and links to many sources of advice on its website, including advice on funding sources.

TechDis (www.techdis.ac.uk/) is a service that aims to improve provision for disabled staff and students in higher and further education through technology. It has many resources related to developing broadly accessible digital resources.

Conclusion

Collaboration is increasingly a factor in all aspects of work in libraries, archives and museums, and is becoming almost a prerequisite for digitization initiatives at a local, national and international level. However, such projects may become a flashpoint for any tensions that exist between the 'two cultures' – technologists and cultural heritage professionals. Learning to work together at the local level provides a valuable paradigm for making larger, high stakes partnerships work. Taking advantage of the many frameworks that can support collaboration and understanding the advantages of partnerships to all parties will build a foundation for successful collaborations. It is also important to think strategically about collaborations. What sort of partnerships will be advantageous: internal, external, with vendors, or with other cultural heritage institutions? What sort of partnerships will assist in acquiring funding, building capacity, or building collections? Partnerships should always foster the institutional mission of all parties, and understanding and stating such goals at the outset will avoid problems in the long term.

Part 2
Digitizing collections

6

Project planning and funding

The feasibility of an initiative depends on the ability to perform all of the required tasks within a given timeframe, for a given amount of money. Establishing the amount needed and securing it are critical factors.

(Cultuurtechnologie, 2003)

Introduction

This chapter examines:

- the development of project plans and budgets
- the potential role of prototypes
- sources for funding and grants
- the development of grant applications and proposals
- the evaluation of RFPs (requests for proposals)
- funding project sustainability.

Developing a project plan

After selecting collections for digitization, assessing the strategic advantages of digitization and evaluating the opportunity costs to the institution, the next activity to be undertaken is the development of detailed project plans. This planning process is the crucial 'first step' on the digitization path and includes articulating the project's goals and objectives, outlining workflows and developing a budget. These activities inform subsequent attempts to gain funding and set long-term objectives for digitization programmes.

The planning process should be a collaboration of many stakeholders, including users, information providers and staff from all parts of the organization. A broad consultative process at the outset will shape the direction of the project and build consensus and institutional buy-in. Stakeholder studies, such as the user assessments outlined in Chapter 2, are important tools in developing project plans, as are risk assessments, institutional and infrastructure inventories, selection criteria for digitization and job descriptions.

The first objective is to develop a detailed project plan, which will help the project manager assess whether or not the project can be accomplished, and extend the evidence base supporting the project. This document should be able to define clearly the objectives, goals, deliverables and priorities for the project, and express the vision of the project as it fits into the strategic objectives of the institution as a whole. The following outline, suggesting the content of a project plan, is based on project plans developed by HEDS (http://heds.herts.ac.uk/resources/papersF.html), and from UNESCO's *Guidelines for Establishing Digitization Programmes in Libraries and Archives* (UNESCO, IFLA, ICA, 2002).

Introduction

This should include a brief outline of the project background, an analysis of all participants and agreements between all collaborative partners (such as other institutions).

Vision and mission

The vision for a project is the clear, concise description, and an overview of what will be achieved and the core benefits to be conveyed to key stakeholders. Its purpose is to maintain the project's goals and to ensure that 'drifting' of core values does not occur. It also delivers the added benefit of providing an easy marketing phrase or description to those not familiar with the project's scope. It should address the following questions:

- What will be the short-term or immediate benefits and objectives of the project?
- What are the changes to participants and their institutions that will be effected by the project?
- Who will the users be and what will this project enable them to do that is not presently possible?
- What materials and collections are to be digitized?
- What are the long-term, strategic benefits of the project?

Needs assessment

This is where existing policies and practices are outlined, especially with regard to preservation and access. What shortcomings or constraints to scholarship and outreach presently exist? What are the expected outcomes of the project (specific digital products, services or skills) and how will the project meet these needs?

Activities

What are the steps that will be taken to achieve the project's goals? What is the intended workflow of the project? Project activities might include general computer training for staff, training in digital conversion techniques, digital conversion of original source materials, post-digitization processing and analysis of content, modifying cataloguing procedures for indexing and metadata capture, web design and publishing, and negotiating with copyright holders. What are the technical assumptions that will drive this work? What equipment will be required?

Quality assessment and performance indicators.

How do participants ensure that project goals are met within the resources and time available? Without quality assurance in place then the standard of work is difficult to assess accurately or just becomes a matter of opinion. Without performance indicators or set deliverables then the progress of the project to plan cannot be easily measured. It will be necessary to carry out sample scans or imaging activities to assess time-and-motion estimates. What rate of image capture can be expected for the different media involved – what scan results can be expected for scanning paper, or capturing fragile source materials? What rate of metadata capture is achievable? What overall production rates are possible, taking all the factors affecting the project (location, staff, original source materials, etc.) into consideration? These results can be based upon sample scanning activities.

Project personnel

Who will be responsible for the various components of a project? What skills, experience or training will be required for each activity? Who will be responsible for the completion of each part of the project?

Timeframe for the project

How long will each component of the project take? What are the anticipated start and end dates? Are there factors that will constrain these calculations and can they be anticipated? Do some activities require the completion of other phases of the project (for example, does cataloguing have to be completed before scanning can start)? Does the timeframe include the possibility of delays, such as those typical at the start-up phase?

Project life cycle

What plans exist for the preservation and sustainability of the digital resources?

Evaluation

How will evaluation of the digital resources be undertaken? What measures exist to demonstrate the project has succeeded? How are user perceptions and expectations of the project to be addressed? (See Chapter 8 for a discussion of evaluation.)

Prototype projects

It is often advisable to carry out a small pilot (or prototype) project in order to explore the feasibility of various ideas, and to support the detailed project planning documents by developing a better understanding of how all the elements of the project will fit together.

Developing a prototype will involve working on a carefully selected, representative sample of materials and defining some project 'outcomes' that can be accomplished in a short time. This will enable the project manager to have a clearer picture of important elements of the project: how long it will take to digitize documents, images or moving image material; the process of obtaining copyright permissions where necessary; the rate of metadata capture, and the complexity required of metadata schema reconciling training requirements and skills gaps. This will form the basis of useful time-and-motion studies, establishing realistic work rates, and identifying efficiencies in the workflow that might speed progress along. A pilot study will also facilitate the development of a cost model, as many aspects of the workflow, as discussed in Chapter 4, will need to be tested out in order to fully understand all related costs (A. Smith, 2001c), and establish if collaborations and partnerships will work on a larger scale.

There are a number of ways to develop such projects – as an in-house planning exercise, carried out by librarians, curators or subject specialists using just the technological resources already available in house (for example, in computer labs, or IT departments), or by first obtaining a small planning grant to develop the prototype. Such grants may be available from internal resources, as many institutions will see such expenditure as 'seed money' that may attract bigger grants if the pilot is carried out successfully. Some external funders may award small planning grants to develop ideas in anticipation of funding a larger project based on the completion of a successful prototype.

Developing cost models; project budgets

Developing an itemized budget is an important part of planning, and will indicate whether or not a project is feasible. Resources such as the document produced by HEDS, *Costing a Digitisation Project*

(HEDS, 2003), can be very useful, and the section on costs in Chapter 4 of this book is intended to offer guidance on the factors to be considered. Cost models should be comprehensive, and incorporate all aspects of a project, broken down into operational, organizational and staffing costs (UNESCO, IFLA and ICA, 2002).

Operational costs include equipment, such as computers, scanners, printers, digital cameras and peripherals; materials, including stationery, preservation storage materials, and software; transport, including transport to project meetings for the advisory board and project participants, transport and training costs for project staff; and services, such as maintenance contacts, conservation of originals, training, and consultancy.

Organizational costs include costs incurred by, or paid to, the host institution. These include cost share for the salaries of project managers or administrators who are employed for a proportion of their time on the project; organizational overhead costs, such as the cost of office space, utilities; and network access and other related costs. Most institutions will set a percentage that must be added to project budgets as indirect costs, usually between 30 and 50% of the total budget.

Staffing costs are usually the highest project cost to be anticipated, and the more human intervention required at any stage of the project, the greater the cost. Staff may be full time, part time, consultants or contract staff. Staff salaries will have to be adjusted to include an allowance for benefits, pensions or national insurance contributions where appropriate, usually adding about 20–30% to base salaries.

Most importantly, cost models should be realistic and include costs for everything that the project may require, at all stages of the project life cycle. This may make a project look expensive, but is crucial. It is also necessary to project the costs of sustaining the project for several years into the future, and consider the costs related to long-term access and preservation. Different sources of funding will often be required for different 'line items'. Never underestimate costs – it will be difficult to meet shortfalls and funding agencies will recognize this as a weakness in your proposal. It is advisable to include everything and have the agency decide that you should seek alternative funds for particular items or activities.

Finding funds for digital collections

May all your problems be technical.

(Jim Gray, quoted in Lesk, 2002)

After developing detailed project plans and budgets, these documents can be used as the basis for applications for funding digitization initiatives. Fundraising should always be pursued in a strategic fashion and should be part of an institutional digitization strategy. It will be necessary to have a clear understanding of the vision, aims and objectives of the project and how it will enhance the institution's objectives (Deegan and Tanner, 2002). This is an important consideration, as digitization will be often driven by the availability of funding opportunities and can be opportunistic. Examples of such opportunities may include internal digitization development programmes, often initiated by senior management to 'make collections available online'; the announcement of a new source of funding or grant cycle (e.g. the UK's NOF-Digitise, which created a new source of funding for many cultural heritage organizations, especially small local archives and collections) which seems too good an opportunity to miss; or when a partner institution makes an overture for collaboration.

Many projects start off with the support of external grant funding, which has been critical to starting major digitization initiatives at many institutions. Developing a project within a set budget and with clearly defined aims and deliverables can reduce some of the risk inherent in new and technologically dependent activities. Attracting grant funding will also lend some legitimacy and stature to new projects among peers, both internal and external. However, grant funding should not be seen as a long-term solution to sustaining digital collections, for which there will ultimately be a need for a substantial institutional commitment (Greenstein and Thorin, 2002).

Two recent surveys on digital collections reported that digital projects obtain their financial backing from a combination of institutional budgets, public grants, private donation or corporate sponsorship (NINCH, 2002), and that there is also an increasing trend for institutions to provide startup funding for digitization from money reallocated by the university librarian from other library purposes. 'As digital library programs mature, reallocated library funding becomes more important, at once reflecting and contributing to the challenges of mainstreaming the digital library' (Greenstein and Thorin, 2002).

However, new patterns of funding are still evolving.

Internal funds

These resources can include internal or specialist funds awarded at the discretion of senior administrators, often for interdisciplinary initiatives. Libraries sometimes have access to discretionary grants to start up digitization projects in collaboration with faculty, or to evaluate the use of digital resources, and some museums are exploring the possibility of making similar grants available to curators to encourage them to develop electronic resources (and to explore the potential of digitization for education, research and outreach) in their field of expertise. At NYU, for example, the library and IT organization support faculty and graduate students developing digital objects designed to enhance teaching and research through its Studio for Digital Projects and Research and its Faculty Technology Center, and plan to give grants to faculty members to develop digital resources. It may even be possible to look to what some administrators call 'budget dust', cost savings that may be available at the end of the year from acquisitions or technology budgets, or salary savings (Greenstein and Thorin, 2002).

Identifying sources of external grants

There are sources of assistance for identifying funding for digitization. Many universities will have a department of development, staffed by experts who can help plan and identity sources of funding from large databases of public and private funding agencies. Individual faculties, schools or planning units may have access to a dedicated development officer or offices which can provide a similar service targeted at particular disciplines or types of projects (for example, many university libraries have their own departments of development). Depending on institutional policies, it may be essential to co-ordinate grant-writing activities through such offices, as they are responsible for ensuring that multiple departments at the same institution do not compete for the same grants.

Universities and libraries can apply for funds from either private foundations or public grant opportunities that are available for their discipline. For archives and museums, government- or centrally funded institutions will be able to apply for central government funds for digitization, such as the grants awarded by JISC, or the Heritage Lottery Fund in the UK, or national funding initiatives in other countries. Small grants may also be available from regional councils to promote local collections and access to digital resources. Grants may also be available under programmes to increase access to digital resources (in the UK, for example, the Scottish Executive funded the Digital Communities Initiative, which provided a computer and one year's free internet access). Information about UK funding opportunities is available at many locations, including the TASI (www.tasi.ac.uk) and UKOLN (www.ukoln.ac.uk) websites. The Arts and Humanities Data Service (AHDS) website (www.ahds.ac.uk) provides information about applying for Arts and Humanities Research Board grants. In Canada, the Federal Government's Canadian Digital Cultural Content Initiative supports content digitization programmes in libraries, museums and archives.

In the USA, funding for digital content creation is less centralized. Limited federal funding is available from agencies such as IMLS (the Institute for Museum and Library Services), NEH (the National Endowment for the Humanities) and the NSF (the National Science Foundation). FIPSE (the Fund for the Improvement of Post Secondary Education) is run by the Department of Education, and is another potential source of funding. The Colorado Digitization Program maintains a list of available funds (www.cdpheritage.org/resource/funding/rsrc_funding.html).

Similar national initiatives exist in many other countries, where state and local governments also offer grants and awards to collaborations. Private foundations have also funded many digital cultural content creation projects. Examples include the Ford Foundation, the Samuel H. Kress Foundation, and the Andrew W. Mellon Foundation, which has been a significant funding source for digital library projects worldwide. Zorich (2003) presents a useful analysis of funding sources for digitization projects, including corporations, foundations and government agencies.

Opportunistic funding

Sometimes, funding will be available for certain types of project that are not necessarily consistent with an overall digitization strategy or institutional mission. Similarly, a project may be proposed that is politically desirable to the senior administration, but which will be of limited interest to the broad user community. It is important to be able to identify such 'gift horses' when they appear and to be able to evaluate the advantages and disadvantages of doing the project.

The advantages are that doing any digitization project can build experience and the prestige of the organization and may present a useful opportunity for research and development into specific tools or applications (such as audiovisual digitization or interface design) that require an investment of time or money that is seldom available. They may also provide an opportunity to be a 'good citizen', by committing resources to a project that is important for institutional prestige overall. As Abby Smith explains, 'even vanity projects, if managed properly, will bring money into the library for digitization and provide the kind of training and hands-on experience that is necessary to develop digital library infrastructure and expertise', especially if there is a firm commitment that all costs involved – including not just digitization, but cataloguing and preservation – are adequately covered (A. Smith, 2001c).

However, such projects can be a distraction in focus or resources. If the terms under which the work is funded are not negotiated clearly, the institution may find itself responsible for expending valuable resources on low-priority projects. Institutions should avoid deliberately seeking funding for such initiatives.

Donor-driven funding is a familiar issue in collections development – generous donations to an institution may come with stipulations about the type of materials to purchase, or even a particular scholarly direction to take. The high public profile of digital collections, and the sense that digitization is the 'latest thing', can make digitization attractive to donors interested in funding vanity projects which match their own priorities or agendas – agendas which may contradict institutional policies on digitization (for example, the decision to digitize materials that are to be used for teaching a core curriculum). Although it is always difficult to turn down money, there is a need to be cautious about investing resources (including staff time) in such projects, as they may cost more in the long term if they do not accurately reflect the strategic goals that exist for the institution.

'*Cherry picking*' or picking out the most attractive materials in a collection for digitization, is often undertaken to raise the profile of an institution, and to attract funding. Special collections are perceived as more compelling to funding agencies, given their rarity and value, regardless of how relevant their content may be to present-day scholarship or the overall research and teaching mission of the institution. Special projects are often driven by motives such as fundraising or public relations, and there is a concern that they can divert resources from more academically significant projects or from the core mission of the institution (A. Smith, 2001c).

'*Low-hanging fruit*', to continue the agricultural metaphor, refers to projects that require 'only' a small investment to develop or complete a resource. These may be legacy projects, projects already under way that need some institutional support to be completed, or small faculty initiatives to digitize some key collections for a particular constituency (e.g. a special collection that is used to teach a particular course). These can be a good opportunity to build a 'critical mass' of digital content and to develop buy-in from the community. However, such projects have to be very carefully managed – they will take up resources and require some sort of commitment to sustainability. It is necessary to undertake a very careful analysis of the resources required to bring these projects to completion, and to stick to a project outline carefully to avoid 'project drift' – a phenomenon where projects consume more time, resources and attention than was ever intended.

Developing grant applications

Securing external funding will depend on an ability to write persuasive grant proposals, as well as the use of marketing and promotional activities to convince funders of the merit of the proposal and the ability of the institution to complete the project successfully (Greenstein and Thorin, 2002). These skills will require some practice in the case of the former, and experience in networking and outreach in the case of the latter. It can be argued that self-promotion does not often come easily to many who work in the cultural heritage sector, so such activities may seem daunting. However, assistance is available from a number of resources.

A development office or office of sponsored programmes can provide some form of assistance – if not in actually crafting the proposal, they should be able to assist with checking budgets and proofreading. For institutions that do not have access to such resources internally, some helpful documents are available on a number of websites, including that of the North East Document Conservation Center (NEDCC), which provides information on sources of funding as well as grant-writing tips (www.nedcc.org/welcome/grants.htm). The Colorado Digitization Program also maintains a list of links to resources on grant writing (www.cdpheritage.org/resource/funding/rsrc_funding.html).

Most importantly, in the USA federal funding agencies will have a programme officer attached to the particular funding source that you are applying for. The programme officer's job is to ensure that there is a level playing field of applicants for the funds available, and that all applicants have access to the same information about what the agency is looking for. Consequently, programme officers will have a high profile (they are usually named on the agencies' websites) and will be fairly easy to contact. Having identified the officer, it is important to involve them early and often throughout the process of developing a proposal. They will be the best source of advice about all aspects of the funding initiative and what a proposal should and should not include.

Foundations will also have programme officers, but they may well have a slightly different remit. Nonetheless, it will be equally important to maintain a collegial relationship with foundation staff and make contact with them where appropriate throughout the grant-writing process.

Evaluating requests for proposals

Developing proposals takes a great deal of time and energy, so it is important only to apply for grants where there is a likelihood of success. Examine the funding agency's requests for proposals (RFPs) carefully to establish that this is indeed the right opportunity to fund a proposed project. First, ensure that any eligibility requirements can be met. These may include requirements on the nature of the collection to be digitized (is this a national or international initiative?), the goal and purpose of the project (education, research, or public accessibility?), and the institutional commitment required (is there a cost-sharing, or matching-funds requirement?).

Next, establish what the grant will cover and what activities will need to be funded from other resources. Will the grant allocate funding for personnel and physical resources to maintain and provide networked access to these materials during the course of the project? What about plans for maintaining access into the future? What portion of the project will the funding request support? If the funding opportunity doesn't support all phases of the project, what additional funding sources are available to complete the project? Will it be possible to divide aspects of the project into modules which can be supported by different agencies, an approach which may lead to a stronger proposal?

Particular points to look out for include the following:

- Will the grant cover equipment costs? Are hardware and software covered? Does it prohibit expenses related to infrastructure development?
- Will the grant support the conversion of existing catalogues, inventories or finding aids? Are there stipulations on the access requirements for the digital resources – for example, must they be freely available to the public?
- Will the grant support the development of websites and outreach activities to publicize the project?
- Does the grant stipulate that a sustainability plan be included in the proposal?
- Will the project have to have a collaborative component? Does the collaboration have to be local, national or international? Is there a community outreach component?

- Does the grant require that the digital resources be deposited in a national repository (e.g. AHDS), and is this acceptable to permissions holders and all project partners?
- Are there stipulations for particular standards to be used (e.g. some NEH initiatives stipulate the use of the TEI)?
- Is there a preference for outreach, education or pure research as an objective? (Ross and Economou, 1998).

Grant conditions may be onerous and it may be necessary to change the focus of a project considerably in order to qualify. It is essential to the long-term success of the project that compromises should not be made on any aspect of the project that makes it difficult to complete the work or makes any party uncomfortable. There is no grant large enough that will compensate for the derailing of a project (with the attendant loss of prestige to the institution) because of unhappy partnerships between ill suited collaborators, a significant shift in focus regarding the collections or in user focus (for example, many funding agencies require that the project will collaborate with participants from schools). Exploring such compromises may be another significant reason to carry out a small prototype project, which might establish if certain aspects of a project can or cannot be made to work.

Developing the proposal

In terms of crafting the proposal, there are no magic solutions or subliminal buzzwords that will lead to the development of a winning proposal, but there are some general guidelines that will help.

First, examine all available material concerning the request for proposals, including supporting materials and examples of successfully funded proposals, if they are available. Review very carefully every detail, including directions on proposal length, closing date and any formatting details that are mentioned (is there, for example, a preferred font size?). Make sure that all requested documents and appendices are included, such as budget justifications, resumés of project participants, and letters of commitment (and allow plenty of time to obtain such materials from all project participants). Ensure that the description of the project makes the goals and objectives clear to someone unfamiliar with the content and try to anticipate any questions that reviewers will have. Include a detailed justification for the project, explaining why it will be important to the intended audience. Include representative samples of the collection where possible.

If the project has developed a prototype, it may well be helpful to include reference to this in the proposal. However, some words of caution – make sure that the prototype is truly an effective demonstration of what is planned for the larger proposal. Prototypes generally lend themselves best to an actual demonstration in the presence of developers and funders, which will allow an opportunity to answer any questions about the project. Unless the prototype is absolutely self-explanatory, it is not a good idea to merely include a URL to such materials (if nothing else, the site will inevitably be examined by reviewers on a day that the website is down for maintenance).

It will also be important to ensure that the proposal includes a detailed evaluation plan and assessment strategies for all stages of the project, an outline of the project workflow and project management plan, a detailed description of the methodology involved, including production processes, resolution, scanning rates, etc., and an overview of plans for long-term access to the materials, including preservation strategies.

A crucial component of all applications will be the ability to demonstrate persuasively that the applicant can complete the project successfully. Obviously, a proven track record is the best way to indicate this, but a lack of experience need not preclude developing a successful proposal. There are two strategies that will overcome this perceived weakness in a proposal. The first is to show a clear understanding of every step in the digitization process and to describe the workflows accurately. This will demonstrate to the funding agency that the applicant understands the technical and managerial aspects of the project and how best to tackle these issues throughout the digital life cycle. It will also demonstrate an awareness that digitization is not a simple process. A second approach is to develop partnerships with experts in the field who have experience in all aspects of such projects. This may take the form of collaborating with a partner institution or it may simply mean including well known experts in the field to be on a project's advisory committee. It may also be possible to contract experts to provide advice on specific components of a project on an hourly or daily basis at an agreed rate.

The most important advice is to not give up at the first hurdle. There is a great deal of competition for available funds and not all proposals will be successful initially. For example, Indiana University Library applied unsuccessfully three times for relatively small amounts of funding from the Library of Congress/Ameritech competition. Three years after their first attempt, an expanded version of their proposal was funded by a $3 million grant from the National Science Foundation (Greenstein and Thorin, 2002). It is important to be creative and flexible about developing proposals and to be prepared to apply for funding from many different sources. It may also be advisable to develop a portfolio of project proposals so that they can be swiftly reconfigured and updated if there is an opportunity for funding from a new resource.

Sustainability

Ensuring long-term access to digital collections depends on careful life-cycle management. How does the library budget for not only the creation of the digital scans but also for the metadata, storage capacity, preservation tools (e.g., refreshing, migration), and user support – the sorts of things that are routinely budgeted for book acquisitions? How much of the program is supported by grant funding and how much by base funding? If the program is currently grant supported, what plans exist to make it self-sustaining? A sustainable digitization strategy may well include the creation of digital surrogates that serve short-term needs and do not demand long-term support. The crucial thing is to anticipate what support, if any, will be needed.

(A. Smith, 2001c)

Ironically, it is easier to attract funds for new, start-up projects than to attract funding to continue to provide access to resources with a proven track record of access and use. In the 'rush to digitize' of the past 20 years, many initiatives did not express concerns about sustainability, hoping that income would continue to materialize in the future (NINCH, 2002). As digitization activities mature, we are no longer in the experimental, start-up phase, and there is a need to examine long-term financial planning for digitization and the potential for sustaining projects through revenue generation.

One should ensure that a provision is made for a continuity of funding because maintenance, exploitation costs and revisions are crucial, but sometimes overlooked. An initiative which comes to a complete stop will not be considered a success, therefore some vision of a continuing development and innovation should be present in the definition of the initiative. It should be budgeted and its funding should be secured for it to be sustainable.

(Cultuurtechnologie, 2003)

Some models for sustaining digital resources have been suggested, such as the following by Kate Wittenberg, of the Electronic Publishing Initiative at Columbia (www.epic.columbia.edu):

1   Institutional subscriptions. This can be a good source of revenue, as long as a project makes clear what the subscription covers, and who should be charged – schools, colleges, individual users? This model will require the support of marketing, billing and accounting staff.
2   Individual sales of images, publications and other materials. This should be seen as a supplementary source of revenue only, except in rare cases when advertisers or commercial users might be targeted for particular collections.
3   Institutional support from the host institution. Projects will be strengthened if they are supported as a core part of the organizational infrastructure, but such arrangements usually have to be set in place at the very start of a project, rather than just before a grant runs out. Unfortunately, many institutions are rigidly organized, and it is extremely hard to get 'interdisciplinary' projects under way, especially given the complex decision-making processes and necessary buy-in at libraries and universities (Wittenberg, 2003).

All of the above models have a number of qualifications and questions, and will have to be thought out very early on in the project life cycle. No part of the project can be in an experimental phase when resources are launched, but how can we judge when materials are ready for release to subscribers? Should they be released incrementally as editorial modifications are completed, although this will mean that the whole body of work isn't available? How will project partners be involved in matters relating to revenues, collaboration, intellectual property protection? What kind of staff are needed for sustainable business models and at what phase in the project – for example, marketing people may be required at launch and during the first year.

Business models will only recover a small portion of costs and the full expenditure associated with developing digital resources cannot be fully recovered by sustainability programmes at this time. As described in Chapter 1, the economics of digitization projects relate to hidden, unseen costs and intangibles such as the value of information, which cannot be translated into cash savings. Digitization is a relatively new endeavour, so we cannot accurately predict future cost recovery, or opportunities for saving costs. Digitization – and the long-term maintenance of electronic resources – is still more expensive than maintaining paper collections and the future of electronic information is littered with little time bombs (such as the cost of long-term preservation, and the unpredictability of future copyright legislation) that may trip up even the best laid digital sustainability plans. This is another reason why digitization projects must be driven by the collections, research and educational goals and opportunities for the institution rather than economic models.

Conclusion

Planning and finding funds for digitization are activities that go hand in hand, and equal attention should be devoted to each activity, as they are mutually interconnected in so many ways. However, the two activities are often connected in a symbiotic fashion; plans for the scope of the project will be dictated by the funds available, and the timeframe available for planning a project will be limited by the amount of time available to develop a grant proposal. Consequently, the importance of developing a portfolio of small, prototype projects should be stressed. Developing such materials will be an important way for people from all parts of an institution to talk about possibilities for digitization, and developing small projects can be an important way to identify what sort of digitization projects will be successful.

7

Managing a digitization project

Introduction

Understanding the digitization process is the best way to develop a sound basis for digital project management. This requires an understanding of all aspects of the digitization process, both technical (what equipment to buy, what standards to use) and administrative (managing people and workflows, and assessing quality). In particular, it will necessitate a precise understanding of all the issues involved at each stage of the imaging process. This knowledge will enable the project manager to make informed decisions about selecting appropriate digitization strategies for their own collections.

Project planning requires the development of comprehensive workflows appropriate to the original source materials and the desired objectives and project goals. Project management will necessitate the implementation of these plans within the constraints of the time and budget that are to be invested in the project. In addition to the expected workflow and components of running a digitization project, selection decisions and related issues (such as cataloguing, assessing the condition of originals, etc.) will add to the costs of such projects and the time they will take to complete.

The first part of this chapter focuses on identifying the core goals of the project and how they will affect the decisions that are made at each point of the digitization workflow. The second part outlines the technical workflow, technical choices, and management of the digitization life cycle. It is important to recognize that the digitization chain is not a straightforward linear series of actions – many activities will happen in parallel and at different stages of the project – and no single set of guidelines can be appropriate for all circumstances. There will be many components of the digitization chain, and these will change over time. However, the core elements of a technology project that have to be managed are:

- the handling, preparation and intellectual content of the original source materials
- the technology and processes that enable the source materials to be digitized and delivered to end-users
- the long-term maintenance and distribution of the electronic resources to ensure that they are useful over the long term.

Other sources of advice

Much excellent work has been produced on the detailed technical aspects of digitizing images and it is not the intent of this book to duplicate this advice. Instead, the reader is encouraged to consult some of these existing resources. These include *Moving Theory into Practice: a digital imaging tutorial* (Cornell University Library, Research Department, 2002). This tutorial offers base-level information on the use of digital imaging to convert and make accessible cultural heritage materials. It also introduces some concepts advocated by Cornell University Library, in particular the value of benchmarking requirements before undertaking a digital initiative. The reader will find technical information, formulas and reality checks on all aspects of digital imaging. A book accompanies the tutorial and expands on many of the key themes, including an integrated approach to digital imaging, and an emphasis on managing projects for preservation and access (Kenney and Rieger, 2000).

Other essential reading includes the recent *Digital Imaging: a practical handbook* by S. Lee (2001a) and *The NINCH Guide to Good Practice* (NINCH, 2002). Other online resources include *An Introduction to Making Digital Image Archives*, by the Technical Advisory Service for

Images (TASI, 2003), and the Research Libraries Group's Guides to Quality in Digital Resource Imaging (RLG, 2000).

Project planning and technology

> The best-managed projects have clear goals. Brainstorming, the first phase of project management, is the time to talk about outcomes. 'Starting at the end' is an effective way to ensure smooth beginnings. Too often there is a tendency to dive right into the questions of technology – e.g., which scanner should I buy? – before articulating the purposes that digital reformatting must serve.
>
> (S. Chapman, 2000)

Articulating the purposes of the project, and the way that the digital imaging processes chosen will create resources that will fulfil these goals, is the best way to plan a digitization project and will make it easier to narrow the choices of scanning technologies and techniques from a constantly expanding selection of equipment and software. Technology should always be assessed with an eye to the objectives of the project, rather than framing the goals of the project in terms of what is technologically available or possible. The factors that will influence these decisions are:

- the reasons for digitization
- the materials to be digitized, especially their condition and informational content
- the level of fidelity to the original that is required
- the technical and financial resources that are available to the project, and the scale of the project
- the potential uses and users of the digital objects
- any specific desired outcomes for the physical objects that are to be digitized.

These considerations will influence the decisions taken throughout the digital life cycle, especially questions of usage and the quality that is required of the digital objects. A frequent concern is how to achieve the proper balance between quality and rate of production. Having a clear vision of the use of the digital materials and the quality required will help to focus such decisions. It is always preferable to reach a well defined and objective measure of affordable quality for the whole digitization chain, and to determine how many objects can be digitized at an acceptable rate of quality in the time available, allocating a longer time span to digitization if necessary. For all projects, 'It is better to set modest goals than to create unrealistic expectations' (Serenson Colet, 2000).

There are a number of approaches to representing original content that correlate the outcomes of the project to the requirements of the end-users and the level of fidelity to the original.

The first is often referred to as benchmarking and is a stringent approach that supposes that end-users of digital resources will have the same requirements and expectations as the users and creators of the original source materials. As such, this requires a careful assessment of the originals to ensure that digital reproductions will replicate the unique attributes of the originals as carefully as possible, by faithfully conveying such qualities and attributes as organization and presentation, size and dimension, and detail, tone and colour (S. Chapman, 2000).

Another approach is to anticipate the needs of the end-users, and to base digitization decisions on these criteria. This will necessitate predicting the hardware and software systems and network access available to the end-users, and implementing digitization decisions based on these factors. For example, are the users researchers who need to magnify or zoom in on materials for detailed image or paleographical analysis? Or will they need to print out copies, or compare several versions of a document or image on screen at the same time? How legible do the materials need to be? It is important to remember, however, that if projects are conceptualized from the perspective of the users of today, it may be difficult to expand the scope of the project for other uses or purposes that may arise.

The best approach is one that will enable the project manager to 'scan once and for all purposes' by creating a fully documented high-quality 'digital master' from which all other versions (e.g. compressed versions for accessing via the web) can be derived. This digital master file should be created at the highest resolution and bit depth that is both affordable and practical, preserving to the greatest extent possible the authenticity and integrity of the original information. The digital master file will become an archive version of the data – it remains as pure a representation of the original as possible. Ideally, multiple copies should be stored on different media types and in more than one geographical location, thus providing a degree of protection against data corruption, media failure and physical damage to equipment. Creating a digital master minimizes the need to digitize again in the future and thus saves the original from excessive handling. It also prolongs the usefulness of the digital archive, which should serve the widest possible range of users and uses, including some that may be unforeseen or unknowable (Frey and Süsstrunk, 1999). This master file should be the source for every other digital copy required, such as low-resolution surrogate files for web delivery or high-resolution copies distributed for archival quality printing. All images used for purposes like viewing and printing should be produced as surrogates from the original archived images. Enhancements such as colour corrections and resizing should be performed on these surrogate images to ensure that they are appropriate for the uses intended. While surrogate images can be produced as part of the capture process, this can require large amounts of storage and processing time. Alternatively, a separate surrogate image production environment can be set up as an extension of the image capture process. From the user's perspective, working with lower resolution web files allows browsing and fast access. The lower resolution and image quality also means that the images cannot be distributed illegally for commercial publication.

As such, this comprehensive approach is consistent with the 'digital ecology' movement, which recognizes that decisions taken at the very outset of a project will inform the long-term use and preservation of the digital materials. This is based on the understanding that digital projects have a 'life cycle', and that there will be a need to plan for not just the creation of the digital files, but their long term-management and possible conversion to another format for re-use (Lawrence et al., 2000).

Digital preservation issues must also be observed when producing digital content, and declaring an intended life-span for the objects will also help the decision-making process.

The project manager

The project manager will be responsible for balancing all these requirements and overseeing all aspects of a project: the 'product' or outcome; the schedule, which will have start dates, end dates and a series of milestone deadlines in between; and its resources: people, budgets, equipment, and source materials. These elements will have to be co-ordinated from the planning stages to implementation of the finished product. Activities will include developing and organizing the project team, supervising all elements of the project workflow, managing the project's resources (including staff and budget) and co-ordinating outreach activities with all stakeholders, including the steering committee or advisory board and funders. Project managers will have to set targets for all aspects of the project and ensure that these are met. They will often be a conduit for the technical and academic aspects of the project, responsible for interpreting academic or project goals and ensuring that the technical specifications meet these goals, and that the technology chosen will be suitable for cultural heritage collections. Consequently, they will be responsible for most of the decision points throughout the project workflow and for allocating all activities to other members of the project team, such as technical staff, evaluation teams and content experts.

The project will be more successful if the project manager is able to build, support and maintain a team that can work well together, which can be difficult when project staff are located in disparate venues, or when participants from different backgrounds with no experience of working together have to collaborate (such as computer scientists and humanists, web programmers and conservation staff, and librarians and IT staff). Good project management is essentially about communication, and sometimes translation – if all participants in the project understand the intended outcomes of the project and the importance of their role, and have a respect for all other activities required to accomplish the initiative, there will be a greater impetus to work together to achieve these goals (S. Chapman, 2000). Regular meetings and discussions, open communications and working to agreed targets, deadlines and expenditures will be crucial in accomplishing such collaboration, as is maintaining staff interest in the project.

Managers should monitor every step of the process, and document all aspects in order that the invaluable experience gained by doing digital projects becomes a resource for the whole institution. Quality documentation outlining the rationale, methodologies, systems, staffing models, costs and lessons learned from a project should be an outcome of every digital project, enabling future managers of digital collections to interpret why things were created in a particular way and what needs to be done to maintain, or even to improve, the digital objects (S. Chapman, 2000). Having documentation will also address the issue of 'legacy projects' – projects created by staff who have since left the institution, or which have languished for the want of attention since they were launched. Developing good documentation will mean that each digital project can be a 'feasibility study' (or a risk assessment exercise!) for the next.

Consistent staffing and management is the best way to ensure the longevity of digital projects. A project manager may manage many smaller projects simultaneously and therefore develop a broad understanding of the institutional factors affecting the implementation and operation of digitization initiatives, and the factors that will facilitate or hinder efforts to mainstream such activities. Consequently, individuals who fill such positions are an extremely valuable resource for the whole organization. Nonetheless, many project managers are often hired on short-term, externally funded contracts, and leave at the end of a project. Emphasis should always be placed on finding, hiring and, most importantly, retaining a good project manager. Their skills will be crucial to the successful completion of digital projects and the successful implementation of digital programmes.

The steering committee or advisory boards

Projects should consider assembling a steering committee or advisory group consisting of stakeholders and experts from within and outside the host institution. The group can consist of representatives of all aspects of the project: subject or discipline specialists, senior administrators, IT staff, conservation and preservation staff, evaluation experts, and experts who have participated in or managed similar projects at other institutions. It is important to think strategically about who should be on the steering committee – it is an excellent opportunity to include senior members of staff at the host institution in the ongoing progress of the project. Including specialists in areas such as evaluation, dissemination and conservation is a good way to obtain ongoing expert advice throughout the course of the project. It is advisable to identify some key members of this group at the very early planning stages of the project and there should be an indication of who will be on this committee in any applications for funding. Project budgets should include the full costs of committee meetings, including travel costs and stipends where appropriate.

The functions of this group should be set out at the start of the project. These may include overseeing the project on behalf of funders, general project advice and oversight, reviewing progress reports, acting as advocates for the project and promoting it, and providing expert assistance where required. The group should meet on a regular if infrequent basis, and these meetings will be a useful opportunity for project staff and managers to report on progress and expenditure and to receive guidance and advice on various aspects of the project. A designated chair of the group should convene the meetings and ensure that the group is fulfilling the functions that are required of it.

Many funding agencies will mandate that such a group is convened, and some will require that a representative of the granting organization or agency is present at their meetings. Other funding agencies will ask that the project manager and other representatives meet with them on a regular basis to provide updates and progress reports.

Meetings with a project advisory board or funding agency should not be seen as an onerous requirement, but as a valuable opportunity to air ideas and gain support for particular approaches, and to obtain input and guidance from experts who will have a broad perspective on project management and implementation. The group will often be able to identify any concerns before they become problems, troubleshoot any issues, and strategize about political or institutional concerns such as dissemination and sustainability. Regular reports written for the group can provide a valuable record of the project.

Why digitization projects fail

As we have seen in the discussion on risk management (see Chapter 4), one of the most important aspects of planning a project is anticipating areas that may cause problems throughout the course of the project.

In a survey of risk factors for technology projects, the following reasons were identified as the cause of project failure (defined as going over budget, failing to complete the project on time, or otherwise failing to meet stated expectations):

32% – inadequate project management and control
20% – lack of communication
17% – failure to define objectives
17% – lack of familiarity with project scope and complexity
14% – incorrect technology, project size & other.

(Tanner, 2001b).

Digitization projects present many classic management issues: they are complex and costly, and often have an alarming tendency to manifest 'project drift' away from the original goals and objectives. This is a problem inherent in the very nature of technology-based projects – it is extremely likely that during the anticipated time to be spent on a project (be it six months or several years), some exciting new technology will come out that will benefit the project enormously. However, even minor changes in equipment, software, personnel and procedures between pilot projects and production projects can cause unexpected results. The project manager will have to steer this path carefully. Because of the complexity and expense of digitization projects, and because they take up so much management time, they can easily skew other priorities. A common perception is that other programmes and initiatives may suffer if the digitization programme or project starts to take up more resources than originally intended.

Effective project management is the key to keeping things on track and to ensuring that the project does not deviate from its stated goals or schedule. Some of the skills and activities that will help this process include:

- communication
- close management of staff resources
- implementing a good steering or advisory committee
- developing specifications based on the best advice obtainable, and fully tested with the people who will do the work
- regular and efficient quality control
- using cross-discipline teams to manage projects, to draw on a range of views and experience (Webb, 2000).

Another potential problem is loss of momentum from project conceptualization to funding to completion – there may be long time lags, and the project manager will have to keep enthusiasm for the project going as people become distracted by other priorities. There are a number of strategies to combat this by making the work of the project staff more interesting. The University of Michigan reports that staff engaged in the relatively tedious and repetitive tasks involved in the scanning of journals for the Making of America project were encouraged to work on different parts of the project's workflow, in order to break some of the monotony of only working on, say, scanning or metadata creation (Bonn, 2001). Other approaches are to encourage and support faculty use of the emerging digital materials in teaching, and by emphasizing as many technological 'advanced research' aspects of the project as possible in order to keep participants interested and engaged.

Managing the digital workflow/digitization process

The digital life cycle

The digital life cycle has many components. It is necessary to understand all these elements, and how they are connected, in order to see how a digital project can be managed. This approach is known as the 'holistic' approach to digitization – decisions taken about one aspect of a project will affect the entire digital life cycle. The components of running a digitization project cannot be presented as a straightforward 'recipe' to be followed, via a linear series of actions – many activities will happen in parallel and at different stages of the project, and many activities can overlap. The project manager will have to co-ordinate these activities and the people responsible for them, and maintain the project's momentum if there are long gaps between activities. It will also be important to understand how these activities impact on one another – for example, if copyright clearance will take a long time to complete, it will be unwise to purchase equipment for scanning until permissions have been cleared. There will be local collections and institutional considerations that affect the sequence of many of these activities, especially policies and procedures related to conservation and physical control of the original materials.

The workflow for a digitization project will consist of all or some of the following activities:

- Articulation of the project goals and intentions.
- Selection of materials for digitization.
- Copyright clearance, rights management research, plans and strategies for managing rights and permissions, development of rights and permissions metadata (administrative metadata).
- Preparation of source materials. This may include moving them to the digitization centre, conservation assessment, or treatment, such as re-housing or remounting.
- Creating catalogue records, finding aids or other pointers to a digital object or collection (descriptive metadata).
- Digital image production. This will include choosing digital capture devices, setting up imaging equipment, scanning source materials to create digital masters and associated technical metadata, and processing master images to create derivatives for screen or print (using image-processing tools, or optical character recognition tools where appropriate).
- Quality control for source materials and digital images, transfer of sources to original or new location, re-housing materials, updating catalogue records as necessary.
- Creation of structural metadata.
- Creation of full text and mark-up where required.
- File management; loading and delivering content to a database or repository.
- Integration of digital images and metadata into an image database.
- Delivery to users, using techniques ranging from developing web

pages to using an automated delivery system such as a database.
- Advertising, promotion, user evaluation.
- Long-term preservation, including migration and conversion (S. Chapman, 2000).

The project manager will have to allocate a cost to each of these activities. Costs can often be projected using the results of prototyping and feasibility tests, as outlined in Chapter 6. Selection decisions and related issues – cataloguing, assessing the condition of originals, etc. – will add to both the costs and the schedule. What will be harder to anticipate than monetary costs will be the amount of time that is to be spent on each activity.

Possible risks associated with each of these activities will also have to be identified and managed. These include managing intellectual property issues, the abilities and experience of staff, the available technologies and their capacity and limitations (including tools for delivery of the digital content), the amount of work to be done versus the available time or money, and the possibilities of delays and how they affect the overall life cycle of the project if activities are interdependent.

Delivery of materials

Before starting a digitization project, it is essential to consider access and delivery options. Technical decisions taken early on in the planning process will affect the quality of information that can be delivered to remote users, and this is an area where testing and end-user evaluation is crucial. Many projects make the mistake of not assessing anticipated users until very late in project – often shortly before the project is launched – rather than evaluating users at the outset. It will also be necessary to consider questions of security, authenticity and authentication. Not all content will be for public access, and copyright and licensing restrictions may mean that restrictions have to be placed on content delivery. Tools such as those emerging from Internet 2's Shibboleth project may be useful in this regard. Shibboleth is developing architectures, policy structures, practical technologies and an open-source implementation to support inter-institutional sharing of online resources subject to a series of access controls (http://shibboleth. internet2.edu/).

Key issues related to the delivery of materials include:

- *Graphic design.* Is a project team member able to design a user interface that is appealing and easy to use, and enables all the 'scholarly primitives' end-users may need: discovering (browsing, searching), annotating, comparing, referring, sampling, illustrating and representing (Unsworth 2000). For example, the maps at www.davidrumsey.com fulfil many of these criteria.
- *Amount of information.* How much information is to be delivered? Are there large images, audio or moving image files? In which case, how will the users download these files? Are thumbnails to be presented for ease of browsing – which will necessitate creating an additional surrogate image as a JPEG, GIF or PNG file.
- *Organization of information.* How is access to the information presented? Is it a logical approach to the content? How many 'layers' of information do end-users have to go through in order to reach the core content (see Goldman and Wadman, 2003)?
- *Types of metadata.* What metadata is used? Is it sufficient for end-users to be able to find the digital resources and navigate their way throughout the information?
- *Types of media.* Are plug-ins or additional tools required? Will users find it easy to access these? Is content to be streamed or downloaded? If streaming is to be used (for copyright reasons, for example), can access to the site be guaranteed, especially if the content is to be used for teaching or other activities that require certain access? Are standard formats used for downloads (e.g. MPEG2 or MPEG4, QuickTime)? Do search tools meet the needs of end-users?
- *Accessibility.* Are there multilingual issues? – Is a mark-up system like Unicode required to support multilingual searches? Is accessibility for the disabled or partially sighted anticipated through the use of tools like the Bobby standard?

A useful overview of the attributes of delivery systems for digital materials that should be considered is the International Council of Museums (ICOM) guide to *Multimedia Evaluative Criteria* (ICOM, 1997). Although developed with a museums audience in mind, it is an extremely comprehensive overview of all the factors that will affect the delivery of digital content.

Evaluation

It will be important to ensure that strategies are in place to evaluate end-users of the digital materials. This should take place:

- before the project has begun, to assess possible audiences for such materials and their expectations and abilities (front-end evaluation)
- throughout the development of a project, to assess the content, design and usability of the resources (formative evaluation)
- at the completion of a project, to assess the effectiveness of the delivery system in conveying the desired message of the content to the desired audience (summative evaluation).

Any evaluation should involve groups of users who approximate the intended audience for the finished project, whether they be students, schoolchildren, members of the public, or academics.

The attributes of delivery systems that should be assessed include:

- ease of use and accessibility
- functionality: how well does the system work? Are the interfaces intuitive?
- consistency of content and finding aids
- navigation and control for the end-user
- help and documentation
- the time taken to access, download and search the material.

Quantitative targets and models can help in setting parameters for these objectives, and monitoring their development throughout the course of the project (Keene, 1998).

Assessment and preparation of materials for scanning

The shape, size and condition of the original source materials will influence the decisions about which capture method to choose. Primary source materials in museums, archives and libraries consist of a variety of data formats (texts, images and sound or moving image), and the digital capture of that data needs to be carefully considered in relation both to the content and to the substrates on which the material is carried. Sound, moving image and fragile or rare material will be addressed in more detail in Chapters 8 and 9.

Anything that can be photographed can be digitized, and some materials can be photographed or digitized with more accuracy to the original than others (Deegan and Tanner, 2002). However, the attributes of the original materials will influence the decisions made about the type of digital imaging equipment and methods to be used:

Format. Materials can be bound or loose leaf, printed or handwritten, and colour or black and white, or a combination of these, such as pages with both print and images. A collection may include materials in a variety of formats, including manuscripts, three-dimensional objects and images. Can materials be laid flat for scanning, or is some sort of cradle required? Can the original materials be scanned, or does a surrogate image (e.g. a photograph or microfilm) have to be created?

Size. Materials will come in a variety of shapes and sizes, from small manuscript fragments to oversized maps or posters, banners or flags.

Detail. There will be questions concerning the level of detail in the originals, such as tonal range, that must be captured, and the level of detail that is to be delivered to the end-users.

Preparation of materials. When is the best time to repair and replace materials? Should this be factored into the workflow? How can a balance be struck between usability, cost and the best representation of the artifact? (For example, should blank pages at the beginning and end of each volume be included?) Post digitization, should the original volumes be kept? For how long? And what is the best way to collaborate with others on cost-effective physical and virtual preservation and giving access to digitally reformatted volumes?

If the collection to be digitized consists of a large variety of original materials, it may be appropriate to outsource the digitization of some materials, and do the rest in house. For example, if only a small number of materials need special attention (e.g., they are oversized, or three dimensional), and the rest can be scanned on a flatbed scanner, the unique materials may be outsourced and the rest done in house. Exceptions, such as taking the time to digitize the occasional image, or to handle special preservation concerns, always increase costs.

Handling and preparation of original materials

Preparation and handling costs add a significant cost to the project budget – in some cases, as much as 30–50% of the project total (Tanner, 2001). If these costs are not anticipated, they will jeopardize a project's budget.

The movement of materials, especially if they are to be digitized off site, can take a great deal of preparation. They will have to be inventoried and packed, and insured against damage if they are especially rare or valuable. The materials may also have to be disbound, unstapled, cleaned or remounted prior to digitization (for example, the Afghan Papers project at NYU is carrying out preservation treatment on every item in the collection prior to digitization).

Each item to be digitized should be catalogued and a unique identifier assigned, which may correspond to the file name of the digital object. It may also be necessary to develop indexing, cataloguing or metadata schema. If applicable, the cost of clearing copyright and obtaining permission to digitize the collections can be the largest preparation cost. For an example of a quantification of how much time and money can be spent on copyright clearance, see Cave, Deegan and Heinink's (2000) report on copyright clearance workflows. They estimate that the cost of simply doing the administrative work of clearing permissions was £5–6 per document during the first year, dropping to £2–3 per document in subsequent years. The time spent on the project was that of a staff member two days a week. Recent assessments by staff on this project suggest that these original cost estimates are probably too low. Similarly, New York Public Library is still developing rights management methodologies for its African Diaspora digitization project, and a half-time staff position is dedicated to clearing and managing copyright for these materials.

The role of surrogate images in the digitization workflow

At the project planning stage, the project manager will have to address two key questions regarding the role of surrogate image formats in the digitization workflow:

- In cases where the original material exists, should digitization be from this original (e.g. black and white or colour photographs, negatives, glass plate negatives, manuscripts, drawings, prints or maps) or from a surrogate image (slides, transparencies, copy prints, microfilm)?
- What, if any, is the role of microfilming in the project workflow?

It may not be possible to digitize directly from the original – its condition or accessibility may preclude the material being handled or exposed directly to scanning or digital photography for conservation reasons. Similarly, digital imaging technologies may not be adequate to cope with certain types of originals, such as oversized maps, banners or posters or three-dimensional objects.

Sometimes, only a secondary image will be available. This is often the case in projects to reconstruct or reunify 'lost' collections, and is frequently the case in photography or slide libraries, where slides are often retained over original photographic prints for quality reasons (the art historical community prefers slides to prints). The quality of negatives can vary greatly, although they are the first generation of an image, there may be substantial differences between the negative and the print, especially in fine arts photography, where artists will spend a great deal of time in the darkroom creating prints (the work of Ansel Adams is one of the best examples of this). The results of this work will be lost if the negative, not the print, is scanned (Serensen Colet, 2000).

However, working with an intermediary may result in a loss of quality. Any copying process may result in the loss of quality between the original and the surrogate, as an operator will have to make decisions about focus and colour based on the individual's ability to perceive the full light spectrum. A scan from a surrogate will only be as good as the surrogate, not the original, and this proposition is demonstrated by some useful comparisons and research carried out by the Digital Image Archive of Medieval Music, a collaborative project between the University of Oxford and Royal Holloway, University of London (www.diamm.ac.uk/).

In cases where it is nonetheless necessary to create an intermediary for scanning, the advances in digital capture (especially digital photography) mean that a digital record can be created that is at least equal to, and occasionally better than, a good photographic copy (and eliminates the expense of this additional step). If direct digital capture is selected as an option, it will be important to create an imaging environment that replicates the care and attention of preservation photography – for example, camera angles, lighting and exposure rates should be given as much attention as with traditional photography, and a professional photographer should be employed to operate the digital capture device.

What, if any, is the role of microfilming in the project workflow?

There will often be a role for microfilming in the project workflow. Stuart Lee (2001a) concludes that there are four situations in which it is necessary.

- if the collection already consists of a good stock of film surrogates, and if the quality of these is deemed to be acceptable
- to match preservation needs, if a conservation decision has been made to make a film copy of an item
- if traditional photography is deemed to pose less of a threat to the original
- if the original cannot be digitized using the equipment available, for example because of constraints of size in the case of maps, etc., or if there are time efficiencies to be gained by filming the materials rather than scanning, as may be the case if working with bound volumes.

Microfilm provides a stable format, with a very long life (estimates range from 200–500 years if the materials are stored and handled properly); it is platform independent and accessible via lens-based hardware. It can be used as a source for re-mastering or digitizing throughout the course of its life cycle, and will not require migration or refreshing.

Filming is a well established technique, with existing workflows and reliable vendors to choose from, and is considered to be the production process that is most appropriate with regard to the integrity of the originals. This may therefore be a better solution for some projects rather than having to set up a scanning workstation that takes into account preservation conditions and special handling requirements. The use of preservation microfilm standards (notably *RLG Guidelines for Microfilming to Support Digitization* (2003b)) will produce microfilm that can be scanned by most microfilm digitization service bureaux with less handling, and less cost, because it is uniform and therefore easier to scan. The RLG *Guidelines* cover areas such as preparation, targeting and indexing of the film. They suggest a technically rigorous approach to preservation microfilming to make it more amenable to digitization, which will help libraries and archives 'achieve the viable option of using microfilm for preservation and digitization of the film for enhanced access' (Robin Dale, writing in the preface to the 2003 *Guidelines*).

What is emerging as a suggested strategy is hybrid approach, in which a combination of both microfilming and digitization of materials is carried out. This approach recognizes that microfilm has the edge as a preservation format but that digital technologies offer advantages for accessing the content, notably via indexing, searching and browsing.

In practical terms, many projects are finding that both scanning and microfilming often go hand in hand, which can significantly add to the project's workflow and costs. The University of Iowa Libraries reports that a project to digitize part of their special collections had four distinct workflows: preservation photocopying, keying and encoding textual information for full-text searching, cataloguing the individual materials, and digital imaging of the same materials. The pieces resulting from each of these separate workflows had to be re-assembled in physical and digital format in the final phase of the project (Hughes, 2000).

Scan first or film first?

If the hybrid approach of scanning and microfilming is deemed to be necessary, there are two possible approaches, both developed in the context of research carried out for the Brittle Books project, funded by the NEH in the USA:

- the model developed at Cornell University Library, which is to create digital images directly from the originals, and then produce film from the digital images using Computer Output Microfilm or COM (i.e. to scan first)
- the model developed at Yale University Library, which is to first microfilm the original source materials, then scan from the film, i.e. to film first. This model would suit an institution with a great deal of experience in preservation microfilming. One project that is following this model is the Australian Cooperative Digitisation Project 1840–45, also known as Ferguson 1840–45, a collaborative project between the the University of Sydney Library, the State Library of New South Wales, the National Library of Australia and Monash University Library to digitize Australian serials and fiction.

For a discussion of both approaches, and the economics of scanning first versus filming first, see Chapman, Conway and Kenney (1999a) and the CLIR *Working paper* by the same authors (Chapman, Conway and Kenney, 1999b), which provides a decision tree to assist institutions in determining the circumstances under which one would scan first or film first.

Equipment

The types of digitization equipment available include:

- flatbed scanners, which may have sheet-feed attachments for batch scanning of disbound documents
- book, or overhead scanners
- microfilm or transparency scanners
- digital cameras.

These can be categorized as using 'contact' and 'no-contact' methods of image capture, and the choice of equipment will depend on the type of material to be digitized. Contact equipment, such as flatbed scanners, transparency scanners and drum scanners, will necessitate placing an original flat against the scanbed in order to scan the image. This approach will only work if the original is flat (for example, photographic materials, sheets of paper) or can be pressed flat without damage, which may be the case with some books, transparencies or negatives. No-contact equipment includes overhead scanners, book scanners and digital cameras. This approach will be more suitable for fragile materials, oversized materials such as maps or architectural plans, and three-dimensional objects.

If working with a mixed-media collection, it may not be possible to use one scanner for everything. A flatbed that is ideal for high-speed, high-volume paper scanning may not be capable of the resolution required for high-quality scans of transparencies. A digital camera studio set-up is not required for scanning loose-leaf pages or for most photographic materials. Most scanners and digital cameras were designed for large markets such as the business and graphic arts segments, and not to accommodate the specific needs of libraries and archives, so some compromises may be necessary when selecting equipment. For a useful summary of the way that different types of equipment have been used in cultural heritage projects, see Chapman (1999).

Scanners

It is necessary to ensure that the capability of the selected scanner is suitable to the materials to be scanned and to the project's objectives. Both scanners and digital cameras use a CCD (Charge Coupled Device) array as their core compoent. CCD is a a collection of tiny light-sensitive diodes that sweep across an image during capture and, when exposed to light, generate a series of digital signals that are converted into pixel values. The most important factor is the resolution that the scanner is capable of. The scanner will often be listed with a maximum optical resolution and an interpolated or software resolution. The optical resolution is the significant figure: interpolated resolution uses software to 'guess' the values of pixels that are between those that the scanner can optically register. Interpolation should be avoided in an archive-quality scanning exercise. Where resolution is listed as, for example, 600x1200 dpi the maximum optical resolution will be 600 dpi. For more information on these requirements, and many other questions about scanning, see www.scantips.com.

The dynamic range of the scanner describes the tonal density of the information that can be captured. The higher the dynamic range the better, particularly for originals with a large amount of tonal detail (e.g. shadow, or other subtle detail), such as photographic prints and transparencies. Production-level flatbed scanners usually have either an A4- or an A3-sized scanning area; scanners are available for larger materials, but they are more expensive. Transparency scanners are available which can scan strips or mounted 35 mm negative or positive transparencies to high resolutions. Adaptors are available to batch scan up to 50 slides at a time. Scanners range in price from tens to thousands of pounds, and the investment made should be appropriate to the requirements of the project.

Kenney and Rieger, in their digital imaging tutorial (2000), discuss these issued in greater detail, and suggest that the following questions should influence the selection of a scanner:

- Is the scanner compatible with the source material and can it handle the potential range of sizes, document types (single leaf, bound volume) and media (reflective, transparent) and the condition of the originals?
- Can the scanner produce the requisite quality to meet the needs of the project? It is always possible to derive a lower-quality image from a higher-quality one, but no amount of digital magic can accurately restore detail that was never captured to begin with. Factors affecting quality include optical resolution, bit depth, dynamic range, and signal-to-noise ratio (see 'Images: technical details', page 187).
- Will the scanner support the production schedule and conversion budget? Are the manufacturer's throughput claims valid? What are the document-handling capabilities, duty cycle, MTBF (Mean Time Between Failure) and lifetime capacity? What kind of maintenance contracts and service agreements are available (does the manufacturer or distributor offer on-site repair and/or 24-hour replacement to eliminate potential downtime in the schedule if there is an equipment failure (Kenney and Rieger, 2000)?

Scanner specifications can be difficult to interpret and often lack standardization, making meaningful comparisons impossible. For detailed, specific information about selecting digital imaging equipment, see the feasibility study for the JISC Image Digitisation Initiative (Tanner and Robinson, 1998). See also the RLG, CLIR and DLF Guides to 'Quality in Visual Resource Imaging', particularly Guide number 2, *Selecting a Scanner* (Williams, 1998).

The software that runs the scanner is also important. It should be straightforward to use and incorporate an ability to run batch scans to save capture time, where applicable (NOF-Digitise, 2002a).

Digital cameras

Digital cameras are developing for both the home and professional market and are priced from several hundred to thousands of pounds. Home-use cameras are aimed at non-professional users for general photography. There are two kinds of professional digital camera. The first has developed from medical and industrial uses and has all the parts (lens and CCD array) integrated into one single unit, which is connected to, and operated directly from, a computer. The second has the appearance of a traditional camera, but replaces film with a digital CCD array with internal processing and memory, which stores the images until the memory is full, at which point the images can be transferred to a computer. This is known as a digital scanning back. Digital scanning backs are becoming an acceptable replacement for traditional film cameras for professional use. One of their advantages is that they use the lenses and camera body of a traditional professional camera. Both types of digital camera are used in digital imaging projects, although the first type of camera will cost considerably more than the second.

Professional digital camera set-ups will require the operator to at the very least understand the basics of photography and for projects where high-quality images are crucial it is recommended that they have a professional photography background. For information on selecting a digital camera, see the TASI section on digital cameras at www.ukoln.ac.uk/nof/support/help/papers/digitisation_process/.

Network assessment

It will be necessary to establish if the institution's network capacity is adequate to support a large-scale digital imaging project. Networks are probably the least visible portions of the technical infrastructure, managed by unseen systems departments. But nothing can bring a digital imaging initiative to a halt faster than a network that is undersized, too slow, or unreliable, especially if large image files have to be moved around the network for storage and access. A heavily used digital image collection will place even greater demands on your network. Institutions may find that a digital imaging initiative makes demands on an existing network that have implications for the entire organization. A discussion with network administrators about the anticipated network demands (including long-term storage on institutional servers) should take place early in the project-planning stage (Kenney and Rieger, 2000).

Equipment procurement

It will also be necessary to address any weaknesses in your institution's procurement process that may slow down or complicate the acquisition of this equipment. It may be necessary to spend a lot of time researching available scanning equipment, requesting samples, and ensuring that expert advice is taken about what equipment to choose. This process can take a lot of time, and the market for this technology changes very quickly, meaning that purchasing decisions will have to be made quickly. Also factor in the time to set up and test an imaging workstation, and to set targets for image capture.

Other equipment

Other equipment that will need to be considered will include computer hardware (CPUs and monitors) and printers. It is always advisable to buy the highest-quality equipment that is affordable, and to maximize available processor speed, RAM and disk space. Requirments will vary, depending upon the needs of a particular project, and what other purposes (if any) the equipment is to be used for. (While dedicated workstations should be allocated to digital imaging projects this isn't always possible.)

Images: technical details

Image quality

Resolution refers to the number of pixels used to display an image. Resolution affects the level of detail that can be shown in the image file. Lower resolution means that fewer pixels will be used to describe the image, leading to blurring of edges and loss of overall detail in the image (Beamsley, 1999). Resolution is usually expressed in dots per inch (dpi) or pixels per inch (ppi), and relates to the density of information that is captured by the scanning equipment. Broadly speaking, the higher the dpi, the more detail is being captured. The amount of resolution required to obtain a useful image of an item is determined by the size of the original, the amount of detail in the original and the eventual use for the data. For example, a 35 mm transparency will require a higher dpi than a 5x4 print because it is smaller and more detailed. An A4-sized modern printed document that is intended to be processed into a searchable text will need less resolution than a similar-sized colour photographic original. There are also upward limits on resolution – file size is one (increasing resolution will increase the file size) and another is preventing the capture of extraneous information. For example, postcards are often printed on poor-quality paper and if they are scanned at too high a resolution the texture of the paper will be captured and can obscure the content. There is also a point where putting more resolution into the capture process will no longer add value to the information content of the digital output.

Bit-depth, or *dynamic range*, relates to the level of colour that will be captured. A bit is the binary digit that represents the tonal value of the pixel. As an overview, a 1-bit image is black and white (the pixel has 1 bit and is therefore black or white with no shades in between), an 8-bit image has 256 shades of either grey or colour ($2^8 = 256$ shades), and a 24-bit image has millions of shades of colour ($2^{24} = 16,777,216$ shades).

Essentially, the digitized images should be of high enough quality to meet most of the institution's foreseeable needs and to satisfy the demands of researchers seeking access to the collections using high-resolution monitors or advanced printing techniques (NOF-Digitise, 2002a).

Comparisons of suitable resolutions for digital master files for various media types are discussed in the JIDI feasibility study (Tanner and Robisnon, 1998), which contains a useful table of baseline standards of minimum values of resolutions according to original material type. A detailed discussion of resolution and of binary and bit depth can be found on TASI's web pages (www.tasi.ac.uk). A comparative analysis of the different image qualities used in a variety of cultural heritage projects can also be found in the Cornell digital imaging tutorial (Cornell University Library, Research Department, 2002).

File size and compression

Production of high-quality images is much more expensive and takes up much more storage space. File size will affect the amount of work that can be done in a specific time and will affect workflow, especially files that are over 100 Mb in size. However, if the intention is to create an archival master file, compromises cannot be made on file size. Reducing image sizes by a small amount, e.g. from 100 Mb to 80 Mb will not significantly change the number of images one can capture in a given time, as most of the time spent is in other aspects of the workflow, such as setting up the source materials on the scanner or setting up a digital camera, editing the work, processing images and backing up the files. Efficiencies and savings should be gained by assessing where the workflow can be made more efficient, rather than by reducing the image size. However, it will be necessary to research the storage required for back-up and archiving of files, and to assess the cost of storing and backing up the digital images over the long term.

Digital image projects will create expensive requirements in terms of hard disk space and processing power, in order simply to open and edit a file and to view multiple images simultaneously. This will create cost considerations that will have an impact on the overall project budget (Serensen Colet, 2000).

The digital file can be compressed to reduce its size. Compressed files are classified as using either lossy or lossless compression techniques. Lossy compression will reduce the size of the file by a ratio from 10:1 to 50:1, but this reduction is at the expense of some of the file's original data, which will affect the integrity of the image. Lossless compression guarantees that the original data can be restored exactly, and so this is the format that should always be used for compressed master images. Typically, lossless compression results in a compression ratio of about 3:1 or 2:1.

Formats and technology standards

The end products of digitization will be files in a variety of formats, depending on their medium. These will include images in many file formats, electronic text files, digital video or audio, virtual reality or 3-D materials. Managing these files will be easier over the long term if conformity to standard file formats is observed from the outset of the project.

A wide range of technology standards exists, reflecting the long history of the computer industry, which develops and adopts new standards on an ongoing basis. It will be necessary for project managers to acquaint themselves with the community and industry standards for digital media. These standards will change over time, and it is important to maintain an understanding of the field in order to keep up to date with changes in technology. The use of relevant standards will be critical if a project is to share and publish the digital files that it has created. Formats used will also be dependent on what sort of compression is required.

Image standards and formats

TIFF (Tagged Image File Format)

This format is used when creating digital images for long-term use and for maximum information capture. It does not use compression, or, if a compressed form of TIFF is used, it will be lossless, so files saved in the TIFF format will be large, high-resolution and high-quality files. Any scanner or digital camera, and the software used in association with them, will provide the option of saving to the TIFF format. This format is recommended as the acceptable format for saving archival master copies of digital images (Kenney and Rieger, 2000). Because TIFF files are so large, it is impractical to transfer them over networks unless over a specially allocated high-speed network such as Internet 2, or to use them for day-to-day project work.

JPEG (Joint Photographic Experts Group)

This standard is used to deliver images across networks, such as the internet or local networks. JPEG files use lossy compression to reduce the file size, while retraining a reasonable-looking image. Consequently, this file format is not appropriate for master archival files. The use and display of JPEG files is supported by all web browsers and by a large number of desktop applications. JPEG files can be created by image-processing software, which will import a TIFF image and export a JPEG one. The JPEG format is suitable for scanned photographs and complex images.

GIF (Graphics Interchange Format)

This format is used to deliver images over networks, usually the internet. Although the display of GIF images is supported by all web browsers and many applications, it is a proprietary file format, covered by a patent. GIF files utilize lossless file compression to reduce the size of the file. This is the file format recommended for cartoons, icons and similar graphic images. GIF files are created by image-processing software, which imports a TIFF file and exports a GIF image. Because they are compressed, both JPEG and GIF files may be considerably smaller than TIFF files (they can be measured in kilobytes).

PNG (Portable Network Graphics)

PNG images are supported by recent versions of web browsers. PNG files have more efficient compression than GIF or JPEG, and images may look better in this format, but they are a larger file size. Most image-processing applications will offer PNG as a format in which TIFF images can be saved.

Audiovisual standard formats

The formats listed here are the most commonly used for web delivery of audiovisual materials, but this is an area where there is a good deal of commercial development affecting standards. The MATRIX project and the AHDS Performing Arts Data Service provide regularly updated information on developments in audio moving image technologies. There is also an excellent comparative chart of file formats for time-based media in the NINCH Guide to Good Practice (NINCH, 2002).

Audio formats

Audio can be uncompressed, compressed without loss, or compressed with loss. Lossless compression will only reduce the file size by a factor of about 2:1, so if compression is used, it is usually lossy. For uncompressed audio it is necessary to know the number of channels, usually stereo, i.e. two, or mono, i.e. one; the number of bits per sample; and the sampling rate. The CD standard is stereo, 16 bit/sample, 44100 samples per second. In terms of storage, that requires about 10 Mb per minute. (For archival purposes 'CD format' stereo at 16 bits and 44100 samples per second is the minimum accepted, because it corresponds almost exactly to our measured ability to hear.) A .wav file at the same sample depth and rate will take about the same amount of space, as will any uncompressed, or loss-free compressed, audio format.

For 'lossy' compression of both audio and visual recordings, it is difficult to draw useful comparisons about file sizes. While these algorithms are based on theory, there is no *a priori* way to compare the alternatives. Companies that are in this business use extensive listening tests to verify what they think should work. While it is possible to compare the alternatives in terms of file sizes, there is no way to know the cost of lossy compression. A file twice as large may not be twice as better sounding.

For some guidelines of comparisons, see the National Institute of Standards and Technology's publication, *Digital Media File Types: survey of common formats* (http://www.itl.nist.gov/div895/isis/filetypes.html).

WAV

WAV is the standard Windows audio file format, and is supported by recent versions of Windows via the inbuilt Windows Media Player (this comes pre-installed on most Windows computer systems). All audio CDs are in WAV format.

AC3

AC3 comes from Dolby and it is the multi-channel surround sound format commonly used in DVDs. It is sometimes called 5.1 audio.

MP3

Part of the MPEG family of multimedia standards, MP3 files are small in size and produce a quality of sound that will be dependent on the compression selected. Although MP3 does not reach true uncompressed CD quality, the quality will be adequate for many users and this is the preferred format for the delivery of popular music over the internet (such as by Apple's iTunes Music Store, which sells music for downloading). MP3 files can be used by the Windows Media Player. Note that MP3 is a lossy compression technique. AAC, a new audio format that is part of the MPEG4 standard, may well replace MP3 by offering better audio quality and smaller files, thanks to improved compression technology (for more information, see www. apple.com/mpeg4/aac).

Real Audio

This is a commonly used file format, owing to the free availability of Real Audio player software, which can be downloaded from the Progressive Networks website (www.real.com).

Digital video standards

The entertainment and technology industries have a vested interest in developing efficient and interoperable formats for the customer. Consequently, digital video formats are rapidly changing. In addition to the existing standards listed below, the reader is advised that there are emerging standards on the horizon, including DivX (see www.divx.com/), which is an up-and-coming video format, and CODEC (COmpression and DE-Compression tool).

MPEG (Motion Pictures Expert Group)

This format is popular for the publication of video on the internet, as it uses a short download time. A large range of player software, including the Windows Media Player, supports MPEG files. Sound and video may be combined in one file (such as in a motion picture or narrated documentary). MPEGs use psycho-acoustic algorithms to encode the most 'prominent' information only and so MPEG files can be highly compressed, while still maintaining a reasonable quality. MPEG is becoming a dominant standard in the field and MPEG formats are used for DVD video and digital television broadcasts. Like MP3, the quality is selectable depending on the acceptable size of the final file. High-quality DVD can use data rates of up to approximately 7 Mb per second (Mbps). There are different types of MPEG files available: MPEG-1, an early (and now fading) standard; MPEG-2, which is used with DVDs and uses data rates of typically about 8 Mbps, but as low as 2 Mbps for VHS quality; and the emerging MPEG-4 format, used for low bandwidth yet high-quality applications such as cell phone video or streaming broadcasts, anywhere from 64 Kbps to 4 Mbps.

Real Video

This is a proprietary format, developed and supported by progressive networks. It produces a good-quality picture, and files in this format can be played on free RealPlayer software. The quality of the image can be adjusted to take into account the desired file size, which means that the material may be compressed and made available to users with a slower connection.

AVI (Audio Video Interleave)

This is currently the most common format for audio/video data on the PC, and is also very common for audio video delivered over the internet. AVI files are supported by the Windows Media Player and RealPlayer.

QuickTime

QuickTime, originally a dominant video format for the Macintosh platform, is now a multi-format standard that supports and includes many software CODECs, including many of those mentioned in this section.

Quality assurance and quality control

The project manager must develop a rigorous quality control process for three stages of the project: first, during the preparation of specifications for the digital-imaging workflow, defining all imaging objectives (regardless of whether the work is done in house or outsourced); second, during the key stages in the project, such as selection, handling and digital capture; and finally during the image delivery project, to evaluate download times, on-screen resolution, etc. Such quality assurance procedures will guarantee the integrity and consistency of the image acquisition process, and minimize the variation between different operators and different scanning devices. The person responsible for the scanning should not carry out the quality assurance. It will be equally important to verify any recorded information and metadata created against the information accompanying the original.

The quality of digital files is affected by many factors, each of which can be controlled independently: original material, capture device (scanner or technique used), operator, scanning resolution, dynamic range of scanner, post-processing and image manipulation, formats, compression algorithms and final display device. Ultimately, digital image quality will be a tradeoff between final image quality and the capture time required, as well as storage available and file size – that is between final image quality and cost. Higher image quality means accompanying increases in resolution and colour depth, storage and file size, all of which place a larger demand on the whole digitization chain.

Quality control procedures should address the following issues:

- Is the digital file named for the correct original object?
- Does the image include all the information in the original image?
- Does the image accurately represent the qualities of the original?
- Does the image conform to the agreed-upon file standards in the specification?

Other technical considerations to review will include: orientation; cropped and border areas, missing text, page numbers; alignment of image; size, resolution and bit depth of image; file format; details in highlights and shadows; tonal values, including brightness, contrast and sharpness.

An overall evaluation should address the quality of the digital objects as a whole, and assess this quality against the original source materials. Is the digital copy unacceptable, adequate but of diminished quality, comparable in quality to the original or of improved quality?

It will also be necessary to assess the quality of the digital files when they are delivered to the end-user by assessing the images under different display or access conditions (e.g. on a lower resolution monitor, or files delivered via a modem).

The importance of consistency

Consistency is the key to ensuring the quality of digital files. It is necessary to develop a consistent series of processes to ensure that there are no variations in quality, regardless of different devices used for different stages of the digitization workflow, and to achieve consistent results. This can be achieved by using standard tools, such as the image quality charts produced by Kodak, and developing routines for testing the image quality of monitors or display devices, scanners, digital cameras and printers, and for calibrating the imaging equipment. For more detail on image quality, see the work of Frey (1997), which is seminal in this area. In particular Frey suggests that four targets be used for evaluating the results of digitization: tone reproduction, colour reproduction, detail and edge reproduction, and noise. Satisfactory performance in output tests for these four targets will ensure that an acceptable digital surrogate of image information has been created. This is especially important if several parties are responsible for the digitization or image capture. If a vendor is to be used, these results should be agreed in advance (CHIN, 2002).

Management of digital assets

Digital files, including images, metadata and associated materials, will often be stored in a database, image management system, or digital asset management system. There are many commercially available tools that can be used, and selection should be based on the needs of the project. For a discussion of these tools, and suggestions for some tools that can be used, see the NINCH *Guide to Good Practice* section on digital asset management tools (NINCH, 2002). See also the TASI website (www.tasi.ac.uk) for a detailed discussion of image management systems and how they can be used to manage the workflow of digitization projects by providing versioning controls when several staff members are working on the same part of a project.

Metadata

Metadata is, simply, information about information. In the digital context, it is information that describes digital objects and enables users, both present and future, to find, manage, and use digital objects. Metadata is more than just cataloguing information; it should represent the total historic record of the digital object, and should represent the totality of information about the object, including its creators, structure, format, etc. Good metadata creation will be a key component of developing digital materials that are usable and useful for the long term, and therefore a significant investment should be made in the design of metadata schema at the project-planning stages and to ensure that accurate metadata is captured throughout the project. There is an excellent discussion on metadata for resource discovery, description and use in Deegan and Tanner's *Digital Futures* (2002), and the reader is encouraged to consult this for a comprehensive overview of the topic.

Typically, metadata will be stored in some type of database, using a controlled vocabulary or series of keywords developed following conventional guidelines for the content, such as thesauri, classification schemes and authority term lists. Examples include the Library of Congress subject classification schema (http://lcweb.loc.gov/catdir/cpso/lcco/lcco.html), terminology from the Art and Architecture Thesaurus (AAT) and Thesaurus of Geographic Names developed by the Getty Information Institute (www.getty.edu/research/conducting_research/vocabularies/aat/index.html), the International Council of Museums International Committee for Documentation (CIDOC) standards for museums documentation (www.cidoc.icom.org). Using a controlled vocabulary will ensure that users of the digital resources are able to search and browse the resources in a consistent fashion.

A schema that has been used widely as a basic framework for many different types of metadata is the Dublin Core Metadata Element Set

(DCMES; see http://dublincore.org/). This is a generic set of 15 elements applicable to a variety of digital object types. Dublin Core has been adapted by a number of communities, including museums, scientific ('Darwin core') and cultural heritage organizations and moving image archive repositories. Dublin Core was originally intended to facilitate the retrieval of web-based resources, but has since grown in scope to become able to describe almost any object.

The three main types of metadata are:

- descriptive metadata
- administrative/technical metadata
- structural metadata.

METS

The METS (Metadata and Encoding Transmission Standard) schema is an improved new standard for encoding the descriptive, administrative and structural metadata of digital objects, expressed using the XML schema language of the World Wide Web Consortium. The standard is maintained in the Network Development and MARC Standards Office of the Library of Congress, and is being developed as an initiative of the Digital Library Federation. For more information see www.loc.gov/standards/mets/.

For an example of a technical metadata schema, see the NISO Metadata for Images in XML (NISO MIX) project, at www.loc. gov/standards/mix).

Descriptive metadata

This is used for resource discovery and providing intellectual and physical access to the collections. Typical descriptive metadata formats are the MARC (MAchine Readable Cataloguing) format (for more information, see http://lcweb.loc.gov/marc/) and the EAD Document Type Definition (DTD), a standard for encoding archival finding aids using Standard Generalized Markup Language (SGML) and exTensible Markup Language (XML). For more information see http://lcweb.loc.gov/ead/.

Other descriptive metadata schema are the TEI Header, part of the TEI (Text Encoding Initiative; www.tei-c.org/Guidelines2/index.html) which is primarily concerned with describing electronic texts, and the VRA Core Categories, Version 3.0, which is a project of the Visual Resources Association Data Standards Committee. The VRA Core Categories, Version 3.0, consist of a single element set that can be applied as many times as necessary to create records to describe visual materials. See www.vraweb.org/vracore3.htm.

Administrative/technical metadata

This is information that allows a repository to manage its digital collection, e.g. date of scan, resolution, rights information. The appropriate technical and administrative metadata (such as catalogue details, copyright status, capture information, file format, resolution, etc.) will assist the project manager in maintaining and preserving the digital collection. This is particularly important with collections that contain large numbers of surrogate images created from a digital master. Each and every digital object will need its own individual metadata; the use of these tools will help manage the workflow of a digitization project.

Structural metadata

This is metadata relevant to the presentation of a digital object to users, and to the relationships of digital objects to one another and to external resources. The METAe project (the Metadata Engine project) is one initiative that is undertaking research into structural metadata (http://meta-e.uibk.ac.at).

For an excellent overview of metadata in a digital library environment, see the work done by Robin Wedler for the Harvard Library Digitization Initiative, available at http://hul.harvard.edu/ldi/html/metadata.html, and also the Getty Resource *Introduction to Metadata: pathways to digital information* at www.getty.edu/research/conducting_research/standards/intrometadata/2_articles/index.html.

Standards and best practices for digitization

> The best thing about standards is that there are so many to choose from.
> (Gill and Miller, 2002)

The idea of following 'best practices' – accepted, documented methodologies for doing things efficiently and well – is long established in the library, archival and museum world, as well as other sectors, including industry. In relation to the digitization of cultural heritage materials, best practices, like their analogue antecedents, are simply working practices and procedures that can provide a safety net for practitioners as they navigate all aspects of the digitization workflow. Following these markers will give a reasonable expectation of success and add value to projects in terms of their long-term consistency, reliability and interoperability.

Developers of digital collections will have to face many difficult decisions in the course of steering a project to completion. Choices will have to be made about every aspect of the project, including the selection of materials; cataloguing, displaying, archiving and preserving digital materials; technical specifications about hardware, software and file formats; and metadata. Any decisions made will be dependent on many factors – the size of the project's budget, the number of available staff, the scope of the project, the time available and the nature of the institution. Publishers, universities, libraries, archives and government organizations will all have different perspectives and priorities for achievable practice within realistic considerations. Having a single set of canonical standards to guide the decisions that have to be made would be helpful to the project manager, and there is an increasing understanding across the cultural community of the need to apply recognized standards and guidelines to ensure the consistency, reliability and longevity of digital resources. However, technology and institutional requirements change too rapidly for any single set of standards to be applicable. The best solution, as outlined in a series of papers developed by the African Online Digital Library (www.aodl.org/bestpractices.html), is not to work towards rigid standards, but to develop sets of best practices, or current practices, around key topics. These can be then applied or modified according to the needs of specific institutions, collections and projects.

The user will find that there are many standards and guidelines for best practice aimed at different sectors of the cultural heritage community, for example:

- The UK's New Opportunities Fund has established a set of guidelines and working practices for projects funded under its digitization initiative (www.ukoln.ac.uk/nof/support/intro.htm).
- The Arts and Humanities Data Service, another centrally funded initiative in the UK, has developed a series of Guides to Good Practice for humanities digitization projects (www.ahds.ac.uk/creating/guides/index.htm).
- The Digital Library Federation (DLF) maintains a comprehensive list of standards which it has endorsed (www.diglib.org/standards.htm).
- The Canadian Heritage Information network also maintains a list of standards (www.chin.gc.ca/English/Standards/introduction.html).
- One recent initiative to evaluate current practices and use them to develop a set of guidelines for practitioners was *The NINCH Guide to Good Practice in the Digital Representation and Management of Cultural Heritage Materials* (NINCH, 2002). NINCH, the National Initiative for a Networked Cultural Heritage, brought together an interdisciplinary working group and a research team from the University of Glasgow's Humanities Advanced Technology and Information Institute (HATII). Their research underscored that much of what we recognize as good practice has been developed at a grassroots level within the community – often through trial and error.

Examining existing guidelines will allow the extrapolation of the best and most recent standards currently available that can be modified to fit the intended purpose, institution and budget. Using community-accepted standards also allows the possibility of collaboration with other institutions in the future. Many consortia-based projects, such as the Making of America or NOF-Digitise projects, have followed shared sets of technical standards and guidelines, and this can be yet another advantage to working within a collaborative project. The approach of funders to the use of prescribed guidelines varies greatly, although some grant-awarding bodies will mandate the use of a particular set of guidelines or practices. For example, the New Opportunities Fund requires mandatory conformance to a set of specified standards and guidelines as a condition of funding (Miller, Dawson and Perkins, 2001).

Ideally, using best practice should ensure that any investment in digitization will create the best results for the least investment by avoiding redundancy, adding value to the resources created and ensuring that investment in digitization creates content of the broadest use and appeal to multiple and diverse audiences. One way to conceptualize this is to focus on interoperability between and among source materials from different repositories or digitization projects by the use of community-appropriate and widely deployed standards. These standards include means of describing data such as MARC, Dublin Core or the TEI header, means of representing information digitally such as Unicode, JPEG and MPEG, and means of controlling data values, such as AAT or LC subject headings. Long-term access to the materials should ensure the re-use of primary materials beyond the context within which they were first digitized and encourage interdisciplinary re-use and interchange of information across disciplines, methodological boundaries and institutional types. Needs of users with disabilities should be considered and addressed (by using the W3C's *Guidelines for Web Site Accessibility* or similar national guidelines – see www.w3.org/WAI/Policy/).

The implication will therefore be that users can focus on research and enquiry, rather than on the technology, that research results are replicable, and that future enquiry can build on past discoveries To achieve this, reliable, permanent resources must be available (NINCH, 2002).

Identifying good processes

Best practice may well be impossible or impractical for a particular project or institution. There is a broad spectrum of 'acceptable' practice for digitization, encompassing everything from no-frills, low-cost (or no-cost) projects aimed purely at making a collection accessible through to nationally funded, high-profile projects with generous provisions for staff and budget. Doing things the 'best' way can add unacceptable costs or time constraints to the project. This diversity was recognized in a recent IFLA/UNESCO Survey on Digitization and Preservation, which noted an 'almost complete lack of consistency in the handling of digitisation projects, from the type of material selected for digitisation, through the technical processes used, to the methods of consultation and the handling of the digitised collections' (*IFLA/UNESCO Survey*, 1999).

Although the report urges practitioners to look to existing standards and guidelines, it emphasizes that such standards as exist will vary according to the type of material to be digitized and that this is still a relatively new area in which best practice continues to evolve and to be defined. Decisions will be influenced by many local conditions, priorities and considerations, as acknowledged in some pragmatic digitization principles developed at the National Library of Australia, which state that 'Decisions about quality and quantity will be bounded by goals, priorities and available resources . . . Digitisation of collection materials can be a complex and expensive process' (National Library of Australia, 2000).

In a recent essay discussing the *Palestine Post* digitization project, Ron Zweig, the project director, invoked Voltaire's observation that 'the best is the enemy of the good' in describing the dilemma faced by many project developers (Zweig, 1998). Trying to achieve 'best' practice may mean delaying a project until technical standards are agreed upon, until large sums of money are available for digitization, or even until new technologies are invented. It might mean never digitizing, or delaying a project to the frustration of all concerned. Utilizing 'best' practice, or even good practice, may be counterproductive, and it may even constrain the creativity or innovation sometimes required to make things work on a budget. For example, Carnegie Mellon University's Million Book Project was established with the goal of digitizing over 250 million books at a very low cost (see www.library.cmu.edu/Libraries/MBP_FAQ.html) and the project is actively researching cost-effective and efficient OCR methodologies in order to achieve this goal.

What can be more significant is working with the idea of 'good process' – developing a comprehensive workflow for project management that ensures that guidelines are followed and that agreed practices are adhered to. Such guidelines will not just affect digitization – they will concern work methods, staffing, resource management and all aspects of institutional infrastructure. Management will require a focused perspective in order to implement processes to check that work is being done to agreed standards, by regularly examining work that is undertaken, overcoming potential barriers and evaluating outcomes. Managers should plan to use quality assurance processes to identify further refinements to programmes, or possible adaptations of methodologies to suit changing needs, expectations or technologies. The implementation of documented and transparent processes for negotiating a clear path through all aspects of the digitization life cycle will also be a valuable service to the diverse groups of stakeholders and project participants who will have a vested interest, and ongoing role, in the creation and preservation of digital materials.

The key to doing this type of work well and integrating it into the institutional infrastructure is not by merely learning the technology, but rather by applying the technology in specific settings, knowing how to make good decisions when there are alternative paths to follow (which is almost always the case), and working in a more concerted way with colleagues. Again we see that, above all, good management practices, including developing good documentation, are key. For example, the Forced Migration Online Project is a multisite, international project. To ensure consistency in all aspects of digitization and delivery of electronic materials, regardless of the location of the activity, the project has produced carefully documented guidelines for partner institutions to follow (www.forcedmigration.org).

A simple, local solution can be to establish an internal standards committee to review digitization projects and initiatives. Such a group can keep up to date with existing standards and guidelines, ensure that projects are not using proprietary systems and applications, and check to see if proposed projects have already been done elsewhere. A committee of this nature could have representatives from many parts of the organization and therefore provide another venue for interdisciplinary collaboration and communication.

There will ultimately be key elements of good practice that should not be compromised, and the first of these are preservation and access. Every digitization project should ensure widest possible access to the digital materials, including using metadata solutions to ensure that resources can be found by the broadest audience and search tools. They should also incorporate solutions for accessibility by the disabled and test that projects conform to W3C standards. Users can employ tools like Bobby, developed by the Center for Applied Special Technology (CAST; www.cast.org/) in the USA, to test web pages for accessibility. There should also be a clearly stated policy on long-term preservation of, and access to, digital resources – even if resources are not being created for the long term, this should be made obvious to users of the material. In many cases (such as when obtaining European Union funding), these conditions have become mandatory. A long-term commitment by the institution to preserve and maintain the materials that are created is the best way to guarantee the longevity of the project.

In this, as in many other aspects, best practices will be dictated by what an institution is capable of, and will be accomplished by the implementation of key processes by management. Choices will need to be made at each stage in the life cycle of the project, and managers must be able to make these informed choices based on an understanding of the technology involved, an understanding of prioritization of key decisions and planning tasks, and resource and skills management (National Library of Australia, 2002).

Preservation of digital assets

> Preservation is a process to be managed, not a problem to be solved.
>
> (Peterson, 1997)

One crucial aspect of planning is ensuring the long-term preservation and continual access to the digital materials. Hardware, software and the underlying network infrastructures change so rapidly that it is difficult to anticipate how the data of today will be viewed and accessed in the future. Anyone who has ever tried to access word-processed documents created in an early generation word-processing software such as WordStar, or to read databases created on early generations of

Dbase software, will recognize that future users of digital data will have frustrations in reading data created on today's systems. All too often, a lack of preservation strategies means that future users of digital data have to resort to extremes of 'Digital archaeology' in order to read files created on older operating systems or software applications (Ross and Gow, 1999). The best way to ensure long-term access to digital data is to use standard formats and open systems (such as OAIS) wherever possible, and to have a preservation and sustainability strategy for the project. See Deegan and Tanner, 2002, for a detailed discussion of the preservation question; for more information on managing preservation of digital materials, see the Preserving Access to Digital Information (PADI) project pages (www.nla.gov.au/padi/).

There are presently several technical approaches to managing long-term access to digital data. These include:

- *Refreshing*. This involves periodically moving a file from one physical storage medium to another in order to avoid the obsolescence or degradation of the storage medium – for example, moving files from 8-inch disks to 5.25-inch disks, and then from 3.25-inch disks to a network storage device. Refreshing is an ongoing process that will be necessary as long as storage media change.
- *Migration*. This approach requires periodically moving files from one encoded format to another that is more consistent with a more recent computer environment: for example, migrating datasets from Dbase to MYSql, or word-processed files from Word 5 to Word 97, then to Word 2000. Migration will gradually bring files into a narrower variety of standard, contemporary file formats.
- *Emulation*. This is similar to migration, but focuses on the applications software, rather than the files containing the data. Emulation will seek to develop new tools that will re-create the conditions under which the original data were created – by mimicking early operating systems and software applications. The objective is that under emulation, older datasets (say, databases created in Dbase 5) will run on a contemporary computer (Lawrence et al., 2000).

The long-term costs of digitization should be maintained and supported by the host institution, which should make a commitment to the long-term maintenance of digital data at the outset of any digitization initiative. Institutions which commit to preserving information in digital format must also commit to a substantial investment in keeping up with technology. While international standards address physical formats for digital information, this is not the case for software components, including operating systems, databases for search capability, viewing software, or for logical formats where a certain level of risk management still remains (Canadian Council of Archives, 2002).

In addition to the costs of software and hardware to support preservation strategies, it is necessary to develop an economic framework for preservation activities, by developing costing strategies for long-term access and maintenance, as well as the physical costs of storing data in a long-term repository (such as the OCLC digital archive). This will involve factoring in all related costs – upfront, hidden and ongoing – but will enable institutions to develop a better understanding of long-term preservation needs that fit their institutional goals (Sanett, 2003).

The role of good metadata is crucial in helping users of digital collections to find and understand their contents. Besser (2000) outlines three ways in which metadata, if properly used, can assist in the long-term preservation of digital data:

- Metadata can help identify the work, who created it, migrated or reformatted it, and other descriptive information.
- It can provide unique identifying information and links to organizations, files and databases that may have detailed information about the digital content.
- It can describe the technical environment in which the digital files were created, including the equipment used, software, operating systems, compression schema, etc.

Metadata should be comprehensive and detail every aspect of the project, as it will be the key to the long-term discovery of resources. Unfortunately, it is often the case that staff responsible for developing digitization projects are on short-term contracts and are let go at the end of a project's funding cycle, thus 'orphaning' the digital materials. Projects are normally funded only for the creation of digital content, rather than for the long-term life of the data. This makes it extremely difficult to implement any kind of long-term preservation plan, or to be aggressive about digital asset management. This is another argument for situating digitization activities as closely as possible to the core institutional activities, involving permanent members of staff:

> Preservation can only be successfully managed if it is perceived as a core task throughout the institution and if preservation experts are consulted in all activities, including digitization initiatives undertaken in the name of access. It is of paramount importance that the preservation field keeps up the dialogue about the preservation of every initiative. They can bring a perspective of continuity to the discussion and make it clear that there is more to access than turning documents and images into tiffs and terabytes.
> (Lusenet, 1999).

Thinking strategically about digital assets from the outset is the best way to manage the preservation process.

Conclusion

An understanding of the essential attributes of original source materials, both intellectual and artefactual, and an ability to evaluate which of these attributes can be delivered to the end-user, must underpin all aspects of the digital life-cycle. Considering the uses and users of digital content will make it possible to make decisions about all aspects of the project, including quality, presentation, and long-term maintenance and access. These considerations will have to be balanced against the resources that are available for digitization (staff and money, as well the institutional framework that will support the project) in order to make decisions that are appropriate for a particular collection, institution, or situation. Judgements will also be influenced by the nature of the materials to be digitized, the required quality of the digital reproductions, and specific institutional policies and priorities. Setting goals based on these considerations will make it easier to select from a wide range of technologies and methodologies. Subsequent chapters explore these issues in relation to texts, images, audiovisual materials and rare and fragile materials, by describing practices which have been implemented and tested by project managers in a number of prominent initiatives.

8

Digitization of rare and fragile materials

Introduction

> Some resources are too fragile to be consulted. Aging newspapers or palm-leaf manuscripts that break at the slightest flex simply cannot be browsed. In such cases, a digital copy might be provided to improve access, and a microfilm or other photographic surrogate made to ensure long-term survival . . . Sources may also be at risk because of high user demand or extraordinary monetary value. A nation's founding documents, glass-plate negatives of vanished architectural sites, or rare maps may benefit from the creation of digital copies.
>
> (Hazen, Horrell and Merrill-Oldham, 1998)

Many cultural institutions and libraries have undertaken projects to exploit the potential of digital technology for displaying and researching unique and fragile materials. Similarly, many institutions prioritize special collections for digitization because of their value, rareness or uniqueness, and for the attention such high-profile initiatives can draw to the institution.

The case studies and examples in this chapter outline these themes and issues and exemplify the many, interconnected strategic reasons for digitizing rare and fragile collections. They also illustrate how existing practices might inform strategies for managing such projects.

This chapter discusses the nature of the unique materials in special collections and the digitization challenges and opportunities attendant upon these formats, and covers the following issues which must be considered before deciding to initiate such a project:

- the selection criteria for digitization of rare or fragile materials, including a risk-assessment-based approach to evaluating the advantages and disadvantages of undertaking a digitization project
- appropriate digitization methods for rare, priceless or brittle collections, including printed material and visual materials in a variety of formats
- the conservation issues which must be addressed before digitization can take place
- community-accepted 'good practice' for the digitization of rare and fragile materials, including developing a digitization environment, training staff, protecting original materials, acceptable practices for handling materials, exposure to light and managing project workflow.

Digitization and preservation

We cannot at present assure long-term access to digital resources; therefore, digital images cannot serve to replace original materials. Except insofar as surrogates can lessen or eliminate risk to documents, digitization is not a preservation medium.

(Columbia University Libraries, 2001)

Digitization should not be regarded as a viable preservation format. When digital technologies first emerged, it was the naïve hope of many that digitization would solve all known preservation problems. Partly this is because of the very apparent fact that the growth of digitization programmes in many institutions has coincided with cutbacks in preservation budgets: preservation budgets in ARL libraries have remained at the same level since 1993, and the number of staff assigned to preservation is the lowest it has been since the late 1980s. At the same time, demand for access to original source materials has increased. Another infuriating paradox for preservation staff is that although the technology for reformatting for access has greatly improved, the funding for preservation continues to decrease:

> More money now goes to digital reformatting of items to provide access than to microfilming to preserve the low-use brittle books that are rotting on shelves.
>
> (Nichols and Smith, 2001)

Although there are those who maintain that digitization is gaining recognition as an acceptable preservation format, this is not the opinion of this author. There is a spirited, ongoing discussion on this issue, which ultimately recognizes on both sides that there is a need for more research into the long-term preservation of digital materials (see preservation chapter of *NINCH Guide* (2002), at www.nyu.edu/its/humanities/affil/nincn/guide/XIV/ for more detail on this issue).

At this time, microfilming remains the most stable preservation format, and leaders in the field such as Harvard, Cornell, the British Library, the Library of Congress and the North East Document Conservation Center all emphasize the need to develop a conventional preservation plan for original materials prior to digitization. Furthermore, many funding agencies require a preservation plan for original materials before they will fund a digitization project.

However, digitization and preservation efforts are not in competition with each other: digitization efforts have, in many cases, sharpened the focus on some of the preservation issues facing libraries today.

Even microfilming can be controversial, however: one of the better known examples of opposition to this practice demonstrates many of the arguments of library patrons and scholars who believe that no surrogate can ever be an acceptable substitute for an original artifact. When the New York Public Library began to microfilm their newspaper collections, with a view to discarding the originals upon completion of the project, there was an outcry, instigated by an article by Nicholson Baker in the *New Yorker*. Despite the ARL's rebuttal of his arguments, in the form of a 'talking points' piece (ARL, 2000), Baker remains unconvinced that microfilming surrogates can ever be an acceptable substitute for newspapers and periodicals. He argues that while microfilm preserves the intellectual content, it cannot adequately reproduce newspapers in their entirety as cultural artifacts. He has subsequently devoted a great deal of effort to establishing an archive of 19th- and early 20th-century newspapers near his home in Rollinsford, NH.

Baker also addressed a conference dedicated to the topic 'Do we want to keep our newspapers', organized by the Centre for Manuscript and Print Studies at the University of London's School of Advanced Studies. This forum provided a valuable opportunity for librarians and archivists to air and address these issues (see McKitterick, 2002).

These concerns notwithstanding, the practical reality for libraries and archives has always been that deciding what to discard and eliminate is far more pressing than deciding what to save and preserve.

Special collections in the digital age

Primary source materials in museums, archives and libraries consist of a variety of rare and fragile formats, many of which will present special challenges for digitization. Manuscripts of all periods and languages are represented and a variety of formats, including paper, parchment, birch bark, papyrus, lead tablets, wood, stone, etc. Visual materials can be on paper, glass or textiles. These materials come in a wide range of shapes and sizes, from tiny manuscript, papyrus or palm-leaf fragments to large maps, banners or quilts.

Special collections also include time-based media formats for audio and moving image materials, encompassing broadcasts, oral history recordings, ethnographic and performance-based materials and materials for the study of language and music. Other collections will comprise three-dimensional objects, which come in all shapes and sizes, and are not limited to items that live in special collections departments. These include the whole range of museum objects and artefacts, from all genres and periods, such as sculpture; architecture and buildings; archaeological artifacts; scientific objects, machines, and vehicles; and even botanical, natural history materials. However, for a detailed discussion of audio, video and 3-D materials see Chapter 9. The current chapter will focus on more traditional library holdings.

The sheer variety of formats creates many different challenges for working with materials of this nature. In addition to obvious preservation concerns related to handling the materials and exposing them to digitization equipment, which are discussed later in this chapter, there are concerns related to the format, size and age of the materials. Digitization equipment and practices will have to be customized to deal with a variety of specialized formats, and unique materials that may also require specialist attention or conservation treatment.

Materials may have degraded because of their chemical make-up, such as nitrate and diacetate negatives, or because of past library practices, such as dry-mounting photographs on acidic board. They may be oversized, such as large map collections or large-format art and design materials, or textiles. Glass plate negatives, tissue paper (used for architectural drawings) and acid-based paper are extremely fragile and watercolours and transparencies are sensitive to light. The source material may even be dangerous, such as cellulose nitrate film stock, which can ignite and produce toxic smoke while burning.

Materials of a recent vintage (less than 90 years) may also still be within copyright (see Chapter 3), so administration of rights issues will add another layer to the digitization workflow.

Materials do not have to be especially old to be rare or fragile – many of the audio-visual materials in collections will be less than 50 or even 20 years old – but they are degrading at a far faster rate than some collections of Dark Age manuscripts. Photographs are very vulnerable to fading and discoloration, as a quick browse through any family photo album will confirm.

As historical archives develop more and more special collections, there are questions about how they can usefully be presented to the public and to researchers. An example of a project which has embraced digitization to resolve these difficulties is the Women's Library Suffragette Banners (vads.ahds.ac.uk/collections/FSB.html). The Women's Library houses an important collection of early 20th-century suffrage banners, the majority of which were carried on the suffrage march on 17 June 1908. The Library's entire collection of suffrage banners, along with associated artwork, has now been digitized and is available for research on a searchable database. The material is significant to the study of the suffrage movement and women's history, as well as to the broader history of protest and demonstration in the 20th century. The banners are also primary source materials for scholars of art and design of the period, as many of them were designed and created by the artist-based suffrage organizations the Artists' Suffrage League and the Suffrage Atelier. The banners are cotton and velvet textiles, decorated with embroidered and painted designs. They are both fragile and oversized, factors which mean that their use is restricted, even to library patrons.

These factors have given particular digitization challenges, but the project has created a broadly accessible resource which can be searched and examined in detail. The materials are presented online alongside other materials from the collection, including digital representations of fabric swatches and design documents. A non-digital surrogate was also created at the same time as the digitization project, a transparency of all the banners in the collection.

Advantages of digitization of special collections

The two main advantages to digitizing rare and fragile materials are preservation of originals from handling, and access. From an access perspective, many special collections are not presently available, or only available to scholars with pre-approved credentials. This is a concern to many publicly funded institutions, which have an obligation to enable the public to view and consult these collections. Digitization can enable broader access to the original material. In terms of preservation, the creation of digital surrogates can eliminate handling of fragile original materials.

Utah State University's Special Collections and Archives (http://library.usu.edu/Specol/index.html) has a searchable archive of photographs, manuscripts and texts relating to many aspects of the history of the area, as well the archives of the American Folklore Society and the Jack London Society. These materials have been collected for the benefit of the public and are available for use by researchers. Historically, however, the public has not been aware of the research possibilities of archival material or been able to access the collections. Making digitized collections available through the internet publicizes the diverse collections and enables the university to fulfil its obligation as a publicly funded institution to provide access to their collections to members of the public, while also protecting the fragile materials from handling.

Potential benefits also include eliminating the risk of theft. In a recent case, Faulkner letters from the University of Missouri Special Collection were found, not in the University catalogue, but on the online auction site, e-Bay. Some materials will always be tempting to thieves. As bookstores keep their copies of Bukowski, Burroughs and Kerouac under the counter to deter shoplifters, special collections may have to regard digitization as an acceptable alternative to keeping the reading room in a state of lockdown and paying soaring insurance premiums.

This was a factor influencing the Library of Congress's decision to digitize its baseball card collection (http://memory.loc.gov/ammem/bbhtml/bbhome.html). Part of the American Memory Project at the Library of Congress, this collection presents a digitized archive of one of the Library's most popular collections, one which has encountered problems with theft in the past as the collection objects are both covetable and small. The collection consists of 2100 early baseball cards dating from 1887 to 1914. The cards show legendary scenes and figures from baseball history. Cigarette card collector Benjamin K. Edwards preserved these baseball cards in albums with more than 12,000 other cards on many subjects. After his death, Edwards's daughter gave the albums to noted poet and Lincoln biographer Carl Sandburg, who donated them to the Library's Prints and Photographs Division in 1954. The baseball cards are one of the first American Memory pictorial collections whose images have been produced by direct capture with a digital camera at high levels of spatial resolution. Most of the collections of photographs and prints for which digitization began prior to 1998 were digitized via photographic intermediates and, with the exception of the panoramic photographs, at lower levels of resolution. The material is set in historical and cultural context by the 'collection connections' pages, which display information about the collection based on themes of critical thinking, arts and humanities, and US history. The collection can be searched by keyword, team, player, league, city or card set.

As with all materials in the American Memory programme, the images have been digitized with a view to placing them in the public domain. The materials can be freely downloaded, both in high-resolution TIFF format and in a low-resolution JPEG format.

Digitizing special collections to enable advanced research

The British Library's Beowulf project (www.bl.uk/collections/treas-ures/beowulf.html), one of the earliest initiatives to digitize a fragile manuscript for both preservation and access, is still one of the most compelling and exemplary in terms of the great improvements to scholarship the project has facilitated.

The Anglo-Saxon Beowulf manuscript is one of the greatest treas-ures of the British Library and of paramount importance for schol-ars of Old English. The manuscript was badly damaged in the Cotton Library fire of 1731 and in order to protect the brittle and smoke-stained pages, each one was mounted in a protective paper frame in the mid-19th century. In order to have a retaining edge for the frame, the letters around the edge of the verso of each leaf were covered; hundreds of letters were thus obscured from view. Despite continual conservation efforts, by the late 20th century the manu-script itself was becoming too fragile to be handled by scholars. As this manuscript was so crucial to scholarship, as well as being one of the most recognizable and evocative pieces in the Library's col-lection, it was essential to continue to allow scholars and members of the public to view it. In order to preserve the original from han-dling, and to experiment with digital technologies for manuscript scholarship, the British Library began the Beowulf digitization proj-ect in 1993.

The digitization of the manuscript was one of the Library's early worldwide digitization projects. It was carried out by the British Library in collaboration with Professor Kevin Kiernan from the Uni-versity of Kentucky and a team of scholars, curators, conservators, photographers and technical experts. Selected images from the pro-ject were some of the first pictures of medieval manuscripts to be mounted on the internet and publication was completed with the production of a CD-ROM in 1997. Using a high-end Kontron digital camera (manufactured originally for medical imaging), while light-ing each page with fibre-optic lighting, it was possible to capture very high-quality digital images of every page. Subsequent analysis of the digital images using imaging tools and ultra-violet lighting and X-ray style photography revealed letters that had been hidden by the paper borders as well as letters that had been scratched out by scribes. The electronic edition also includes 18th-century transcriptions of the manuscript, collations, a glossarial index and search features.

In this case, digitization offered tremendous added value to the original manuscript in terms of both access and scholarship. Some of those hidden letters represent the only known record of some Old English words. The project subsequently expanded to include a collection of digital images of all the primary evidence of the Beowulf text held in different geographic locations, ranging from the Royal Library in Copenhagen to Houghton Library at Harvard University, thereby creating a new resource and tool that allows enhanced study of the manuscript by re-unifying it with contemporary materials. For an overview of digital manuscript scholarship, see Kiernan, 1994b.

Materials from this project have subsequently been successfully re-purposed. They have, for example, been integrated into the British Library's educational and outreach activities, such as the 'changing language' modules on the origins and uses of language. These modules include copies of the digital images of the manuscript, a transcription of the texts and an examination of key words, as well as audio files of the texts being read. The Beowulf materials area, also a key component of the British Library's Turning the Pages project, is an interactive, kiosk-based display system replicating the physical experience of reading a manuscript and turning the pages, using touch-screen technology and animation. Other manuscripts in the project are the Lindisfarne Gospels, the Diamond Sutra, the Sforza Hours, the Leonardo Notebook, the Golden Haggadah, the Luttrell Psalter, Blackwell's Herbal, the Sherborne Missal and Sultan Baybars' Qur'an.

Developing digitization policies for rare and fragile materials

Digitization is not only costly in monetary terms. It is an extremely invasive process, involving handling original materials, removing them from storage, and exposing them to some degree of light and heat. However, everything that ever happens to an original object compromises it in some way. If that original is both unique and important, while every effort should be made to minimize the damage, every effort should also be made to bring it safely to the widest possible audience. Digitization policies, backed up by risk assessment of the material factors affected by digitization (the age, condition and location of the originals) will provide a useful framework to evaluate the benefits of digitization to a particular special collection, and identify the key decision points for developing digitization workflows. Where none exist, the digitization of fragile and unique materials is a high-stakes activity that can influence and inform their development.

As with any project, the first step will be a survey of the materials in the collection to determine which are most in demand, which are most at risk by handling and which are most valuable for scholarship. The institution can then make an assessment as to whether the benefits of digitization outweigh the risks and costs. A comprehensive survey will also establish whether additional expenses are required to cover such procedures as cataloguing, metadata creation, cleaning or re-housing. This process should establish the intellectual value of the collections, and whether or not there are any rigid institutional policies regarding moving and handling of materials that might preclude or severely restrict digitization activities (for example, insurers may prohibit certain types of work, or the transport of materials to a digitization area). The condition or fragility of the original materials, and their suitability for digitization, will be the first and foremost consideration that must be considered before any of the other selection criteria come into play. Where there is any doubt that digitization may damage the originals, then photographic intermediaries should be scanned instead of the originals. A number of stakeholders should be involved in this selection and evaluation process, including conservation and preservation staff, subject specialists and content experts, and users of the collections. This group should have input into developing risk management models for the digitization process, as they will have the most familiarity with the content and be able to anticipate any potential problems.

As materials are evaluated and prioritized for digitization, there should be an evaluation of the desired outcomes, and an assessment of technological solutions and methods that can be used, working with vendors and digital reformatting experts where appropriate. There will be outcomes that affect the users of the collections (such as improved access) and those that have discernable benefits for the materials in question (such as limiting the movement or handling of the source materials). These should be stated clearly in a digitization policy: Columbia University Library's criteria for digitization (2001), for example, state that digitization should lead to:

- a significant reduction in handling of fragile materials
- access to materials that cannot otherwise be easily used
- protection of materials at high risk of theft or mutilation.

Having a clear understanding of what the digitization project must achieve will make it easier to assess the technological methods and equipment that are to be used. This will help to take into account the physical size, nature and condition of source materials in order to address whether the available means of digitization – from a time, budget and technological perspective – are appropriate. It will also assist in developing realistic budgets: every step of the digitization process should include practices and equipment that guarantee the safe digitization of the originals, and the budget must be adequate for these considerations and any additional steps that they necessitate.

Any digitization policy, or decision matrix, will also have at its core an understanding of the risk factors related to digitization, and guidelines for measuring their probability and impact. The acceptable threshold for risk will be far lower when dealing with unique or valuable materials. This means that institutional policies may well be very restrictive when the need to protect the original is paramount. Brown University Library's *Selection Criteria for Digitization* (2001) advises that the condition of original materials be a factor in deciding whether or not digitization should go ahead: if the materials are in a fragile state, and would be damaged or compromised by digitization, then the project should not be undertaken, and discussions and project planning should end at this point.

Case study: the Smithsonian Institution (www.si.edu/)

> The Smithsonian's goal is not only to digitize its own collections but also to make the public understand what it means to digitize.
>
> (David Allison, curator and chairman of the Smithsonian's Division of Information Technology and Society, at www.si.edu/opa/researchreports/00101/digilab.htm)

There are over 142 million items in the Smithsonian's collections, including Julia Child's kitchen, Playboy Bunny costumes and Apollo 11. With such an embarrassment of riches, the museum's digitization initiatives are not geared towards the complete digitization of all collections. Priorities are set by a collection's popularity, condition and internal demand. By making digital images of highlights of its collections available on the internet, the Institution is able to fulfil its mission of ensuring broadest access to its collections. The Smithsonian's website features many permanent and temporary exhibitions, containing images of objects in the collections of its 16 museums and art galleries. Fourteen of these museums and galleries are in Washington DC and two are in New York City (the Cooper Hewitt Design Museum and the American Indian Museum at the Heyde Centre), but all the collections are displayed as a whole on the website. The digital surrogates are not intended to be a replacement for use of the originals by researchers, but as a way to promote the museums, and to enable visitors to plan their trips to them, particularly during peak holiday seasons. The website contains a great deal of material that is of interest to junior and secondary school teaching.

For researchers, the most valuable materials in the 'virtual' Smithsonian are detailed, annotated guide indexes to the museum's collections, enabling researchers to browse the collection catalogues in great detail. The Ralph Rinzler Folklife Archives and Collections, containing the Moses and Frances Asch (Folkways) Collection and recordings on the Paredon, Cook, Dyer-Bennet, Fast Folk and Monitor labels, can all be searched by artist, title, track and other options in the online databases, many of which contain audio clips of original recordings (see www.folkways.si.edu/).

In addition to increasing access, viewing digital surrogates of museum objects can give virtual visitors a deeper, more focused learning experience. Including contextual and background materials and links to images from other collections and presenting multiple interpretations of museum materials enriches the experience of working with the materials. From the perspective of a museum curator, digitizing popular items that are heavily used for display, research or publication reduces their exposure to exhibit lighting, and the handling required to move them around the museum throughout the construction and moving of exhibits.

Protecting originals: technology solutions

A pressing issue is that of how advanced technology can improve the conservation conditions of fragile collections in museums, libraries and archives. Rather than relying on digital reformatting as a means of preserving access to fragile materials, controlling the storage environment remains the most effective way to extend the usable life of information materials. For valuable research into how the conditions in which collections are maintained can be mitigated by new technology, see the work of organizations like the Image Permanence Institute at Rochester Institute of Technology, USA (www.rit.edu/~661www1/).

Such research goes to the core of using technology for preservation. It envisages solutions such as 'smart' library buildings that monitor environmental conditions, new treatments for brittle books and the use of microchips which can be embedded in objects to monitor their environmental conditions, prevent theft and keep a record of use and circulation.

Case study: brittle books

From the early 1800s, paper was manufactured through processes that leave an acidic content, which gradually breaks down the cellulose fibres of the paper itself. After a period of time, especially in conditions of high temperature, humidity or pollution, the paper becomes extremely fragile, and breaks when folded. A commonly used test to see if paper has become brittle is to fold over the corner of a page and to tug gently at the corner. If the paper has become brittle, the corner will break off. Many libraries, especially research libraries, are now faced with the problem that large parts of their collection, including materials that may be in high demand, are becoming too fragile to put back in circulation. The fact that the paper breaks when folded means that the book cannot withstand the manipulation normally required for re-binding or standard repairs. Page-by-page conservation treatment is expensive and many books affected by this problem are relatively inexpensive, mass-produced materials – their monetary value doesn't justify spending large sums per volume for repair. Consequently, most library policies on brittle books have been to purchase replacement copies, and where this is no longer possible, to make a microfilm copy of the text of the volume – its 'intellectual content'. A master negative is then stored under archival conditions, and the positive copies can be put into circulation. If the volumes have colour plates or unique or valuable illustrations, the plates are de-acidified and put in plastic coverings for future use. Preservation photocopies are also created as paper substitutes for brittle books, although these cannot be used as archival masters, or to create additional copies.

The complexity of this process and its dependence on so many factors – costs, circulation and usage – mean that the rationale for conserving brittle collections has to be extremely pragmatic. Consequently, this is an area that may well benefit from advances in digital imaging technologies. Digitization preserves not only the intellectual content of the original, but can create surrogate images of colour plates, special bindings and printer's marks, and include images of the actual book itself. Digital images can also be duplicated without risk of degradation. They can, of course, be browsed, searched, previewed and manipulated. They can also be printed, e-mailed and imported into other materials.

There are, however, still drawbacks to digitizing this kind of material. Brittle books may well be damaged by scanning or filming – they will have to be disbound to be scanned on any large scale – and the sheer volume of brittle materials in collections means that digitization isn't a cost-effective approach at this time. However, this is an area where technology is making rapid advances and institutions are starting to make significant investments. Recently, the University of Michigan purchased a Zeutscel Omniscan 7000 for the scanning and OCR of brittle books, with the intention that this process will replace microfilming – an important commitment for an institution to make (Schiff, 2002)

Another source of guidance for practitioners and development in this area is the NEH's Brittle Books Program, which was established in 1987 with the aim of saving over three million brittle books. It is a division of the NEH's Department of Preservation and Access, and although its primary focus is still microfilming, the Program also has a focus on developing technologies, methods and standards for the digitization of brittle materials. Pilot projects to develop accurate and cost-effective methods for scanning and digitizing brittle books are now under way at several institutions, including the University of Michigan, Cornell and Harvard. From this Program, the guidelines for practitioners on whether to film or scan originals have been developed. These are discussed in Chapter 7.

In other initiatives, the DLF has put out a call for an international registry of digitized books, which would ease the financial burden of libraries who find that they have to make copies of brittle books that are not necessarily valuable, and which are in mass circulation:

> Suppose . . . that your library contains a lot of 'brittle books,' volumes deteriorating because of the chemical fragility of their paper. But your budget will not cover the cost of microfilming or digitizing all of them. Existing registries indicate that other libraries already have microfilmed some of the same texts but not all. If a digital registry existed, you could check it also. There you could find out which titles among your brittle books might already have been digitized in a high-quality format, or were scheduled to be, and whether commitments to long-term maintenance of durable, reproducible digital texts – and 'artifact' copies of the original books – had been made by one or more libraries elsewhere.
>
> Their commitments would reduce the number of volumes on which you would need to spend money for preservation copying, conservation treatment, and even library storage space. Your online catalog could provide links to the copies that were digitized and maintained elsewhere. And your own digital investments, if identified in the registry, could save

money in turn for other libraries.

Through a digital registry, libraries could expand access while reducing redundant effort and expense for preservation as well as digitization. Because texts identified in a digital registry would be electronically accessible anywhere, libraries could additionally control costs by not duplicating their acquisitions.

(DLF, 2002)

Good practice for the digitization of rare and fragile materials

The following discussion is based upon accepted conservation practice in memory institutions, which has evolved over decades of well documented experience and practice. This expertise and experience has informed the development of good practice for handling rare and fragile materials during digitization projects. It is important to recognize that, though digitization is relatively new, many of the attendant processes are not, and they are already well documented by experts in the field.

Workflows and methods can be adjusted to lessen the risks, and special equipment such as cold lights, cradles and exposure limits can be used. Where necessary, curatorial staff should prepare the material and also monitor the process until they are happy with procedures. There should always be adequate supervision of staff working with such materials.

It is also worth mentioning that if the digitization workflow includes conservation treatment of the originals, or housing, the digitization process can be a valuable opportunity to actually treat, conserve and improve the storage conditions of original materials. The logic is that if originals have to be handled at all, the opportunity should be seized to treat them at the same time.

Of primary concern is that the digitization pay closest attention to controlling the two areas over which control is possible – handling the materials, and the physical environment in which scanning is carried out.

Handling materials

Handling a fragile object is one of the easiest ways to damage it.

While many projects hope that digitization will prevent handling of fragile materials in the long run, as Steven Chapman observes: 'digital images do not make themselves' (S. Chapman, 2000). The process of digitization requires that materials be touched and moved, in many cases for the first time in centuries. This may well be the very first time that all the pages in a manuscript or folio have been turned. Handling processes vary greatly, depending on the value of the source materials and the proximity of conservation staff to the project. Some projects consider it acceptable practice to disbind or open volumes 180 degrees so they can be flattened on a scanner. Other projects have to be extremely cautious with the source materials – special cradles may be built to mount source materials. Often, materials will have to be handled for two separate processes – once for processing and cataloguing, and again for imaging.

Variables that can be controlled in handling materials include the behaviours and actions of the staff charged with working with the materials. A detailed overview of how to control the conditions under which special collections are digitized is *Audiovisual Archives*, edited by Helen P. Harrison (1997), which discusses the storage, handling and preservation of audiovisual archives and photographic collections. A summary of the good housekeeping recommendations in this report includes the following elements of exercising caution when working with fragile materials:

- Always have clean hands when examining such materials, and preferably use talc-free latex gloves
- Use two hands to hold the photograph or sheet of paper or vellum, and, if possible, support it with a piece of stiff card. Avoid touching the surface.
- Do not stack up loose materials – nothing should be placed on top of the source materials.
- Take care when removing materials from their folders or other housings: for example, remove envelopes from negatives and not vice versa. If a photograph, slide or negative appears stuck in its container, do not attempt to remove it.
- Support albums or books with cradles to protect their structure and with book snakes to hold the album open at the relevant page.

- Do not attempt to flatten rolled or curled prints, sheets or pages.

Environment

The process of digitization itself creates many conservation challenges, and preservation departments will also have guidelines for each institution to follow – it is often the case that a preservation-ready environment may already exist at your institution, so refer to internal resources that may exist.

It is crucial to ensure that the scanning environment is adequate to protect the materials selected for digitization. There will be considerations about the location and conditions affecting the space to be used:

- Check temperature and relative humidity regularly. Also check for signs of deterioration such as mould.
- Avoid storing archives in basements, which are prone to flooding.
- In storage and display areas, lights should be fitted with UV filters. Perspex provides a better protection against UV light than glass.
- Never place source materials near a heat source, such as hot pipes, or hang them above a radiator, or in direct sunlight.
- Keep originals out of freshly painted rooms and away from freshly painted objects for at least two weeks and preferably four weeks. Fresh paints may emit peroxides which can cause damage to photographs.
- Keep copying machines away from the collections. Ozone, produced by electrostatic copy machines, is very damaging.
- Do not allow photographs or their containers to come into contact with household cleaners containing ammonia or chlorine.
- The digitization area must be as clean and dust free as practical, and the capture devices and computers should be cleaned regularly, yet kept free of residues from cleaning materials.
- Food, drink and smoke should be kept out of the digitization area.
- There should be ample table space, and space for easy access to the equipment and source material.
- Avoid the use of ink, especially felt-tip pens: use a soft pencil. Do

not use adhesive tapes, staples, pins, metal paper clips and rubber bands.

- Slides/transparencies should be cleaned often with a puff brush.
- Textiles should be kept in darkness for as long as possible.

All aspects of the physical environment should be kept consistent, and when environmental control is feasible, specifications can range from the wall sockets (using line conditioners to control voltage) to the ceilings (requirements for paint colour and indirect lighting to create calibrated viewing environments), and from the HVAC (heating, ventilation and air conditioning) system to the furniture (S. Chapman, 1999).

Furthermore, in cases where collections may not be moved – for example, materials that reside in a university special collection or archive – the digitization equipment (and staff, their filing cabinets, desks and other accessories) may have to be moved into an already cramped or overcrowded environment and their working conditions will have to conform to the required preservation conditions for the duration of the project.

Staffing issues

It is essential that project staff be fully trained in all aspects of protecting the materials they are working with and maintaining a secure environment for handling materials. This can be especially difficult for smaller projects where staff must multitask – web design specialists must sometimes double up as imaging or conservation project staff. There are some resources available for staff training – NEDCC workshops, preservation workshops, and Library of Congress White Papers (e.g. lcweb2.loc.gov/ammem). However, a clearinghouse for information about conservation and how technical advances can make digitization less traumatic for fragile materials is badly needed.

Another important issue is the question of who is actually doing the digitization – photography of special collections is always undertaken by a photographer and it is advisable that digital imaging staff also have an imaging sensibility and familiarity with the materials they are working with. It is not a good idea to assign scanning of special collections to technical staff alone.

The deployment of staff, and overall accountability of time expended, is another issue – conservators can find themselves distracted from their primary responsibilities in order to spend time overseeing scanning staff.

Outsourcing

Outsourcing of fragile materials is a controversial topic, and again, one of risk assessment. Outsourcing is generally not recommended for fragile or irreplaceable materials, which may require careful chaperoning by conservation staff at every stage of a digitization project. The HEDS/JIDI Feasibility Study explicitly advises against outsourcing the following formats to commercial bureaux:

* original art works
* textiles, including colour swatches or materials
* early printed materials
* book bindings, including tooled book covers
* large-format originals.

If, however, it is necessary to outsource any materials, it is essential to arrange adequate insurance cover, packing and handling, and transportation (Tanner and Robinson, 1998).

Controlled-environment imaging labs have been created at the Denver Public Library, the National Archives and Records Administration, the Museum of Modern Art, the Library of Congress, and selected service bureaux in the USA. If a project were able to use such a facility, the risks of transportation and loss of direct physical control could possibly be justifiable.

It is sometimes possible to gain the benefits of outsourcing while maintaining the originals *in situ*: some suppliers will capture materials on-site, though this should only be negotiated with very experienced companies, and conservation staff may still need to be on hand for much of the process.

Some institutions have made a specific commitment to setting up a digital imaging environment. Harvard College Library established such a facility in 1999 in order to meet the growing demand for digitizing capabilities in-house. The development of this facility was primarily driven by the institutional commitment to digitize special collections, including unique materials for which handling and security were of concern. What resulted was a 'one-stop shop' for materials preparation, digital image processing and quality control, metadata creation, file management and storage. Curators and preservation staff as well a digital reformatting experts were all stakeholders in the development of the facility, and all have a vested interest in its success (for more detailed information about this facility, see its description in Chapter 10).

Equipment and methods

There are several capture methods that are applicable in the context of special collections. The computer industry is driven by the business and entertainment market, and it is their needs that dictate emerging research and technologies. Archives, special collections and preservation departments are simply not a large enough market for computer hardware to be adapted to their specialist needs, so it will be necessary to make do with the generically available technological tools.

Of the different scanning options available at this time, only flatbed scanners (preferably overhead scanners) and digital cameras are suitable for fragile materials. However, this does not mean that options are limited: the underlying technology is changing rapidly, meaning that far more control and choice over image capture are possible than ever before. For example, digital camera technologies are emerging which give the operator more flexibility, such as digital camera backs and filtering mechanisms (for UV light). On the other hand, a scanner is a controlled and enclosed system – there is no need to worry about changing lenses, flash exposures, or special lighting.

It is important to recognize that there is no 'best' approach and indeed no 'best' camera or scanner for image digitization. No single device can accommodate the wide range of physical formats in library, archives and museum collections because the expertise of the camera or scanner operator varies considerably and because handling guidelines, image quality requirements, budgets and timetables are project specific. To look for examples in the field, NARA prefers to use scanners for fragile materials, whereas Harvard uses digital cameras. The question of whether a scanner or digital camera is 'better' as a capture device is again an issue that depends on which approach works best for the needs of the project, and the demands presented by the materials to be digitized.

Many projects have developed cradles – often custom made – for materials such as glass slides, manuscripts and books that cannot be opened 180 degrees. The Goettingen Gutenberg Bible digitization project commissioned specially made cradles to allow entirely contact-free scanning (see www.gutenbergdigital.de/), and it is not unheard of for impecunious slide libraries to fashion very effective home-made cradles made of cardboard for scanning glass slides.

As with all digitization initiatives, it will be necessary to ensure that the materials are scanned 'once and for all purposes'. In order to avoid having to do multiple scans of the same object as technology improves over time, it is essential to ensure that the equipment's dynamic range, optical resolution, bit depth, maximum scanning area and software interface are at the optimal settings and capabilities affordable (see Chapter 7). In addition, benchmarking should be carried out and test images put through various output scenarios. Colour accuracy and the maintenance of image information within scans should be ensured by the use of colour profiling, standard colour patches and rigorous quality assurance procedures.

Light exposure during scanning

Heat and light exposure can have a negative impact on fragile materials, although assessing the exact scale of the damage is still an inexact science. More research needs to be carried out on the potential damage to fragile materials caused by scanning, especially when some longer scans can take up to 20 minutes.

However, some recent research has suggested that high-end digital capture exposes an object to the same amount of light as two days' lighting under average gallery conditions (Blackwell, 2000). These findings are consistent with guidelines issued by the Smithsonian in 1996, on minimal light exposure during imaging: www.nmnh.si.edu/cris/techrpts/imagopts/section8.html.

Unlike libraries and archives, which may keep their artifacts and precious materials out of the public eye for many years, museums have a joint obligation to preserve and present their materials, and often these two missions are at odds. Wear and tear of providing public access to collections – especially by mounting exhibitions, when objects will be displayed in galleries for long periods of time – can severely impact the integrity of fragile artifacts. Therefore, for a museum, the issue of exposing an object to digital photography in order that the original can be preserved is often a necessary evil.

A more concrete threat to rare and fragile materials is heat, which causes discernible damage. Both scanners and computers produce a great deal of heat, so it is important to ensure that the scanning environment is adequately air-conditioned, with both cooling and air circulation necessary. Avoid any devices that use infra-red heat.

Metadata and standards

In addition to using conventional metadata schema for administrative purposes, it can be necessary to expend extra time and labour in developing descriptive and structural metadata that will adequately describe the content of rich and unique originals and ensure that they will be found by users. As the Duke website's history of the Database of Documentary Papyri project recounts:

> This is an essential point: the production of large sets of images for the Internet has to go hand in hand with the production of large sets of descriptive data. Without the catalog records the images of the Duke papyri would not only be meaningless, but also inaccessible. . . . That the DPA provides both content and pictures in fully searchable and browsable form is the result of more painstaking work than meets the eye. Eventually only four months out of a total of sixty-four months of work will have been spent on the DPA proper. The rest of the time was spent conserving, transcribing, interpreting, cataloging and imaging the papyri.
>
> (Minnen, 1995)

It may also be necessary to develop enriched metadata to describe unique and detailed aspects of the collection, as demand for 'content-rich' searching increases. For example, many slide libraries and image archives are realizing that traditional metadata schemas like Dublin Core and MDA are inadequate for compositional research, visual rhetoric and other advanced uses of digitized collections.

Unique metadata and markup schema have been developed for historic and archival materials – the Encoded Archival Description schema is an SGML-based standard finding aid used by archives. It is supported by the Library of Congress and the Society of American Archivists and was used for the Making of America project.

The TEI (the Text Encoding Initiative) is an SGML-based schema developed for literary, linguistic and historical materials. Using the TEI enables the unique characteristics of these materials to be marked up, or tagged, for searching and cross referencing. The Canterbury Tales Project and the Civil War Archive at the University of Virginia both use the TEI standard.

The use of standards for creating and preserving digital resources that can be found, broadly used and re-purposed in the future is a theme that is discussed extensively in Chapter 7, but it is worth re-iterating in the context of digitizing rare and fragile materials. The very nature of these materials means that digitization should only be done once and done well. Re-digitization, on the grounds that the materials were not scanned at the optimal bit depth, that a lossy compression format was used, or that the digital file was saved in a proprietary format will not be viewed favourably by the preservation and conservation team at any institution.

Delivery issues for specialist materials

As with any project, delivery considerations should be paramount when planning to digitize special collections. Because the stakes can be so much higher (in terms of both cost and risk) when digitizing rare and fragile collections, it is particularly important to evaluate whether or not digital delivery will be able to represent the full content of the original, both artifactual and intellectual. It will be necessary to understand how end-users will use the digital versions and the level of image quality that that implies, whether the materials will display well digitally on current and future platforms and networked environments.

Contextual and authentic representation of special collections post-digitization is a key issue. Materials should be presented in such a way that they can be understood in their context – institutionally, historically and culturally. Present technologies mean that programming is required to design web pages or other 'background' for these materials.

Authenticity is vital in the context of special collections: digitization must strive to preserve to the greatest extent possible the authenticity and integrity of the original information, as it is imperative that users have as much faith in a digital surrogate image as they would in the original (Ostrow, 1998).

Materials should be easily identifiable as the collection of the institution that holds them. This is important not just from a public relations perspective, but also in managing the digital assets and ensuring that they are not improperly or illegally used. It may be necessary to develop a digital watermarking scheme (see Chapter 3). Watermarking is a technology to watch, although such schemes have been tested by institutions such as the University of Michigan's Digital Library Production Services only to be rejected as ineffective and costly. As yet there is no system that works well enough to wholeheartedly recommend its adoption. There is no recognized standard format and only proprietary systems are currently available.

Conclusion

The digitization and delivery of rare, fragile and older materials can be extremely rewarding for archives, libraries and museums. It can promote access to valuable sources and eliminate handling of the original materials while raising the profile of the institution. As the case studies in this chapter have shown, digitization projects have been undertaken on almost all manner of objects and artifacts in special collections.

New resources and technologies are making such projects more and more feasible, as lower-cost yet high-quality digital imaging technologies become more accessible and as digitization practices become more streamlined and less experimental. Scanners and digital cameras are being developed that are capable of producing extremely high-quality images, yet at the same time are becoming more and more 'archive friendly', by producing less light and heat. There are many technological developments to watch: 3-D imaging techniques and tools for depicting spatial objects are improving and becoming more user friendly. Cheaper disk storage and less complex film digitization technologies are making the digitization of rare and fragile moving image collections far more feasible for smaller institutions.

Despite the best efforts of organizations like Harvard University's Digital Imaging Group, the Matrix Project at the University of Michigan and the Higher Education Digitization Service, there is no one point of contact for up-to-the-minute expertise and guidance on this topic. A clearinghouse for information about digitization resources for special collections is badly needed. At this time, the community-wide expertise that has been developed by practitioners in the field is disseminated by means of publications like the Research Libraries Group's *Diginews*, and the Library of Congress's White Papers. It is vitally important to rely on the guidance of experts in developing projects. Observing good practice is the key to ensuring that digitization does not have to be done again in the future.

Whatever changes in technology and digitization practice come about, it remains true that at some point, objects will have to be handled in order to be digitized. Handling rare, old and fragile materials is still the easiest way to damage them and a decision to digitize will be a question of evaluating all of the risks involved before deciding whether or not to proceed. However, longstanding guidelines for handling such materials do exist, and they have evolved from the centuries-long traditions and practices of preservation and conservation experts. Guidelines for handling materials for digitization have now been developed based on this expertise and knowledge so it is possible to minimize the potential risk of digitization. This process can also ensure that any preservation treatment which may be necessary, or cataloguing of underlying source materials, can take place in tandem where appropriate.

When deciding to digitize, it is important to think strategically by asking how digitization will be effective in the context of the collection. Creating a specialist digitization centre in-house for this type of material can be a good way to make these projects a more high-profile component of the institutional mission. It can also help to build bridges between departments at the institution. This issue of digital preservation is discussed in detail in Chapter 7, in the context of building and sustaining a digital library for the long term.

Given the enormous investment in projects of this nature, it is crucial to ensure the long-term care and preservation of the digital objects that have been created, in order to ensure their long term accessibility and interoperability.

Digitization of audio and moving image collections

Introduction

This chapter will discuss the variety of formats that contain audio and visual materials and the importance of audio and moving image collections for research and access, and will address some of the problems in digitizing these materials. It will also present an overview of current practices, with suggestions for sources of expertise on this emerging field.

Increasingly, libraries, archives and museums of all sizes are being asked to preserve and maintain access to collections of moving image and audio materials. These materials encompass broadcasts, oral history recordings, ethnographic and performance-based materials and materials for the study of language and music.

The need to preserve and disseminate our audiovisual heritage has been identified as an area of particular concern at the national level in Europe and the USA. The European Union has recently funded a number of audiovisual digitization and preservation initiatives, including ARCHIMEDIA (www.ledoux.be/archimedia/) and a number of initiatives under the auspices of the Digital Heritage and Cultural Content Programmme, part of the Information Society Technologies Programme (IST; www.cordis.lu/ist/). These include ECHO: European Chronicles On-line.

In the USA, the issue was articulated in a statement prepared by the Association of Research Libraries, CLIR and the National

Humanities Alliance in support of the National Endowment for the Humanities, the year 2000 statement to the US Senate's appropriations sub-committees:

> Of growing concern to all in the humanities is how to ensure the preservation of the fragile historical record of the twentieth century captured in film, video, television, recorded sound, and other audio or visual forms of information. These media have given us an unprecedented means by which we can capture the experience of a diverse American culture with a vividness and faithfulness that print often cannot match and give us a rich, multidimensional portrait of ourselves and our times. Regrettably, while widely accessible to Americans of all cultural, linguistic, and ethnic backgrounds, these media are hard to preserve. Yet without access to the rich heritage that audio and visual resources document, there are large segments of the American democratic experiment that will not survive to become part of the historical record. Without such audiovisual records, we would not be able to create documentary histories of baseball, slavery, the Civil War, or the immigrants' odyssey through Ellis Island. Institutions large and small across America are preserving these resources.
>
> (ARL, 1999)

The value of audiovisual collections to scholarship

Audio and moving image source materials are valuable for many types of research. They are the primary source materials for the study of contemporary history and recent political affairs. Our understanding of such material is increasingly dependent upon the archives of news organizations, which pioneered the use of audio recordings and then film for recording and broadcasting. It would be difficult to imagine how certain recent events could be studied without access to film or audio recordings, including the study of recent elections around the world, when so much of contemporary politics is carried out under the scrutiny of the broadcast media.

In addition, a growing number of important archives and collections of recorded material are being established, such as the video archives of recordings of the testimonies of Holocaust survivors collected by the Survivors of the Shoah Visual History Foundation. Many sound and moving image recordings by anthropologists contribute to our understanding of indigenous cultures and dying languages, sometimes providing the last remaining record of languages and folk traditions. Small archives and local history collections around the world are recognizing that recordings of the spoken word, music and performance are important primary source materials. For example, on the Hebridean island of Tiree, on the west of Scotland, a community archive and museum called An Iodhlann is developing a collection of materials related to all aspects of the island's history and culture. One of their most significant collections is a series of audio cassettes with recordings of song, music and the spoken word, preserving access to Gaelic language and tradition. Such collections are becoming common in many small local museums and libraries.

As the discipline of media studies grows in significance, the study of film and television draws upon a rich archive of dramatic productions made over the last century. Film is also a powerful tool for depicting historical buildings or archaeological sites, as it can allow the presentation of three-dimensional spaces and objects, without the need to create full virtual reality content.

Audiovisual formats

Watching film or listening to audio requires the use of a huge variety of playback and storage devices compared to what is required to appreciate a book or painting.

A recent survey (NINCH, 2002) identified the following formats that have been used for time-based media in the relatively short period of time since recording technologies began. Since Edison recorded the words 'Mary had a little lamb' on a tinfoil cylinder phonograph in 1877:

- Sounds have been recorded on wax or celluloid cylinders, magnetic coated wire drums or reels, 78 rpm shellac resin disc, 45 rpm and 33 rpm vinyl discs, reel to reel magnetic tape, compact cassette, 4 and 8 track cassette cartridges, and compact discs.
- Moving images for personal and broadcast use have been recorded on 8 mm and Super 8 film, 16 mm and 35 mm ¼", ½", 1", and 2" reel to reel video tape, ¾" (U-Matic) tape or cassette

and 8 mm videocassette in both VHS and Betamax format. Digital video has been recorded on DVCAM, DVCPRO, DVCPRO 50, Digital S, and Digital Betacam.

See also the Center for Media History, at the University of New Mexico, for a comprehensive timeline of all communications formats (www.mediahistory.umn.edu/index2.html).

Providing access to a variety of such material is an enormous undertaking, which will require staff with expertise to maintain all the playback equipment. Use of such recordings will usually require a visit to the research centre that maintains the collection in order to be able to use the materials. For example, visitors to the Rogers and Hammerstein Archives of Recorded Sound at New York Public Library (www.nypl.org/research/lpa/rha/rha.html) can have access to one of the world's richest collections of recorded sound. Virtually every format developed to record sound, including wax cylinders, acetate and aluminum discs, magnetic wire recordings, 78 rpm recordings, audiocassettes, compact discs and digital audio tape, can be found in the Archives. Rarities in the collection include the Mapleson Cylinders, recorded at the Metropolitan Opera House in 1901–3 with singers including the De Reszke brothers, Milka Ternina and Lillian Nordica; Irving Berlin singing his own songs; and thousands of other rare recordings. Because the originals are so fragile, the user may never handle them. Instead, the user makes a request to listen to a particular piece, and a sound engineer sets up the equipment in a basement storage area. Then the recordings are piped into specially designed listening and viewing booths; subsequent communications take place directly between the listener and audio technician through computer terminals stationed in each booth.

Providing access to old film stock has just as many conservation and delivery considerations. It may even be dangerous, especially in the case of nitrate film stock, which can ignite. The digitization of film and audio recordings is therefore extremely advantageous for preventing the handling of the originals, and may even be urgently required.

It is estimated that up to 80% of silent films made in the USA have been lost, as have 50% of films made in the era of nitrate film stock, that is before 1950 (CLIR, 2001). The crisis of preserving such content is exacerbated by the fact that even though there is an urgent need to preserve such materials, moving image is especially difficult to digitize as playback devices for the originals may have become obsolete or impossible to operate. The sheer scope of playback devices required, and the proliferation of technology in this field over the past 120 years makes preservation of recorded materials especially challenging.

One initiative to address this concern is Memorarchiv (www. memeriav.ch/). This project seeks to digitize the radio, film and television archives of Switzerland, many of which are in a dangerously fragile condition. Degradation of the format is coupled with the loss of mechanisms to read and play materials – as Betamax video recorders, 8-track tape players and analogue cassette players go the way of the gramophone, many projects are transferring audio and video materials directly to digital format, which is becoming, by definition, a preservation format.

Funding limitations mean that the archive is restricted to digitizing on a pragmatic basis: the primary focus has to be on materials that require urgent measures before they are completely unusable, such a lacquer disks and nitrate film, and on materials that are perceived as vitally important to the culture and heritage of Switzerland. However, the archive seeks to maintain a balance of materials: film, sound, video and photograph, as well as an equitable balance between Swiss linguistic regions, states and communities. The archive works with partner institutions – often broadcast and heritage institutions. These partners commit matching funds and labour, and commit to providing long term-preservation of the material and guaranteeing wise public access to it.

Advantages of digitization

Digitization has other advantages beyond prevention of handling of the originals. It also enhances access, by allowing the originals to be viewed in a consistent, computer-readable format. And it enables enhanced access by allowing comparison, searching and editing of the original. Access via the internet makes the materials accessible to a far-reaching audience.

Consequently, there has been much investigation into the digitization of moving image and audio source materials, and their online delivery. The availability of digital video editing software at the desktop (applications like iMovie and iDVD, and desktop multimedia bundles of various kinds supplied by vendors now come pre-installed on most Windows and Macintosh computers), as well as of relatively inexpensive still and video digital camera equipment, has created a great interest and enthusiasm for developing multimedia resources. The technology required is now accessible and attractive to small or pilot digitization projects, and to small institutions.

Challenges

Technology

This is an emerging field. It is important to keep up to date with expert advice and to be aware of standards and best practices. This is an area where it may be advisable to consider outsourcing digitization activities, as the capital purchases required to develop an in-house system will represent a significant investment and will only be cost efficient for institutions that plan to develop a comprehensive audiovisual digitization initiative.

A further concern is that the file sizes of the digital objects are very large, far more so than the file sizes of text or image files. This has serious implications for the storage and delivery of audio and moving image content over the long term. Project managers should seek expert advice on calculating storage requirements, but some general examples may be helpful: CD quality (i.e. uncompressed) audio is 520 Mb per hour (i.e. 74 minutes requires 640 Mb of 16-bit 44 kHz audio). One hour of DVD-quality video (which is compressed by about a factor of five and not considered archival quality) is 13 Gb per hour, although this varies according to the format used, for example, MPEG format may be 4 Gb per hour. One hour of broadcast-quality video, which would be the best archival choice, following the standard called ITU-R BT.601-4 (also formerly known as CCIR-601 in the USA) is 75.6 Gb per hour.

Such high data rates, and the resulting large files, cannot be used for day-to-day work in anything other than specialist environments, so as with images, it will be necessary to develop an uncompressed archival master copy at an optimal data rate, with a compressed version for delivery to the end-user and for day-to-day viewing. It is also notoriously time-consuming to quality check digital audio against the original analogue material. However, the technology is changing at a rapid rate, and what is difficult or expensive today may be easily accessible in the near future.

The requirements of the end-user will also have to be considered, and their expectations managed. Delivery of audio and visual content will require specialized equipment for online delivery, such as specialized displays, powerful computers, high-speed network connections and appropriate software. Audiovisual files require a great deal of bandwidth – large files cannot be transmitted over a 56 Kb modem connection at a speed that is practical for the user. Broadband or high-speed network access is required for mass delivery of full-length films or significant quantities of recorded sound.

These issues should all be taken into consideration when tailoring a user interface for access to audio and moving image content. Access should be provided to any plug-ins or specialist software (such as media players) that will be required, and it may be necessary to provide compressed versions of the content for users who only have access to a slow internet connection. It will also be necessary to design interfaces that enable the user to browse or search the content, which may involve designing a bespoke interface.

An initiative that is experimenting with interface issues is Informedia, at Carnegie Mellon University (www.informedia.cs.cmu.edu/). Informedia's focus is research into digital libraries for video materials, especially broadcast news and documentaries. The Cable News Network, the British Open University and a public television station in Pittsburgh, WQED, provide their content. Each programme is segmented into short sections (such as interviews, or the items in a news broadcast). The Informedia programme is developing tools for indexing the video materials so that they can be searched and browsed by the end-user. In particular, a tool has been developed called 'video skimming', which will use automatic methods to extract important words and images, which are then presented in a video abstract form that is browsable by the user (W. Arms, 2000).

Copyright

Another major consideration is that of copyright. Most archives do not retain the rights to the majority of items in their video and audio collections and existing deposit agreements are unlikely to cover online access. New agreements will have to be negotiated to provide online access to any material that is still within copyright. Managing the rights to a large scale digitization project of a sound or film archive will be as challenging as the digitization itself, as film resources may be subject to multiple and cascading rights restrictions, such as mechanical, performative and underlying rights. Musical soundtracks are especially fraught with difficulty when negotiating the rights for networked delivery (Owen, Pearson and Arnold, 2000).

Sources of expertise

There are a number of sources of specialist advice on issues related to audiovisual digitization:

- Duke University maintains a very useful website with information about video digitization (http://cit.duke.edu/).
- The MATRIX Center at Michigan State University is host to the National Gallery of the Spoken Word and maintains information on many aspects of audio digitization (http://matrix.msu.edu/).
- The Performing Arts Data Service at the University of Glasgow (www.ahds.ac.uk/performing arts) is the AHDS specialist subject centre for all aspects of the digitization of performance. The staff of PADS can advise members of the UK higher education community on recorded performance, metadata for archives, and storage issues.
- The British Universities Film and Video Council (www.bufvc.ac.uk/) promotes the uses of moving image in research and teaching in the UK and can provide some advice on delivering moving images online.
- The NINCH Guide to Best Practice has a section on audio and

video digitization, with a detailed discussion of playback devices and file formats.

Digitizing audio and video

More and more video digitization is now done on a camcorder rather than the computer, i.e. shooting is on a mini-DV camera to a tape which is already digital. The video is then moved to the computer via an external device such as firewire, I-Link or IEEE 1304.

If conversion from an analogue audio or video source is required, the original can be viewed on a TV or listened to on a hi-fi audio player to identify the clips or section that is to be digitized. Once the section for digitization has been identified, the playback device is connected to the capture device that is to be used for conversion to the digital format. This is usually accomplished by connecting the playback device to an integrated capture card in the computer, sometimes via a connection to a device known as a 'breakout box'. The audio or video capture card in the computer will convert the analogue source to digital. Separate cards and computers are recommended for audio and video, as each card will require different quality settings, their own input–output settings and discrete software to control the digitization (Deegan and Tanner, 2004).

Film digitization can also be carried out directly from analogue film sources, but this approach requires specialist expertise and equipment. The *NINCH Guide* (2000) suggests the following methods of transferring film to digital: via a transfer box or a multiplexer, or by using a chain film scanner to digitize directly from 8, 16 or 35 mm film. The latter option scans the films and digitizes at the scanner, passing the digital signal to the computer. An important advantage is that the analogue to digital conversion is done at the camera, rather than on the computer, creating less opportunity for 'noise' to be added by the process. However, these are all still extremely expensive options, which makes it impractical for most institutions to consider purchasing such systems. Work of this specificity would usually be outsourced to a vendor. Simpler, and cheaper, solutions include using systems to transfer the film images on to analogue video tape (VHS or Beta) and then performing digitization on the video feed. This technique is known as telecine, and is the most heavily used technique available at this time, although there is a resulting loss of quality (see www.ericksonarchival.com/ for an example of supplier).

Audio digitization is less of a challenge, as many audio formats are still supported. It is still possible to purchase cassette players and hi-fi systems that will play 45, 33 and 78 rpm records. Such devices can be connected to a computer and recorded via an internal sound card. For older formats, such as wax cylinders, an external microphone can record the sound on to an intermediary format that can be digitized. Reel-to-reel tapes, wire recorders or cartridge players (such as 4-track or 8-track systems) often have an analogue signal-out connection, or they can be modified by sound engineers to provide a direct sound output, which is then connected to a digital capture device.

Because digitization techniques vary depending on the hardware platform available, as well as the available skills and expertise, it is important to take expert advice at the outset of any project of this nature. Sound engineers and film experts may be required to interpret what in the original content (especially background noise or frame speed) should be represented in the digital format. It will also be necessary to take advice on editing. The investment involved in setting up a workstation for in-house digitization will be significant, and may be beyond the resources of many small projects. Unless there are specific reasons to develop this expertise in house, it may well be easier to outsource digitization to one of the many vendors who convert audio and film to digital format. As with any digitization project, it is unlikely that it will be possible to re-digitize the materials again, so it is always advisable to digitize at the best quality possible and affordable. This may mean outsourcing, rather than compromising on quality in order to be able to use in-house tools.

The use of standard formats will also be important: audiovisual standard formats are introduced in Chapter 7, page 189 onwards.

Post-capture processing

After digitization, significant post-processing may be required. This may include editing the data to exclude background noise using digital noise-reduction techniques, or compressing the files for online delivery. Editing tools, such as Final CutPro, Adobe Premiere or Imovie, may be required to edit video content into smaller segments.

Compression will also be required for viewing or listening to files online, using a process of Compression and DE-Compression (CODEC). This will involve initial compression at the production end using a suitable CODEC to gain the desired file size, frames per second, transmission rate and quality. Compression will be a difficult balancing act between achieving the smallest file size and retaining suitable quality (Deegan and Tanner, 2004). The format and compression to be used will be dependent upon the expected usage patterns and the intended user base, and the issue of informational content is an important one in the delivery of digitized audio and visual material. If the file size can be adjusted to deliver highly compressed video, the resulting file will be of a poor quality, but accessible to a wider audience. Whether or not this is important is a decision that must be based on the information that should be transmitted to the end-user. Some projects will give the user the option of downloading a large file (for delivery over a high-speed network) or a smaller, compressed file that can be downloaded via a modem. The video archive of the Hemispheric Institute of Performance and Politics at New York University uses this approach, delivering digital video files in either Real Video or QuickTime format, in three different files sizes – high, medium or low. This requires that six different files be created, which increases the time it will take to do the project.

Media outlets such as the BBC Online, have taken the decision to compress Real Video files in such a way that the video appears jerky, because it is transmitted in a very low frame rate format.

There are many other online film outlets, and it may be instructive to look at them to see what kind of choices they have made regarding formats and quality:

- www.thebitscreen.com/home.htm
- www.ifilm.com/
- www.loc.gov/rr/mopic/ndlmps.html
- http://atomfilms.com
- www.archive.org/movies/movies.php.

The content will then be saved in an appropriate file format, such as QuickTime, or Real Audio/Video, or a generic DivX or MPEG format. Video and audio will be streamed directly to the user, or downloaded then viewed locally. This will depend on the file size, available bandwidth and copyright considerations. Streaming is a suitable delivery option for live broadcasts, such as lectures and performances. For an example of the use of streaming media for education, see the BoxMind project at the University of Bath, at www.boxmind.com. This project is developing tools to integrate audio and moving image content into teaching and learning materials. Streaming is also an option that can protect rights holders, as it does not make a copy of the file on to the desktop. If copyright is an issue, it may be possible to digitize only small samples of the material.

Setting up a digitization centre

As discussed above, it will often be more appropriate to outsource moving image and audio digitization initiatives, as the equipment purchases can be particularly expensive. If an institution wishes to set up a preservation-level digitization centre to work with valuable or unique materials, it will be necessary to take advice from preservation experts with a great deal of experience in this area, and to have such expertise on hand throughout the duration of the project. Unlike other source materials, in addition to the need to protect fragile originals, there can be dangers inherent in the process. For example, cellulose nitrate film, produced mainly between 1889 and 1939 (although some production continued until 1950), can be very dangerous as it is highly inflammable and may spontaneously ignite in certain conditions. Any nitrate film in a collection should be isolated and removed to a cool, dry, well ventilated area until it can be copied. The greatest risk is with large amounts of old, densely packed film (which may ignite at temperatures as low as 48°C). Once cellulose nitrate begins to burn, it very quickly produces highly toxic fumes, as well as smoke and heat. If the archive buildings or contents are insured, the policy may prohibit the storage of cellulose nitrate film (Harrison, 1997).

Case study: an in-house digitization suite

Some institutions are developing specialist suites for general purpose audio and video digitization. The equipment available for audio/video digitization at NYU's Arts Technology Group's Studio, an interdisciplinary centre for faculty who are creating electronic resources for teaching and research, is typical of the equipment that is required for digitization and post-capture processing. This centre, part of the University's central Information Technology Services, provides the following equipment for the Macintosh platform:

General resources

- six video editing systems for short quality video pieces using the mini-DV standard and Apple's FinalCutPro or Adobe Premier editing software
- three ProTools audio systems with Roland MIDI keyboards
- medium format archival and non-archival printers.

Supported processes

- high-quality scanning of positive and negative film and reflective film
- film recording in 35 mm, 120, and 4x5 colour formats
- large format printing with archival and non-archival output.

Additional resources

- two video-editing booths for advanced students and faculty working on large video post-production projects; primarily used to edit analogue Betacam SP source materials, in addition to mini-DV, DVCAM, and DVC-Pro digital formats.

Supported media

- DVD-R, CD-RW, mini-DV, DVCAM, and DAT
- video dubbing rack format: DVCAM, Betacam SP, Hi-8, S-VHS, VHS, mini-DV.

Audio: a preservation concern

The standard format for audio CDs of 16 bits and 44.1 kHz (with resulting data rates of 1.4 Mb per second) was developed by Phillips and Sony in the 1980 *Red Book* document, and was patented. However, the patent for this specification has expired and new formats are emerging. These include Super-Audio Compact Disk (SACD) and DVD-Audio (DVD-A). These will store audio at 24-bit 96 kHz, producing significantly higher-fidelity audio than CD. It is unclear which format will ultimately replace the CD format, and this is comparable to the battle over VHS versus Betamax as a standard for video. However, it is expected that both SADC and DVD-A disks will also have CD format encoding, so will be backwardly compatible. Although these technology and formats are yet to mature (and so it is presently inappropriate to suggest them for archival purposes), there is little question that 24-bit audio will become the industry standard for domestic usage over the next decade.

Metadata

As with all media types, appropriate metadata will be essential to guaranteeing the creation of a 'well-formed digital object that will survive for the long term' (Deegan and Tanner, 2004), as well as access to the materials. All data must be documented properly to ensure that future curators and users understand the materials that they are dealing with. The creator of digital objects must expend almost as much effort on the development of appropriate metadata as on the digitization itself. The time and effort expended on metadata creation at the outset of a project will save an enormous amount of subsequent work. Retrospective metadata creation and input is often unworkable and always frustrating.

For audio and visual materials, technical metadata will include information about the date of digitization, equipment and software used, file format, sampling rate, compression, etc. Administrative metadata will also include information about any copyright issues, including any citation requirements of the original, as well as preservation metadata, such as information about migration of obsolete file formats. Because a great deal of digitization activity may have relied upon proprietary formats or emerging standards, documentation about the file formats used is essential to the future use and discovery of the content. Descriptive metadata will include the attributes of the content itself, and will require extensive information including details regarding the title, creator, subject, language, and keywords related to the content.

PADS have carried out a good deal of research into the issue of metadata for digitized moving image materials, and have developed a modified Dublin Core metadata set which addresses many of the issues in describing such content, by developing qualifiers to the 15 basic elements of the Dublin Core. For example, is the 'creator' of a film the director, the producer, or another figure? A full-length feature film can include many 'creators', and the PADS system anticipates this kind of ambiguity in film (Owen, Pearson and Arnold, 2000). The Metadata Encoding and Transmission System (METS) can also be used for audio and visual content, and the MPEG-7 metadata schema is often used for audiovisual materials.

Case studies

Hemispheric Institute of Performance and Politics (http:/hemi.nyu.edu)

The Hemispheric Institute for Performance and Politics at NYU collects and produces materials related to the study of performance and politics in the Americas. In 2001, the Institute collaborated with the Arts Technology Group and The Humanities Computing Group at the University's Information Technology Services (ITS) to develop a prototype for an online, searchable archive of this video material. The prototype set about developing a digitization workflow for a sample of the video collections, developing metadata for cataloguing the performance and designing a web interface for the archive testbed. The Arts Technology Group at one of the University's multimedia computer facilities digitized the video. Footage was digitized using Final Cut Pro and then compressed using Media Cleaner Pro, and the digital output was dubbed where necessary. Each file was then compressed into real audio and QuickTime formats for user delivery. The metadata schema developed by the Performing Arts Data Service for moving image was used (see previous section). Both the video files and the metadata were stored in MySQL databases living on central servers. They were accessed via a website which includes a search feature. This searches the metadata for keywords relating to the material and then presents the user with the option of downloading the file as a small, medium or large file in either QuickTime or Real Video format (giving the user six choices to allow for a variety of network access conditions, crucial for a project which has a large user base in the countries of the south).

National Library of Norway, Sound and Image Archive (www.nb.no/)

A copyright library, the National Library of Norway receives legal deposit materials from all national radio and television broadcasts (17,000 audio- and videotapes annually). The Library is committed to managing and preserving the archives of this material, working in co-operation with NRK, formerly the only national broadcaster, to preserve existing archives of pre-1990 material. Around 2000 television programmes from 1960 to 1990 have been deposited on digital tape at the Library.

The Music Section handles collections of both historic recordings and legal deposit material since 1990. More than 25,000 items cover the Norwegian heritage through 100 years of recorded music. Examples of collections are recordings from the Norwegian State Academy of Music, the Norwegian Collection of Folk Music (University of Oslo), the Norwegian Jazz Archives and the Norwegian Council for Cultural Affairs.

The Film Section collects, archives and preserves films of national historical importance. Most existing film material on nitrate stock produced before 1953 has been transferred to purpose-built nitrate vaults. Parts of the film commercials collection will be used in a project that is intended to give online access to digital versions, limited to Nordic film students.

The Photography Section is primarily concerned with the preservation of important photographic collections in Norway. Nitrate and other older materials are converted on to new film in 70 mm format.

The owners of the photographic collections are offered duplicate negatives and/or high-quality digital images of their collections. Some 700,000 photographic items have been deposited. About 120,000 photographic units have been digitized to be displayed and can be found in the database Galleri Nor on the internet (http://www.nb.nor/gallerinor).

The Library is using digitization of sound and image archives to preserve fragile and vulnerable materials (e.g. volatile nitrate-based film stock) or materials that need special handling or obsolete playback devices. The challenge here is to produce a high-quality digital version.

The highest priorities in the selection of materials for digitization are:

• teaching and learning potential (e.g. what the National Library can do with the materials — can they be made available to schools?)
• research significance
• enhancing access
• preservation (this criterion is becoming more and more important over recent years and higher on the list of priorities).

3-D objects and artefacts

Collections will often include three-dimensional materials, and the representation of these materials in a digital format can be desirable for access and research. The digitization of three-dimensional materials is of particular interest to museums, but many other institutions are seeking to experiment with digitization of 3D materials from all periods of history, and related to all genres and areas of research. Archaeologists in particular are benefiting from developing interactive digitized models of excavations, depicting the locations of artefacts and materials as they are found. With present technologies, it is not possible to create a 'true' facsimile, but there are 3-D techniques that can give some good representations of 3-D materials. A great deal of research in this area is coming from the museum communities, such as the research projects of the Smithsonian's imaging departments. However, this technology is still emerging, and may require the use of proprietary formats and applications, including the user interface level (Rowe, 2002).

The creation and publication of three-dimensional material can be a powerful method for representing cultural heritage content. 3-D models are increasingly used in museums, and they are also useful for the study of buildings and archaeological sites. Such models support the interactive manipulation of objects, and the exploration of landscapes, which can be an important tool for research, as well as representing all sides of fragile objects. There is information about 3-D technologies on the website of the Web3D consortium, at www.web3d.org, and www.3dsite.com. Many interesting examples can be found of projects which exploring this technology for the representation of cultural heritage content. These include the Pompey project at Cambridge University, which was an important early initiative to reconstruct an early Roman theatre. The EU has funded the Theatron project (Theatre History in Europe: Architectural and Textual Resources Online www.theatron.org/) to build on some of the work developed by this initiative, which features interactive real time walkthroughs of highly accurate 3-D models of present and past theatres. Another project that has developed 3-D models for research and access is the Cistercian Abbeys project at the University of Sheffield (http://cistercians.shef.ac.uk/). The project explores the history and architecture of the Cistercian order in Britain, focusing on five Cistercian abbeys in Yorkshire. A central component of the project is the set of three-dimensional reconstructions of the five abbeys and their outbuildings. These are accompanied by texts explaining the history and importance of the Cistercian order and their abbeys.

VRML is the 'official' standard for the modelling of virtual reality and 3-D material. Because the use of 3-D tools is presently mostly the bailiwick of specialists, its take-up has been sporadic. It has not yet become part of the pre-installed suite of tools on computers (in the manner that QuickTime or Windows media players come pre-installed on new Macintosh or Windows computers).

However, some excellent examples of 3-D models are available. In addition to those listed above, many museums have developed 3-D models, which they can put online for remote access, or make available to visitors in viewing kiosks within the museum itself. The Hunterian Museum at Glasgow University has experimented with this format for depicting the Egyptian sarcophagus and mummy in their collection. VRML content cannot be 'streamed' to the end-user because of the file sizes involved. Rather, the material is downloaded as a compressed (zip) file then viewed locally. VRML is an accurate 3-D technology available at this time as a development environment for small-scale projects.

The Smithsonian's imaging departments have experimented with 3-D photography and VRML imaging, and written several position papers on this topic. To create 3-D images, an object is set on a rotating table and photographed with a digital camera. It is rotated 10 degrees, and another picture is taken. Thirty-six pictures are taken per object; once the images are electronically stitched together, they appear as a single image on the screen that can be manipulated by computer users in a variety of ways. For example, the compass used by early American explorers Lewis and Clark has been digitized in such a way that it is seen not just from multiple angles but also opening and closing. It took 108 photographs to offer this effect, 36 for each of the three positions in which it is shown.

Shockwave 3D is a new technology that allows 3-D models to be imported into the software application Macromedia Director (the industry standard for publishing interactive content) online or on a CD-ROM. 3-D interactive content can be published as a shockwave file and viewed by anyone with access to the free, cross-platform Shockwave viewer plug-in.

Conclusion

It may seem that the biggest challenge to the digitization of moving image and audio materials is the fact that both the digitization technology and the large amounts of storage required are expensive. While this is true at this time, it may not always be so. There is encouragement to be drawn from the investment – and vested interests – of the entertainment and media industries in advancing digital technologies for the delivery of digital media at the desktop. We have already seen enormous advances – the desktop video editing systems that come pre-installed on many new computers rival, for many users, the expensive Avid editing suites of just a few years ago, and computer companies are in fierce competition with one another to deliver better and more user-friendly systems for the desktop. Unfortunately, this does not mean that digitization of audio and moving images is not still fraught with difficulties. The biggest obstacle remains copyright, and this will be the case for some time. Because so many moving image and audio materials are still within copyright, permissions will have to be cleared and managed before any significant investment is made in digitization of audio or moving image materials.

10

Digitization of text and images

Introduction

In all digitization projects, the shape, size and condition of the primary source material will dictate how faithful to the original the digital surrogate can be. This is especially true of the materials held by special collections. Decisions about the approach to be taken will always depend on the nature and requirements of the project, the anticipated outcomes and uses of the digital reproductions, and the available infrastructure, budget schedule and staff. Textual and image collections held by libraries, archives and museums are likely to include a large variety of formats, all of which present challenges for digitization.

Textual materials will include documents that are both in manuscript and printed form. Manuscripts from all periods and languages will be written on a huge variety of surfaces, including paper, parchment, papyrus, tablets, wood and stone, and will have script or character issues. Handwritten materials will include ancient and early modern manuscripts, including illuminated pages, letters, diaries and musical manuscripts, presenting a great deal of variation in scripts and character sets. Palaeographic interpretation will often be required and automated recognition of characters will not be possible. Manuscripts come in all shapes and sizes, they may be in bound volumes, and they may also include images, such as marginalia, illustrations or sketches, embedded in the text. Printed works from the last 500 years also present a huge variety of formats, including books, journals, newspapers, letters, typescript, grey literature and musical scores. They may be bound or loose leaf, printed on paper or parchment, and they will include incunabula, which present the same problems as manuscripts. They present a huge range of font and typesetting issues, will often have visual images embedded in the text, and come in a variety of shapes and sizes.

Still images of visual materials may be on many different kinds of substrates, including canvas, paper, glass, textiles, stone, etc. They will include manuscript images, paintings, drawings, engineering and architectural drawings, photographs, maps, stained glass and fabrics, as well as modern formats such as Geographic Information Systems (GIS) data, Landsat (Land Remote Sensing Satellite) images and satellite images depicting land surface features in images of the earth's surface (Deegan and Tanner, 2004).

All the formats listed above will have special digital capture requirements, and the nature of the originals will affect the planning of the digitization workflows and the related costs. It is important to note that most collections are not homogeneous, and will include materials in different formats. It is rare for a project to set about digitizing just texts, or just images – often, it will be necessary to use a variety of text and image capture techniques for different types of material. As with all digitization projects, it will be necessary to assess the source materials at the outset and plan appropriate strategies for:

- the preparation, transfer and handling procedures for the originals, as well as any rights management or licensing issues
- all aspects of the digital imaging process, including choosing digital capture devices appropriate to the originals
- creating administrative, structural and technical metadata
- post-digitization processing of the digital images to create derivatives for screen or print, using image-processing tools, or optical character recognition tools where appropriate, and creating markup where required
- delivery to users, using techniques ranging from developing web pages to using an automated delivery system such as a database
- long-term preservation, including migration and conversion of the digital objects.

This chapter will discuss these issues with reference to a number of case studies of text and image digitization projects.

Managing the digitization of text

Textual materials may be the core elements of a collection and the primary focus of a digitization project. Even if this is not the case, many projects are a hybrid of different media formats, so textual materials (explanatory essays, background reading, navigation instructions) of some sort will usually be required. In this context, 'text' refers to any material where the intellectual content to be conveyed is textual. Items may be handwritten or machine-printed, single-leaf or bound, original materials or surrogates (e.g. microfilm, photocopies) and in any language (S. Chapman, 2003b).

Digitization of text can be especially advantageous for scholarship and research. Electronic texts can be searched, browsed and collated, which is important for the study of languages and literatures. Humanists have been digitizing and analysing text since the advent of the earliest computer systems, with early pioneers in the late 1940s exemplified by researchers like Roberto Busa, a scholar of biblical texts who developed a system of entering text on punch-card systems for processing on mainframe computers in order to produce concordances of Aquinas. Significant investments have been made in developing online text collections such as the Oxford Text Archive, and the Electronic Text Center at the University of Virginia.

Handling

An analysis of the condition of the original materials, and the planned outcomes for the original source materials after digitization, will inform the processes that can be used during digitization and assist the project manager in deciding which digitization equipment should be used (including scanners and digital cameras, lighting, copystands and specialist cradles). As with all materials, the more rare or fragile the originals, the more restrictions that will be imposed on the digitization staff and workflows. Such restrictions will increase the cost of digitization both in terms of the time that is spent on the digitization processes and the equipment and peripherals that must be purchased. These issues are presented in greater detail in Chapter 8.

Many textual materials will be in bound volumes, so one of the principal considerations will be whether or not the originals can be disbound for production document scanning (i.e. autofeeding), a method that significantly lowers scanning costs, as scanning books is far more expensive than scanning single pages. If materials can be disbound, it may be necessary to re-bind them after digitization, which can add an additional layer of costs to the process. If materials are in book form and cannot be disbound, then they may be scanned using a flatbed scanner, but only if it is acceptable for the operator to turn over pages and have the materials make direct contact with the scanner platen. If this is unacceptable, then the options will be limited to the use of overhead scanners or digital cameras, using the appropriate cradles to hold the volumes in place. In cases where the material is extremely fragile, it may be better to microfilm first, then scan from the microfilm (S. Chapman, 2003b).

Technical issues in text digitization

There are a number of ways to approach the conversion of full-text documents, depending on the documents themselves and the uses to which they are likely to be put. Essentially, these can be summarized as processes that produce machine-readable and machine-viewable electronic text. An image of a page is machine displayable, and will depict all the original features of the original source. However, it cannot be processed or edited, as although it can be read by the human eye, it is not machine readable. With machine-readable text, however, the computer can read every individual entity, as well as formatting instructions and other codes that may be embedded in the digital file. Machine-readable texts, therefore, have a good deal more flexibility (Deegan and Tanner, 2004).

An imaging approach: creation of page images

Page images are pictorial reproductions of analogue source materials, produced by scanning or digital photography. Like photocopies, page images are not searchable, and like photographs, page images may be created either to replicate or merely to approximate the appearance of the originals. Page images may be created from text in any language, on any type of substrate; the images that are produced may be black and white, greyscale, or colour. Many projects are now using this method of digitization, and this chapter will review a number of these throughout the world. These will illustrate the various decisions made regarding all aspects of text digitization, including mark-up, metadata and the different techniques used to link index and image.

A full-text conversion approach

'Full text' resources are machine readable and fully searchable. This approach is the more expensive option and so it is important to evaluate whether a full-text conversion route is appropriate for the project in hand. If this method is chosen, then there are two main ways to achieve text of the desired accuracy (99.95%). The first of these is optical character recognition (OCR) of a page image produced by scanning or digital photography, followed by manual proofing and correction. OCR is a digital-to-digital process, as OCR may only be done from page images, not the originals. Generally speaking, OCR works best from high-quality black-and-white page images. OCR is not available for all languages (for example, there are presently no OCR applications that can read Arabic fonts). The editing that has to be done on OCR'd text can be time consuming. For a detailed description of the OCR process, see Witten and Bainbridge (2003).

The other method of full-text digital capture is rekeying, the process of manually transcribing (typing) text into machine-readable form. Keying may be done from original materials or surrogates such as photocopies, microfilm or page images. Keying is usually outsourced to specialist bureaux, which provide accurate transcriptions by double or triple re-keying, when two or three operators will work on the same text, and then use software to compare the texts with each other. Any differences are highlighted and corrected manually. Specialist bureaux deliver an accurate and reliable service, with costs that are consistently low. One project that is using this approach is the Million Book Project, at the University of Pittsburgh.

Both of these approaches are costly. Deciding which approach to use will include considering what the users of the digital text will require, and what functions need to be delivered, such as searching, browsing or text analysis of the electronic texts. It will often be the case that a hybrid approach – a combination of page images and searchable text – will be required. Steven Chapman, in a comprehensive assessment of managing text digitization (S. Chapman, 2003b), has suggested that the best way to assess which approach to take is to first consider the delivery issues and then to translate these into functional requirements for text digitization projects. The best way do this is to review examples of text digitization projects conducted by libraries and archives in order to see which offer the functionality and results that are required. The various options for the delivery of electronic textual materials are listed below, in ascending order of cost.

Page images

This is delivery of non-searchable facsimile images of each page, for use on screen or in print. These can be in colour or greyscale, and can convey fully the original attributes of the original. This is the most simple and inexpensive method of text digitization, and produces machine-viewable text that is not amenable to any processing or editing. For an example, see the Cornell Historic Math Book Collection (http://cdl.library.cornell.edu/cdl-math-browse.html).

Full text

This option is delivery of fully searchable, accurate transcriptions of texts for use on screen or in print. The text that is produced is machine readable. This is the preferred format for scholars and researchers who may wish to search or conduct text analysis of the original materials. It will also allow the electronic texts to be edited and used in different ways (for example, excerpts can be copied for captions for images). As outlined above, the two methods for capturing full text are transcription or scanning followed by OCR. Transcription is the best option for handwritten materials or printed materials in non-standard fonts. However, full text (whether it is produced by OCR or by keying) will only represent the textual elements and will not convey the original layout or incorporate illustrations.

An example of a transcription project is the Canterbury Tales project. The long-term aim of the project is to determine as thoroughly as possible the textual history of *The Canterbury Tales*, working with the 84 extant manuscripts, as well as four pre-1500 printed editions. These are manually transcribed into computer-readable form using a text editor, and the electronic text is subsequently collated and analysed for manuscript agreements and disagreements.

Documenting the American South (DAS) uses an OCR approach; the project is creating an electronic collection of sources on Southern history, literature and culture based at the University of North Carolina (UNC). It includes over 1200 books and manuscripts, from the colonial period to the early 20th century. After selection and stabilization by staff conservators, the texts are scanned (from either originals or photocopies, depending on the original's physical condition) then put through OCR software. In the case of manuscripts, OCR scans are made of pre-existing typescripts. After scanning, spell-check software is used to review and correct the text file created by OCR. The OCR scans are also subjected to proofreading by graduate assistants and the Digitization Librarian, with an ultimate goal of 99.95% accuracy, the level currently accepted by libraries.

Other projects, such as the Electronic Text Center at the University of Virginia, use a combination of transcription and scanning/OCR to develop full-text materials: OCR is only used on smaller jobs with modern typefaces. For older or large-scale materials, rekeying has proven more effective. For another example of a full-text digitization approach, see Bartleby.com's Great Books Online, at www.bartleby.com.

Page images and hidden full text for searching

While what the end-user sees is a page image of the text, there is a full-text version of the text which 'lives' in the background, for use by a built-in search engine. Search results are presented to the user by providing links to the page images that contain the topic, word, or phrase that has been searched for. An example of this is the Digital

Library of the Forced Migration Online (FMO) project at the Refugee Studies Centre, University of Oxford (www.forcedmigration.org).

Page images and full text for searching and display

This option allows the end-user to choose between viewing either the page images or fully searchable transcriptions, for use on screen or in print. The Institute for Advanced Technology in the Humanities (IATH) Blake Archive, based at the University of Virginia, is an example of this approach. The end-user can look at a page image that is an exact copy of Blake's original works, or select the option to 'click for transcription' to view a full text of the original which can be browsed and searched.

Page images and encoded text for searching and display

As above, the users have the option of viewing a page image or full text for searching, but this option also includes text mark-up using tools such as XML or SGML (see below) to express the structure of the original document, formatting and editorial features (corrections, marginalia, etc.). This option is particularly useful for the digitization of manuscripts or editions, such as the Whitman Archive at IATH. It is the most expensive approach to text digitization and also one that will require involvement of scholars familiar with the original source materials throughout the course of the project (S. Chapman, 2003b).

Mark-up and metadata

Because of the difficulties involved in ensuring that digital text can be represented on different computer systems and exchanged across these systems without loss of formatting, mark-up schemes have been developed by various standards bodies. The Text Encoding Initiative (TEI; www.tei-c.org) has developed a subset of the industry standard Standard General Markup Language (SGML) that is applicable to electronic texts. Similarly, the World Wide Web Consortium (W3C; www.w3c.org) has developed the XML schema, which is used for an increasing number of digital library projects.

For example, the Electronic Text Center at the University of Virginia marks up its texts using SGML in accordance with TEI guidelines using a subset of TEI tags called TEILITE, and more recently, its XML counterpart TEIXLITE.DTD. The Center has been using the TEI guidelines since its inception. For the last several years, the Center has used a programme to convert its TEI headers into MARC records, easing their inclusion into the general library catalogue. In addition, the Center has developed an on-the-fly TEI-to-HTML conversion program to facilitate web browsing. This process eliminates the need for the Center to store HTML copies of its TEI texts on the server.

Texts in the *Documenting the American South* collection are marked up using SGML encoding, according to TEI guidelines, using the TEILITE.DTD, and checked for both conformance and consistency. A fully structured TEI header, a mandatory element of any TEI-conformant text, precedes the encoded electronic text, providing a detailed framework for documenting the electronic text, its source, encoding system and revision history. Following mark-up, the texts are published on the internet in both TEI/SGML and HTML formats. The alternative HTML versions are generated from on-the-fly translations using a Perl script, permitting access to users without SGML browsers. All of the digitized texts also receive individual full-level MARC catalogue records, made available through the OCLC system.

These mark-up systems are the 'glue' that links electronic resources, and enables their interoperability. Similarly, the use of metadata standards such as those outlined in Chapter 7 will enable the long-term management and re-use of electronic textual resources, and make the long-term preservation and migration of electronic content less of a challenge. The development of the Unicode standard offers a way of encoding multilingual materials so that they can be read on different computer systems. Adding complex mark-up or metadata is time consuming and expensive, however, and costs associated with this process will have to be factored into the project budget. For more information, see the Oxford Text Archive.

Digitization of image collections

Many libraries and other cultural institutions hold image and photographic collections, which are of tremendous interest to both the general public and to researchers. Visual history resources are a compelling means of connecting with the past and of recording disappearing cultures, communities and traditions. Photographic collections include a whole range of formats, including photographs on glass plates, negative film, photographic paper, microfilm and microfiche.

The scale of image collections in archives, museums and library collections is vast. The Library of Congress Prints and Photographs Division has over 13 million items, including photographs, cartoons, posters and banners, architectural drawings and ephemera such as baseball cards, badges, etc. Many were acquired as part of large collections and bequests, and have been catalogued by photographer, the institution the materials were obtained from, or donor. Many images are held by the library only as negatives (C. R. Arms, 1999). A survey of photographic materials in Europe carried out by the European Commission on Preservation and Access revealed that the 140 institutions that responded to the survey hold some 120 million photographs, half of which are over 50 years old. This gives some sense of the scale of the world's photographic stock. Around four-fifths of the survey respondents had already begun digitization of their photographic holdings or were planning to digitize in the future, with protection of vulnerable originals being a crucial reason. Digital surrogates are excellent substitutes for photographic originals and can provide almost all the content information that the original can yield (Deegan and Tanner, 2002).

What is particularly compelling about such collections is that they convey important information about the ordinary lives and activities of millions of people. Whereas we only have access to the written historical record from the pre-photography area, visual historical records enormously enrich our understanding of our recent and contemporary history. The photographic collections of the Imperial War Museum in London and Manchester, for example, document events of World War 1 in an accessible way to visitors and researchers. Similarly, initiatives such as the Early Office Museum, with its collection of virtual exhibits and images related to office life from the 1830s to the 1940s, illustrate everyday life for early workers and tell the contemporary viewer a great deal about working life in the period (www.officemuseum.com/photo_gallery_1900s_ii.htm).

Projects intending to digitize large image collections face special considerations. In addition to considering the content, format and physical condition of the material, it is important to evaluate their potential use. These collections are of interest to scholars in a variety of fields, including architectural historians, environmental researchers and social and political historians. However, scholars are no longer the majority audience for many image collections. These are now also used intensively by commercial enterprises such as publishers, news organizations and advertisers. They are used to illustrate both popular and scholarly publications, and browsed by users researching family and local history. The universal reach of digital images on the internet provides a means to respond to this escalating demand for broader access (Ostrow, 1998).

Usage of image archives

The primary reasons for digitizing image collections are:

- to increase and enhance access to the collections
- to ease reproduction of originals
- to preserve the original materials by reducing or eliminating handling of originals
- to facilitate research
- to implement broad licensing arrangements for dissemination of large-scale projects.

Increasing access

Image collections are among the least accessible primary sources available to researchers because of their large size, physical fragility and haphazard cataloguing. Digitizing collections, use of the internet and the development of powerful databases, search engines and online image repositories can facilitate greatly improved and more widespread access to image collections.

Digitizing image collections is likely to have a significant democratizing effect, particularly when the institutions allow access to these from outside their walls. As Walter Benjamin pointed out (Benjamin,

1978), being able to appreciate a work of art in a setting other than a museum is a significant step in the democratization of art. Using digital surrogates may bring the user into even closer proximity to the intellectual content of the original. Interactivity offers the opportunity for participation in many different ways. With the ability to zoom in and zoom out and to compare close-ups, spectators can begin to make their own juxtapositions at various levels. This includes placing close-ups side by side, as well as superimposing images on one another, to discover new relationships between them. By being able to manipulate images in these ways, the spectator is able to participate in activities that previously were almost exclusively within the domain of curators and scholars. These interactive processes engage the viewers and makes them more participants than spectators. Additional techniques such as image processing (which allows the viewer to alter and combine images) offer even further engagement (Besser, 1991).

Remote digital access to a sample of images from a collection can also prepare scholars for subsequent research, if the digital selections are accompanied by a database documenting in detail the scope of a whole collection (and incremental development of a digital collection of this sort often makes the most sense financially).

Facilitating reproduction of originals

Digital copies may be created not only for searching, but also to produce user copies. These can then be distributed via e-mail or on disk. Vancouver's City Archives are experimenting with the digitization and electronic dissemination of many of their historic photo collections, which can subsequently be ordered by users via the city's website.

This is also useful because few institutions actually have photographic duplicates from which they can make user copies. In most cases they have to go back to original negatives or prints. If high-quality digital files are available, this can be avoided. The ease of dissemination of electronic duplicates also creates a powerful argument for the distribution of photographs of commercially available artwork. The format is being developed and tested by many online galleries, e.g. Artists Online (www.artists-online.net/archive/index.shtml).

Preservation of originals

Photographic collections are increasingly at risk because of inherent instabilities in the photographic process; even relatively recent materials like colour prints of the last ten or so years are fading and losing definition. Many holdings are in urgent need of conservation and reformatting (Deegan and Tanner, 2002).

> The number one advantage of digitization from a preservation perspective is that it reduces handling of originals. This goes for all materials, but for photographs the advantage can be very real indeed. The availability of digital surrogates can reduce handling of the originals considerably: the Royal Library of Denmark estimated that to find 3–5 pictures, a user may handle as many as 300 originals. One reason is that photographs are often described only at sub collection level. The second reason is of course that the suitability of a print cannot be judged from a description, one has to see it. The advantage of an image base in which users can check on a screen which photographs they are interested in while the originals remain safely stored is so overwhelming that it should be an argument for every conservator to support digitization.
>
> (Lusenet, 1999)

Improving research/scholarship

Many projects report significant improvements to scholarship and research through digital image enhancement – it is possible to use digital imaging to look at source materials in an entirely new way and to subject the digital surrogate to processes that would be forbidden with an original (e.g. the techniques for the ultra-violet exposure for X-ray analysis of manuscripts that have been carried out on the digital images of the Beowulf manuscript at the British Library). These advantages are often unforeseen or the result of adding emerging technologies to an existing digital surrogate. Enhanced access to digital materials, e.g. complex linking of information, quick and easy retrieval and access, complex, combined searches, the ability to present and manipulate information in a variety of ways, also affords many opportunities to improve use of image collections.

Scanning reveals information previously unseen in photographic materials, especially in black and white photographic materials – glass plate negatives have a very broad tonal range. Higher resolution and density range translates into pulling more information from the original object. See, for example, the Butcher collection of glass plate negatives at the Nebraska State Historical Society, a project which demonstrated that advanced imaging could reveal hitherto unseen portions of negatives. Image recovery is also possible from glass plate negatives damaged by mercuric iodine intensification (Koelling, 2000).

Consequently, an area to watch is the research into advanced imaging tools and technologies emerging from the computer science and engineering communities. These issues were addressed in a workshop jointly sponsored by the Andrew W. Mellon Foundation, the National Science Foundation and the Harvard University Art Museums Digital Imagery for Works of Art, held at Harvard University in November 2001. The workshop was called

> to explore how the research and development agenda of computing, information and imaging scientists might more usefully serve the research needs of art and architecture historians, art curators, conservators, and scholars and practitioners in closely related disciplines. At the same time, we looked for opportunities where applications in the art history domain might inform and push information technology research in new and useful directions.
>
> (Kiernan, Rhyne and Spronk, 2001).

The workshop identified many areas where advanced research might produce useful results, including, colour management, digital capture equipment, and advanced image analysis tools.

Copyright

Copyright and licensing issues related to images are significant and can seem daunting. This is especially a concern for photographic materials: if over 50% of the photographic materials surveyed above are under 70 years old, then copyright restrictions may well apply to their use and distribution. The temptation is either to despair of the cost and effort of obtaining permissions to use such materials and abandon digitization, or to try to operate below the radar of the 'copyright police'. Slide digitization projects often apply the latter approach, by restricting access to campus machines, or even to registered students of a particular class. Such initiatives avoid lawsuits, but result in costly duplication of effort across many campuses. To address these concerns, some initiatives are investigating collaborative models for the publication and use of digital resources in a managed, licensed environment. A few examples include:

- ARTstor (www.artstor.org), created by the Andrew W. Mellon Foundation. It is developing a digital library that will offer collections of art images, descriptive data, and tools for using the collections, to subscribers. Currently, the ARTstor Library has approximately 300,000 images covering art, architecture and archaeology.
- BiblioVault (www.bibliovault.org/), based at the Chicago Digital Distribution Center of Chicago University Press, is a digital repository for materials from scholarly publishers, including materials with small print runs. Seventeen university presses are depositing backlist titles, and recent and new books into BiblioVault, which will manage access to these resources by purchasers.
- Electronic Enlightenment (www.e-enlightenment.info), developed by the Voltaire Foundation at the University of Oxford, is providing access to 18th century texts in collaboration with several major publishing houses.
- *Columbia International Affairs Online* (CIAO) (www.ciaonet.org/) is evaluating whether it is possible to provide a cost-effective means for publishing high-quality scholarly material in a particular discipline, by disseminating a wide range of scholarly materials related to international affairs, including working papers, conference proceedings, abstracts from journals, and the full text of books published by Columbia University Press on these topics.

Such initiatives are exploring ways in which communities of users and publishers might create a collaborative environment to create effective and useful digital collections of scholarly materials, while still respecting and observing copyright laws. Many institutions are also investigating the use of Digital Rights Management tools (discussed in

Chapter 3) to monitor and manage controlled access to digital collections, and to implement and manage subscription or licensing arrangements.

Technical issues in image digitization

The digitization methods chosen will depend on the nature of the original materials, and the fidelity to the original that is required. Image digitization projects will often be motivated by a desire to produce digital surrogates that are of the highest possible quality. This is to ensure that the digital images represent as much detail from the original images as possible, and also to create a high-resolution digital master copy that can be used for multiple purposes (Deegan and Tanner, 2004). Consequently, selecting a digitization method will involve balancing these factors against the methods of digital capture, which presently include:

- Flatbed scanners, used for reflective materials, materials that are on loose sheets or materials in bound volumes that can be placed on the scanner. Flatbed scanners are presently capable of delivering up to 2400 dpi. Overhead scanners have the same capacity, but will be more suitable for scanning materials that cannot be placed on the scanner plate.
- Film or slide scanners, which can deliver up to 4000 dpi. Attachments are available for these scanners that will enable the scanning of up to fifty 35 mm slides at a time.
- Digital cameras, which vary enormously in quality, and are suitable for rare and fragile or oversized materials. Digital cameras should be set up professionally, with the same considerations for lighting and positioning as in conventional photography.

Where to set up the imaging project?

In many cases, digital imaging will be outsourced to a specialist bureau but, increasingly, institutions are setting up in-house digitization centres. The goals of these centres are manifold. Having such resources in house means that they are available for many different projects and collections. Provision of the equipment can build expertise in the staff of the institution. It may also even be used to digitize the collections of other institutions on a fee-for-service basis. An example of such a centre is provided below.

Case study: an in-house digital imaging environment

Some institutions have made a specific commitment to setting up a digital imaging environment. Harvard College Library established such a facility in 1999 in order to meet the growing demand for digitizing capabilities in house. The development of this facility was primarily driven by the institutional commitment to digitize special collections, including unique materials for which handling and security were a concern. The concept was the development of a 'one-stop shop' for materials preparation, digital image processing and quality control, metadata creation, file management and storage. Curators, preservation staff as well as digital reformatting experts were all stakeholders in the development of the facility, and all have a vested interest in its success.

The room assigned to this facility is located in a restricted, staff-only area within the Widener Library at Harvard. It is a 650 ft^2 studio, adjacent to the microfilming and photography studios. The design criteria for the space were constrained by a number of requirements, including:

- accommodating document scanning, digital photography, and image processing/quality control workflows in one studio
- achieving an optimal balance between handling and production
- managing colour
- maintaining consistency in processes and products.

A group of experts were involved in developing the specifications for the facility, attempting to control as many of the variables as possible that can affect the quality of a digital image. Lighting finishes, furnishings and laminates were all carefully evaluated for use in the space. ISO 3664: 2000 *Viewing Conditions for Graphic Technology and Photography* was observed as a partial solution to the challenge of achieving consistent colour and detail reproduction for digital images. New electrical, heating and air conditioning systems were installed, as were ceiling-mounted air cleaners.

After refurbishment, the following equipment was installed in the studio:

- a flatbed scanner for documents
- a workstation for colour work and special collections material, including a digital camera system
- a monitor for image processing
- a viewing booth
- colour and black and white printers.

Projects carried out in the facility's first year of operation included digital imaging of 19th-century trade cards, photographs of China, and typescripts from the Nuremburg military tribunals (see Chapman and Comstock, 2000).

Case studies

The following case studies of image digitization projects illustrate the various reasons that have motivated image digitization projects and the different approaches that have been taken by various institutions. The reasons for digitization in these cases range from the creation of searchable indexes for browsing, to more specific developments in image processing. In all cases, however, similar goals and motives influence digitization, namely access to and protection of originals.

The Butcher Collection, Nebraska State Historical Society (www.nebraskahistory.org/index.htm)

With support awarded by the Library of Congress/Ameritech National Digital Library Competition, the Nebraska State Historical Society digitized the Solomon Butcher Photographic Collection in their state-of-the-art digital imaging laboratory housed in the Society's Gerald R. Ford Conservation Center in Omaha, Nebraska. By constructing the laboratory within the existing Conservation Center, it could share the receiving, security, HVAC (heating, ventilation and air conditioning), access control and handling facilities already in place.

The Collection, comprising 3300 6 x 8 in. glass plate negatives, documents European settlement of the American great plains between the years 1886 and 1912. Although the photographs have been used widely in histories of the American West, Butcher was not a master craftsman and the quality and degree of exposure within his plates vary greatly. Some are overexposed and dark while others are underexposed and light, the latter capturing little information at all. In addition, the negatives have a tremendously large tonal range, exceeding that of today's photographic papers and containing information unable to be conveyed through a traditional photographic print. To overcome these limitations, the Nebraska State Historical Society digitized the original in-camera negatives themselves, displaying electronically what Butcher captured at the time of exposure and ultimately increasing the amount of information available within each image, particularly in shadow areas.

The glass plate negatives were scanned at 800 dpi and saved as uncompressed TIFF master files. The master files were checked for quality by both the scanning technician and the curator of photographs. For this process, histograms offered the best indication of the tonal range captured, as well as whether or not a true white and black were used during the set-up of the scan. Failure to establish a true white and black can undermine the tonal fidelity of the scan as well as create pixelation, processes often referred to as clipping and spiking. No modifications were made to the master file and failure during quality inspection resulted in mandatory re-scan. Following successful inspection, the thumbnail and reference files were created. Unlike the master file, these JPEG derivatives were manipulated by increasing tonal contrast to optimize web viewing. The master copies of the images are stored at the Nebraska State Historical Society, service copies having been delivered to the Library of Congress, which has since integrated the collection into its larger American Memory project.

Centre for the Study of Ancient Documents (www.csad.ox.ac.uk/)

In an effort to focus the study of ancient documents occurring within the university, Oxford created the Centre for the Study of Ancient Documents (CSAD) in 1995. Since its establishment, it has developed into a site of both national and international significance. Forming a key component of Oxford's new Classics Centre, the CSAD provides a home for Oxford's epigraphical archive, which includes one of the largest collections of squeezes (paper impressions) of Greek inscriptions in the world. CSAD also contains the Haverfield archive of Roman inscriptions from the UK, and a substantial photographic collection. Current projects include the creation of a digital library of Greek inscriptions, based on the material within its squeeze collection, and a joint initiative with Oxford's Department of Engineering Science to develop a computer-based image-enhancement technique for incised material.

CSAD's inscription-imaging project developed out of an effort to catalogue and re-organize the primary squeeze collection, as well as to make the collection a more accessible research resource. The project, drawing inspiration from similar work undertaken at the University of Michigan and Duke University, aims to create a unified database of papyrological resources including both texts and images. However, inscribed documents tend to be larger than written papyri, necessitating image capture at a lower resolution than the 600 dpi archival standard to create manageable files. During an initial experimentation phase, 150 dpi was found to be adequate for most scholarly purposes. However, in order to maximize the future usefulness of the project, 300 dpi was ultimately selected as the minimum resolution for all scans. Scans are made using flatbed scanners and when inscriptions exceed the scanning area in size, they are stitched together from separate scans. A master scan is stored as an uncompressed TIFF on the University's Hierarchical File Server. While no alterations are made to the master, derivative images are modified using Adobe Photoshop to enhance contrast. The potential of digitally photographing the squeezes has also been explored, and although the results were satisfactory, the flatbed scanners remain the project's preferred image capture method.

Because the quality of a digital surrogate is so closely related to the condition of the original object, CSAD has simultaneously been researching image-enhancement techniques for incised materials with

Oxford's Department of Engineering Science. The project is concentrating on the analysis of the stylus tablets from the Roman fort at Vindolanda in northern England, a collection of approximately 200 texts. Like other stylus tablets, the incisions on the Vindolanda tablets are difficult to read because they are often incomplete, as well as undermined by woodgrain and surface damage. The project has created several methods for increasing legibility, including the removal of the woodgrain by aligning the tablets in a specific direction during image capture, ensuring a consistent direction of the woodgrain, which can then be masked out. To distinguish incisions from other surface markings, the project has developed a system of photographing the same tablet numerous times as a light source moves over the tablet, casting shadows to highlight the incisions. This process closely models a manual technique, developed by scholars, that uses light and shadows, yet benefits from computerized recording of the information, freeing the historian from having to remember when the incisions have been found as the light moves over the tablet. Both methods have greatly increased the legibility of the tablets for scholars, and exemplify the significance of Oxford's Centre for the Study of Ancient Documents to the field of humanities-based digitization.

The Corpus Vitrearum Medii Aevi (www.kcl.ac.uk/humanities/cch/cvma/xml2/index2.htm)

The Corpus Vitrearum Medii Aevi (CVMA), established in 1949, is an international research project dedicated to the publication of all medieval stained glass. In the UK, the project is a British Academy research project, funded by the Arts and Humanities Research Board and hosted by the University of London's Courtauld Institute of Art. Although the CVMA is primarily committed to publication in book form, it has recently been exploring the potential benefits of digitization and electronic publishing for its nearly 30,000 photographic images, housed at the National Monuments and Records Centre in Swindon. The photographs, gathered over the last 30 years, document stained glass from the eighth century to 1540, with 65 book volumes published thus far.

A six-month 1999 pilot study, funded by the Arts and Humanities

Research Board, saw the digitization of 3600 images. Of these, most were in colour, but a representative sample of black-and-white images was included, as well as of all of the various formats within the collection to assess how they would scan. Scanning was outsourced to the Higher Education Digitization Service (HEDS). The pilot-study images were scanned at various resolutions, generating both high-resolution masters, saved as uncompressed TIFFS, and lower-resolution JPEGs and thumbnails.

In addition to scanning, important components of CVMA's pilot study included the creation of a Filemaker Pro database and a prototype website. Over a period of four months, information about the scanned images was entered into the database. Because of the nature of a pilot study, with its time and economic constraints, the information entered in the database was much simpler than a full catalogue entry within a traditional published volume. However, experimentation was also undertaken to explore the addition of themes beyond the interpretive and authoritative information within the published volumes. An advisory group from the CVMA, as well as the National Monuments and Records Centre, identified a range of simple themes that would be useful for searching, including the history of the glass, simple formal analysis and subject matter. This process allowed important questions about the potential benefits of digitization to be raised. Ultimately, it was realized that digitization offered two primary benefits to the CVMA's existing programme of publication: the process created a series of high-resolution masters easily duplicated and published in the traditional volumes, and secondly, when combined with the database and website, provided a more convenient public search tool with subsequent educational benefits.

Since the pilot study's completion, CVMA has begun a three-year project to scan a further 9000 items, including transparencies and photographic prints. Like the pilot study, the project will be managed by HEDS, with an ultimate goal of creating high-quality digital masters that represent as closely as possible the information content of the original. The digital masters will be stored as uncompressed TIFFs. High-resolution copies will be available for order, with JPEGs available freely on the web.

The Huntington Archive of Buddhist and Related Art
(http://kaladarshan.arts.ohio-state.edu)

The Huntington Archive of Buddhist and Related Art, housed at Ohio State University, contains nearly 300,000 original slides and photographs of art and architecture throughout Asia. The Archive originated from the personal resource collection of photographs taken by art historians John and Susan Huntington during nearly three decades of research. Formalized in 1986, the Archive focuses primarily on Buddhist materials from 3000 BC to the present. Hindu, Jain, Islamic and other related works are also represented. In addition, the Huntington Archive holds the world's largest photographic collection of Nepalese art and architecture, marking the only formal collection that photographically records Nepal's artistic heritage. Other countries represented within the Archive include India, Afghanistan, Pakistan, Bangladesh, Sri Lanka, China, Japan, Thailand, Indonesia and Myanmar (Burma). The Archive documents the art and architecture of these countries *in situ*, as well as that found in major museums around the world.

Its unique material, combined with a focus on scholarly research and classroom teaching, made the Huntington Archive a logical choice as a charter collection for the Andrew W. Mellon Foundation's ArtSTOR initiative. ArtSTOR, modelled after the Foundation's successful JSTOR project, which serves as a centralized repository for scholarly journals, will be a database of high-quality digital images and scholarly materials intended to assist researchers in the study of art, architecture and other humanities fields. Currently in a testing phase, ArtSTOR will eventually provide full access to students, teachers and scholars at educational and cultural institutions on a site-licence basis.

In conjunction with the Archive's participation in ArtSTOR, the Mellon Foundation awarded a grant to digitize 10,000 photographs from its collection. The Archive used a portion of the grant to hire additional staff, including a picture editor, scanning technician, image corrector, image controller and cataloguer. Additional support for digitization and cataloguing has been received from numerous other funding bodies, including the National Endowment for the Humanities, resulting in nearly 80,000 images digitized thus far. An equal number have been catalogued within a text-based database, of which an online version is currently under construction. Conceived of as a public research tool, the online database will be fully searchable, containing both digital images and accompanying data. A partial test version of the database is being launched in late 2003.

The Archive is also a member of the Electronic Cultural Atlas Initiative (ECAI), a consortium of hundreds of networked digital projects created by libraries, museums and archives. ECAI, housed at the University of California at Berkeley, enforces strict metadata standards to create a controlled online catalogue of geographical data held by its participating members. In the case of the Huntington Archive, information about religious practices throughout Asia is made available to the scholarly community by adhering to ECAI's descriptive standards, greatly expanding the potential audience for its collection.

With its participation in the ArtSTOR and ECAI initiatives, the Archive is truly an exceptional model for the educational partnerships that can be developed through digitization, transforming a unique personal collection into a premier global resource.

IATH and the William Blake Archive (www.blakearchive.org)

The University of Virginia's Institute for Advanced Technology in the Humanities (IATH) began in 1992 with a major grant from IBM to foster computer-based humanities research. Today, IATH operates as a research unit within UVA, cultivating partnerships between scholars and computer professionals, and developing special-purpose software to meet the needs of humanities researchers. One of the Institute's major software developments is an image-annotation tool called Inote, which allows descriptive information to be added to specific portions of a digital image (see below for further details).

An example of a project incorporating IATH's image-annotation software can be found in the William Blake Archive, a collaborative initiative unifying access to a vast array of disparate visual and literary works that would otherwise be restricted because of their rarity, value and extreme fragility. Available freely on the web since 1996, the Archive contains fully searchable and scaleable electronic editions of Blake's illuminated manuscripts, as well as extensive transcriptions, image descriptions and bibliographic information. The Archive, which now totals over 4000 images, also contains substantial examples of Blake's paintings, drawings, prints, manuscripts and rare typographic works. Included is a fully searchable version of David V. Erdman's *Complete Poetry and Prose of William Blake*, the standard printed reference, as well as detailed lists documenting the complete Blake holdings of the collections from which the contents are drawn. These elements make the Archive a truly robust resource.

Most often, the digital images within the Archive are scanned from transparencies, which include colour bars and grey scales to ensure colour fidelity. The transparencies have been verified for colour accuracy against the original by the editor responsible for colour-correcting the digital image, as well as the photographer. The baseline standard for all scanned images is 24-bit colour and a resolution of 300 dpi, which are scaled against the source dimensions of the original artifact so as to display at true size with a 100 dpi screen resolution. During the scanning process, a project assistant completes a form known as the Image Production (IP) record. This record contains detailed technical data about the creation of the digital file and becomes the basis for the Image Information record that is inserted into each image as metadata. Colour corrections are made against the original transparency using Adobe Photoshop and saved on CD-ROM as TIFF images. No colour corrections are made to the master image files.

Acting as a model for both digital reproduction and electronic editing, the project is also important for its implementation of the image-annotation Java applet Inote, developed at IATH. Inote permits the appendage of textual notes to selected regions of a particular image by constructing a grid overlay upon the image. The user can click on various sectors to retrieve annotations about that portion of the image, which are generated directly from the SGML-encoded descriptions prepared by the editors. Because the annotations are image specific, not general descriptions of works within the collection, comparisons can be made between various copies of the same work. This type of plate-specific description that Inote enables had never been attempted before.

A second innovative Java applet utilized by the Blake Archive is Imagesizer, a sophisticated image manipulation tool that automatically resizes all viewed images in accordance with the user's monitor resolution to appear at true size. Should the user prefer images with consistent proportions other than true size, such as twice the normal size, Imagesizer is capable of re-scaling all subsequent images to those preferences on the fly. The applet also permits users to enlarge or reduce the image within the on-screen display area, as well as to view the Image Information record's textual metadata embedded within each digital image file.

Both applets, which have provided a pioneering level of functionality to the Blake Archive, are available for public distribution.

The Victoria and Albert Museum (www.vam.ac.uk)

London's Victoria and Albert Museum is the world's largest museum of decorative arts, home to 145 galleries that include national collections of sculpture, furniture, fashion and photographs. In November 2001, the Museum opened its largest gallery project in 50 years, a series of 15 rooms that serve as a chronological survey of the history of design in the UK from 1500 to 1900. An important aim of the British Galleries, which took seven years to complete, was the incorporation of multiple forms of interpretation. To meet this objective, a series of 18 web-based applications, served to 40 kiosks, were developed in conjunction with curators, educators and an external agency. During this process, a decision was made to employ a multimedia manager to serve as a conduit between the V&A and the external agency, Oyster Partners, who would be developing the applications.

The project itself was broken into three main stages: prototyping, full development and acceptance. During the initial prototyping and testing stage, which lasted for 18 months, a series of 20 lectures, seminars, workshops and presentations were conducted and attended by the external design team, as well as V&A staff. This process permitted an open exchange of ideas regarding the final interactives. Content was then provided by the V&A staff and the design firm began to work up screen designs. Following agreement on several variations of screen designs, working prototypes were built and installed for public testing. Public testing resulted in the need for redesign of several elements. After new designs were generated, a second round of public testing took place. Following this process, the V&A prepared the final content, which included over 13,000 images for the interactives and 25,000 images for a database of the collection.

Several different types of interactives mark the final product of the collaboration. Nine of the kiosks, located throughout the galleries, educate about various design styles. Two additional kiosks address the social and political history depicted within specific paintings. Four kiosks contain design exercises, allowing visitors to create their own designs using objects within the V&A collection, including a coat of arms, monogram, bookplate and textile. One kiosk helps visitors understand the process of dating objects and two additional kiosks are located in study rooms, granting access to all of the various applications. One kiosk allows visitors to contribute to ongoing debate between other visitors and museum staff as well as contribute to a changing series of online history projects, and the remaining kiosks contain a searchable database of objects within the British Galleries.

Since the opening of the British Galleries, the V&A has seen a 300% visitor increase and received a British Academy of Film and Television Arts nomination for best use of new media. However, the interactives are not the only point at which the museum is exploring the potential benefits of digitization. The V&A's Photographic Studio has been using a digital camera to produce rotational movies and panoramic gallery views for the museum's website. And the institution has joined the Artiste Consortium, a joint initiative aimed at creating web-based applications for the automatic indexing and retrieval of high-resolution art images by pictorial content and information. The Consortium, funded by the European Union, will result in a system that can be used for publishing, collections management and training applications.

Conclusion

Many projects around the world have experimented with the digitization of text and image. Because the materials created by these projects can be so useful for research and study, the advantages of developing such resources are clearly apparent. Large scale text digitization projects of journals, linguistic corpora and literary works have created a body of work that can be searched, collated and analysed for authorship and the development of literary and linguistic patterns. Similarly, the advantages of image digitization are immediately compelling: when 'a picture paints a thousand words', the appeal of digitized image collections can be seen as extremely advantageous for the user, especially if the images are linked to a searchable database, or other delivery system.

Much work has already been done in this field, and a critical mass of content has already been created, creating exemplar projects that can be emulated. In negotiating the planning path for the digitization of tests and images, the reader will benefit from careful examination of the case studies presented here. While the technology is more established than that for audio and moving image digitization, there are still challenges to overcome in developing digitization plans for projects of this nature. The digitization process will have to managed very carefully.

Despite the promise of technology, it will not be possible to digitize everything in a collection, and so judicious selection policies will have to be implemented. This will be especially difficult when working with large photographic archives, which may contain thousands (or even millions) of original materials. Visual resources curators and slide librarians will have to be involved in the selection process. Rights management – both clearing permissions to digitize and managing the rights over the long term – will be important. Issues of authenticity and accuracy will be equally important: the physical properties of digital images do not provide evidence of their authenticity. Both texts and images can be manipulated when they are in digital form; and an institution will have to establish how the integrity of digital images is to be maintained. The high resolution and file size of archival master digital images will place demands on equipment and institutional networks which will have to be anticipated and managed. It cannot be emphasized enough that detailed planning will have to address all these issues at the outset.

Conclusion

Institutions must create and manage their digital collections properly to ensure their long-term value and utility and to protect the investment that has been made in them.

(Kenney, 1998)

Libraries, archives and museums of all types and all sizes are creating multilingual and multicultural digital content at a dramatic rate. This is a small – but significant – component of the global information explosion described by Deegan and Tanner (2002) in *Digital Futures*, which also addresses the management and use of digital resources in this context. A recent survey conducted by the School of Information Management and Systems at the University of California at Berkeley contends that the total information output around the world would require 1.5 billion gigabytes of storage, and that 93% of this is already stored digitally (Gill and Miller, 2002). The audience for this data is similarly expanding. That the creation of digital collections can have many positive outcomes for scholarship, access and preservation of original materials has been seen in the many examples and case studies described in this book. Information and communication technologies can also direct public interest to the original collections, by providing narrative and contextual materials alongside computer assisted displays and exhibits (Mulrenin and Geser, 2001).

Ideally, the goal of digitization initiatives should be to develop interoperable and sustainable resources that can be regarded as institutional assets, of as much value to the users of the collections as their analogue antecedents. This would sharpen the focus on creating and developing them for the long term (Kenney, 1998). For this to be the case, institutions will have to support digital programmes set up to develop resources that can be delivered to users and managed in a useful and consistent fashion over time:

> to be viable in the long run a digital library must be more than a collection of digital objects that can be efficiently stored and transported. Just as the traditional library evolved to provide services to make its contents more accessible to its users, the effective digital library must develop a range of services to assist its users in finding, understanding, and using its contents.
>
> (Geisler et al., 2002)

The services and tools to ensure this must manage and maintain access to digital content to the broadest possible audience. They must support Unsworth's 'scholarly primitives' (2000): the discovery, annotation, comparison, referencing, sampling, illustrating and representing of digital content for scholarly purposes, as well as the use of tools that will enable the resource discovery of all digital content, in a manner equivalent to the serendipity of browsing the stacks for primary source materials. They must provide access consistently over the long term, so that reliability of access to digital files can be guaranteed (no more '404 file not found' when using an online slide collection in a lecture, or demonstrating an online audio stream at a conference). Creating and managing such tools – many of which have not been fully developed at this time – will require an expensive and technically demanding infrastructure, and enforce new skills, working practices and funding models in cultural heritage institutions.

However, no matter how good the tools that support the discovery and use of digital collections, they will only be useful if the digital objects have been developed in such a way that their future preservation and access has been anticipated. This means taking a strategic approach to digitization initiatives, One way to think 'strategically' is to follow a sporting metaphor: the successful player of a game is not one who merely sees where other players are positioned, but one who sees situations arising; where every player is positioned at a given time in the course of a game, and what this will mean. It is a question of watching, not where the play is at a given time, but where it is going (Groen, 1999). This type of metaphor (one of working in an environment that approximates a fast moving game, or, possibly more accurately, taking aim at a series of moving targets) is often invoked by administrators, as it identifies one of the key difficulties of working with any sort of technology. Activity in (or on) the field is changing so rapidly that it is almost impossible to anticipate future developments, yet at the same time there is a rush of momentum to exploit the technology. In some cases there is also pressure to jump on the digitization bandwagon. Thinking strategically will identify some core policies and priorities. If we ensure that these priorities are in place, and manage and manipulate the way that they evolve over time, then developing the agility required to follow the moving target of technology will be less of a challenge.

Strategic questions will come into play at all stages of the digital life cycle: when planning projects; while running digitization projects; and while sustaining projects over the long term. The key consideration is that the same foresight that goes into building and sustaining conventional collections should go into the development of digital materials. Political and strategic implications need to be factored in. We shouldn't just digitize because we can. This will be true no matter how the original project plan came about. Zorich (2003) has examined the history behind the establishment of a significant number of digital cultural heritage initiatives in the USA, and reports that the minority (of which JSTOR is one), emerged from detailed studies and needs assessments, whereas a far more significant number had their genesis in 'hallway brainstorming' between colleagues, identifying an opportunity, or gap in the available knowledge. But regardless of how a project is conceived, the following are the 'moving targets' that should always be considered:

- **Copyright** should be managed and careful attention should be paid to all aspects of the legal framework, whether working with materials that are in the public domain, invoking fair use or obtaining permission to use materials that are within copyright.

The copyright of digital materials should be managed and protected. The management of intellectual property is potentially the greatest challenge to the development of digital collections.

- **Selection** policies should be consistent with the overall development principles of collections, and also with the overall institutional mission, using the type of decision matrices outlined in Chapter 2. Selection policies should incorporate an assessment of the users of digital collections: who will find these materials useful? What is the demand for digital surrogates of analogue resources? It is important to foreground the involvement of key constituents and stakeholders in the decision-making process: these will include faculty (at universities and research institutions) and members of the public (in the case of public libraries, archives, and museums). What are their needs, and are the digital resources that have been created useful to them? Will they have a say in choosing what is selected for digitization?

- The readiness of **institutional frameworks** to support digitization initiatives and maintain digital collections should be assessed at the outset of the project. This will involve understanding the institution's capacity for digitization, by assessment of whether staffing, the technological framework and available network are adequate, and, if they are not, evaluating whether digitization will help to build this capacity. It should also be ascertained whether digital programmes have similar priorities to the overall institutional mission. One way to gauge this commitment is by looking at the 'cost share' that the host institution is prepared to provide, and the overhead that they charge, when preparing funding applications.

- Strategies should be in place for the long-term **preservation** of digital resources. We lack the luxury of technological stability, so we must plan for emulation and/or migration of resources in the future. One of the best ways to ensure longevity of resources is by implementing community-wide 'best' practices wherever possible in their creation; and by ensuring the use of good metadata for describing all aspects of digital objects: technical, administrative, structural and preservation.

- There must be a clear understanding of all the **costs** that are involved in developing and maintaining digital projects. These include not just the costs related to digitization, but also to the long-term management and storage of resources. A full understanding of all the costs involved may make it possible to eventually develop institutional strategies for recovering some of the costs of digitization, and to see where the costs for digitization should come from: rarely should such initiatives be funded from the acquisitions budget. As seen in the section on costs in Chapter 4, Puglia's position is that approximately one third of a project's costs will be actual digitization (i.e. scanning or digital imaging). In the discussion on managing the digitization project, we have seen that a very small part of the time allocated to a project will be spent on actual digitization, and that most of the time will be spent on selection, preparation, metadata creation, and the like. Creating cost models that will illustrate these factors is very empowering, as is the development of prototype projects to further explore such issues.

- Good **project management** of the digital workflows involved in creating all digital objects, including well-defined and measurable objectives for each stage of the project, is essential. Complete documentation of the whole process should be readily available.

- **Sustainability** is another key consideration. Deanna Marcum, writing in the introduction to Zorich (2003), notes that digitization efforts 'rise and fall on the waves of external funding', and that digital programmes must have a business plan in order to survive over the long term. However, few of the digital cultural heritage initiatives surveyed in Thorin's report have been able to achieve, let alone maintain, sustainability. Several reasons for this are given, including the present economic downturn, which has not only depleted the core budgets of many libraries, museums and universities, but also impacted on granting agencies and other sources of funding. The endowments of many foundations have been affected by the stock market decline, and corporations are not as lavish with grants as they once were. Moreover, funding agencies are reluctant to commit ongoing resources to projects, and to support the ongoing provision of digital resources, no matter how worthwhile they may be. Most importantly, however, most host institutions still treat digital projects as special initiatives, rather than ongoing programmes with a dedicated commitment of staff, funding and management structure over the long-term.

- Underpinning almost all of these factors will be the question of **risk assessment** and management. What is the degree of risk involved in a particular activity? Is this an acceptable figure? What are the plans and procedures that are to be implemented for controlling and monitoring risk? Every stage of a project – from planning, through deciding what materials can be safely digitized, to selecting a preservation strategy – will involve elements of risk. Anticipating and planning for such risks will mean that negative outcomes can be avoided.

The integration of digital programmes into the institutional mission of the organization is still, unfortunately, the exception, not the rule, and this lack of commitment makes any other kind of revenue generation (whether through user subscriptions, licensing, or the sale of digitized resources) more difficult. One way to overcome this is to plan digitization projects by carefully evaluating what is to be digitized, and why: sustainable resources, with a stable institutional home, will be those for which there is a definable, quantifiable and robust demand and need. This will create resources that are of sufficient 'value' to justify, and possibly even to recover, the investment expended in their creation.

All of the above considerations will allow institutions to create a policy framework that will support the development of digital collections. None of these are necessarily new issues for libraries, archives and museums, which throughout their history have had to develop and implement policies on selection, copyright, resource management and preservation of analogue resources. The principles that support the development of useful and sustainable digital resources will be very similar to existing policies for analogue originals. Developing and maintaining digital collections will necessitate collaboration and communication between staff and management at every level of the institution to ensure that digitization activities are consistent with the institutional mission and policies. Digital resources will not replace analogue collections, but should complement and augment analogue originals. They will often lead users to the original collections, and provide enhanced access for scholarship and research. Digital resources can add value to cultural heritage collections, for the benefit of the entire organization and its patrons.

Bibliography

Allen, L. (1997) *Digitising the Collections: LISWA's strategic directions: 'Western Stories'*, www.nla.gov.au/niac/meetings/liswa.html.

American Assembly (2002) *Art, Technology and Intellectual Property*, Columbia University.

Archives and Information Consulting Services (2003) *Definitions of Archival Terms*, www.mannon.org/archives/arcdef.htm.

The Archive-Skills Consultancy (2003) *Useful Links: digital records and archives*, www.archive-skills.com/links4.htm.

ARL (Association of Research Libraries), The Council on Library and Information Resources, and The National Humanities Alliance (1999) *Statement on the FY-2000 Appropriations for the National Endowment for the Humanities*, www.arl.org/info/letters/neh00.html.

ARL (Association of Research Libraries) (2000) *Talking Points in Response to Nicholson Baker's Article in the 24 July* New Yorker, www.arl.org/preserv/baker1.html.

Arms, C. R. (1999) Getting the Picture: Observations from the Library of Congress on Providing Online Access to Pictorial Images, *Library Trends*, **48** (2), 379–409, http://memory.loc.gov/ammem/techdocs/libt1999/libt1999.html.

Arms, W. (2000) *Digital Libraries*, MIT Press.

Arts and Humanities Data Service Executive (2001) *A Strategic Policy Framework for Creating and Preserving Digital Collections*, www.ukoln.ac.uk/services/elib/papers/supporting/pdf/framework.pdf.

Ayris, P. (1999) Guidance for Selecting Materials for Digitisation, *Joint RLG*

and NPO Preservation Conference Guidelines for Digital Imaging,
www.rlg.org/preserv/joint/ayris.html.

Barton, M. and Harford Walker, J. (2003) Building a Business Plan for
DSpace, MIT Libraries' Digital Institutional Repository, *JoDI – Journal of
Digital Information*, **4** (2).

Beacham, R. and Denard, H. (2003) The Pompey Project: digital research
and virtual reconstruction of Rome's first theatre, *Computers and the
Humanities*, **37** (1), 129–39.

Beam, C. (2003) Fathom.com Shuts Down As Columbia Withdraws.
Columbia deemed the online learning venture too great a financial
risk, *Columbia Daily Spectator* (28 January).

Beamsley, T. (1999) Securing Digital Image Assets in Museums and
Libraries: a risk management approach, *Library Trends*, **48** (2), 359–78.

Benjamin, W. (1978) *Reflections: essays, aphorisms, autobiographical writings*,
translated by Edmund Jephcott, edited by Peter Demetz, Harcourt
Brace Jovanovich.

Bennett, N. and Sandore, B. (2001) The Illinois Digital Cultural Heritage
Community: museums and libraries collaborate to build a database for
the elementary school classroom, *Spectra – a Publication of the Museum
Computer Network*, **5** (1), 48–55.

Besser, H. (1991) Advanced Applications of Imaging: fine arts, *Journal of
the American Society of Information Science*, (September), 589–96.

Besser, H. (1994) *The Changing Role of Photographic Collections with the
Advent of Digitization*,
www.gseis.ucla.edu/~howard/Papers/eastman.html.

Besser, H. (1996) *Image Database Bibliography*,
http://sunsite.berkeley.edu/Imaging/Databases/Bibliography/.

Besser, H. (1997) *Procedures and Practices for Scanning*,
http://sunsite.berkeley.edu/Imaging/Databases/Scanning/.

Besser, H. (1999) *Implications in Digitizing Special Collections Materials: the
collection, the institution, scholarship, interoperability, longevity*,
http://sunsite.berkeley.edu/Imaging/Databases/Conservation/
RBMS99/ppframe.htm.

Besser, H. (2000) Digital Longevity. In Sitts, M. K. (ed.), *Handbook for
Digital Projects: a management tool for preservation and access*, Northeast
Document Conservation Center (NEDCC).

Besser, H. (2001) Digital Preservation of Moving Image Material?, *The

Moving Image, **1** (2) (Fall).

Besser, H. (2002) The Next Stage: moving from isolated digital collections to interoperable digital libraries, *First Monday*, **7** (6).

Bickner, C. (2003) From Projects to Full Programs: institutional cost issues. Paper delivered at *NINCH Price of Digitization Symposium 2003*, www.ninch.org/forum/price.report.html#cb.

Blackwell, B. (2000) Light Exposure to Sensitive Artworks during Digital Photography, *Spectra – a Publication of the Museum Computer Network*, **26** (2), 24–8.

Bonn, M. (2001) Benchmarking Conversion Costs: a report from the Making of America IV Project, *RLG Diginews*, **5** (5), www.rlg.org/preserv/diginews/diginews5-5.html#feature2.

Brandt, C. and Ndoye, M. L. (2002) *Building Partnerships for African Digital Libraries: the West African Digital Library Network (WADiLiN)*, www.iatul.org/conference/proceedings/vol12/.

Brandt, L., Gregg, V. and Stendebach, S. (2002) The National Science Foundation Digital Government Research Program's Role in the Long-Term Preservation of Digital Materials, *RLG Diginews*, **6** (5), www.rlg.org/preserv/diginews/diginews6-5.html#feature2.

Breaks, M. (2001) *SPIS: Shared Preservation in Scotland*, http://scurl.ac.uk/projects/spis/.

Brophy, P. (2001) *The Library in the Twenty-First Century: new services for the information age*, Library Association Publishing.

Brown University Library (2001) *Selection Criteria for Digitization*, www.brown.edu/Facilities/University_Library/digproj/digcolls/selection.html.

Bruya, B. (2002) Editorial: Chinese Collections in the Digital Library: introduction to a special issue, *JoDI – Journal of Digital Information*, **3** (2), http://jodi.ecs.soton.ac.uk/Articles/v03/i02/editorial/.

Buchan, J. (2003) Miss Bell's Lines in the Sand, *The Guardian* (12 March), www.guardian.co.uk/g2/story/0,3604,912266,00.html.

BUILDER (Birmingham University Integrated Library Development and Electronic Resource) (1998) *Annual Report*, http://builder.bham.ac.uk/ar98/html/activities.asp.

Burrows, J. (2003) Questions of Authorship: Attribution and Beyond, *Computers and the Humanities*, **37** (1), 5–32.

Bush, V. (1945) As We May Think, *The Atlantic Monthly*, **176** (1), 101–8, www.theatlantic.com/unbound/flashbks/computer/bushf.htm.

Byrd, S. et al. (2001) Cost/Benefit Analysis for Digital Library Projects: the Virginia Historical Inventory Project (VHI), *The Bottom Line: managing library finances*, **14** (2), 65–75.

CAMILEON (Creative Archiving at Michigan and Leeds: Emulating the Old on the New) (2003) *BBC Domesday*, www.si.umich.edu/CAMILEON/domesday/domesday.html.

Canadian Council of Archives, Preservation Committee (2002) *Digitization and Archives*, www.cdncouncilarchives.ca/digitarc.html.

Cave, M., Deegan, M., and Heinink, L. (2000) Copyright Clearance in the Refugee Studies Centre Digital Library Project, *RLGDiginews*, **4** (5) (15 October).

CDP (Colorado Digitization Program) (2002) *Digitization Resources*, www.cdpheritage.org/resource/.

CDP (Colorado Digitization Program) (2003) *Digitization Glossary*, www.cdpheritage.org/resource/introduction/rsrc_glossary.html.

CDP (Colorado Digitization Program) Advisory Council (1999), Market Segments and Their Information Needs, www.cdpheritage.org/resource/reports/rsrc_users.html.

Cedars (2002) *Cedars Guide to Intellectual Property Rights: executive summary*, Cedars (Curl Exemplars in Digital Archives), www.leeds.ac.uk/cedars/guideto/ipr.

CELT, the Corpus of Electronic Texts. The online resource for Irish history, literature and politics (2003), www.ucc.ie/celt/.

Chapman, C. (2002) *Managing Project Risk and Uncertainty: a constructively simple approach to decision making*, Wiley.

Chapman, C. and Ward, S. (1997) *Project Risk Management: processes, techniques, and insights*, Wiley.

Chapman, S. (1999) *Guidelines for Image Capture*, www.rlg.org/preserv/joint/chapman.html.

Chapman, S. (2000) Considerations for Project Management. In Sitts, M. K. (ed.), *Handbook for Digital Projects: a management tool for preservation and access*, Northeast Document Conservation Center.

Chapman, S. (2003a) Counting the Costs of Digital Preservation: is repository storage affordable?, *JoDI – Journal of Digital Information*, **4** (2).

Chapman, S. (2003b) Managing Text Digitisation, *Online Information*

Review, **27** (1), 17–27.

Chapman, S. and Comstock, W. (2000) Digital Imaging Production Services at the Harvard College Library, *RLG Diginews*, **4** (6), www.rlg.org/preserv/diginews/diginews4-6.html#feature1.

Chapman, S., Conway, P. and Kenney, A. (1999a) Digital Imaging and Preservation Microfilm: the future of the hybrid approach for the preservation of brittle books, *RLG Diginews*, **3** (1), www.rlg.org/preserv/diginews/diginews3-1.html#feature1.

Chapman, S., Conway, P., and Kenney, A. (1999b) Research Project: Digital Imaging and Preservation Microfilm: the future of the hybrid approach for the preservation of brittle books, working paper available at: www.clir.org/pubs/archives/archives.html.

Chapman, S. and Kenney, A. (1996) Digital Conversion of Research Library Materials. A case for full informational capture, *D-Lib Magazine* (October), www.dlib.org/dlib/october96/cornell/10chapman.html.

Charting our Future: a report of the North Carolina State Historical Records Advisory Board (2002), www.ah.dcr.state.nc.us/sections/archives/SHRAB/ChartingReport.pdf.

Child, M. (1999) *Collections, Policies and Preservation*, Northeast Document Conservation Center, www.nedcc.org/plam3/tleaf15.htm.

CHIN (Canadian Heritage Information Network) (2002) *Capture Your Collections: planning and implementing digitization projects*, www.chin.gc.ca/English/Digital_Content/Capture_Collections/.

Clark, S. (1997) Photographic Conservation. In *UNESCO Audiovisual Archives: a practical reader*, National Preservation Office, The British Library, www.unesco.org/webworld/ramp/html/r9704e/r9704e16.htm.

Clark, S. (1999) *Preservation of Photographic Material*, National Preservation Office, The British Library, www.bl.uk/services/preservation/npo3.pdf.

CLIR (Council on Library and Information Resources) (2000) *Collections, Content, and the Web*, www.clir.org/pubs/reports/pub88/contents.html.

CLIR (Council on Library and Information Resources) (2002) *The State of Digital Preservation: an international perspective, conference proceedings*, www.clir.org/pubs/reports/pub107/contents.html.

Colet, L. et al. (2000) *Guides to Quality in Visual Resource Imaging*, Digital Library Federation, Research Libraries Group, www.rlg.org/visguides/.

Columbia University Libraries (2001) *Selection Criteria for Digital Imaging*, www.columbia.edu/cu/libraries/digital/criteria.html.

Coppock, T. (1999a) *Information Technology and Scholarship: applications in the humanities and social sciences*, Oxford University Press for the British Academy.

Coppock, T. (1999b) *Making Information Available in Digital Format. Perspectives from practitioners*, Edinburgh, Stationery Office.

Cornell University Library, Research Department (2002) *Moving Theory into Practice: a digital imaging tutorial*, www.library.cornell.edu/preservation/tutorial.

Cornell University Library (n.d.) *Digital Imaging and Preservation Policy Research*, www.library.cornell.edu/iris/research/dippr.html.

Council of the European Union and the Commission of the European Communities (2000) *eEurope 2002 Action Plan*, http://europa.eu.int/information_society/eeurope/2002/text_en.htm.

Cultuurtechnologie – Monitoring Digitisation of Cultural Heritage in the Netherlands (2003) *Benchmarking Digitisation Initiatives to Identify Best Practice*, www.cultuurtechnologie.net/walkthrough.htm.

Cuneiform Digital Library Initiative (2003) *Method and Conventions*, http://cdli.mpiwg-berlin.mpg.de/.

D'Amato, D. P. and Klopfenstein, R. C. (1996) *Requirements and Options for the Digitization of the Illustration Collections of the National Museum of Natural History*, www.nmnh.si.edu/cris/techrpts/imagopts/.

Deegan, M., Steinvel, E. and King, E. (2002) Digitizing Historic Newspapers: progress and prospects, *RLG Diginews*, **6** (4), www.rlg.org/preserv/diginews/v6_n4_feature2.html.

Deegan, M. and Tanner, S. (2002) *Digital Futures: strategies for the information age*, Library Association Publishing.

Deegan M., and Tanner, S. (2004) Conversion of Primary Sources. In Schreibman, S., Unsworth, J. and Siemens, R. (eds.) *Companion to Digital Humanities*, Blackwells.

Deggeller K. (1999) Conservation of the Audiovisual Heritage: strategies and practices. In *CITRA: Proceedings of the International Conferences of the Round Table on Archives XXXIV: Access to Information. Preservation Issues/ICA*, Budapest, 53–6, www.ica.org/citra/citra.budapest.1999.eng/deggeller.pdf.

Delany, P. and Landow, G. P. (1994) *Hypermedia and Literary Studies*, MIT Press.

DigiCULT (2003) *eEurope: creating cooperation for digitisation,* www.cordis.lu/ist/ka3/digicult/eeurope-overview.htm.

Digital Imaging and Media Technology Initiative (1999) *Questions to Consider before Beginning an Image Database Project,* http://images.library.uiuc.edu/resources/20questns.html.

Digital Imaging and Media Technology Initiative, University of Illinois Library (2003), http://images.library.uiuc.edu/.

Digital Imaging Laboratory (2003) *Safe, State-of-the-Art Scanning for Your Collections,* www.nebraskahistory.org/lib-arch/research/photos/digital/.

Digitizing Primary Sources for the DIAMM Archive: why build a digital and not an analogue archive? (2001), www.diamm.ac.uk/images.html.

Dillon, D. (1999) *Digital Library Collection Development Framework,* University of Texas, www.lib.utexas.edu/admin/cird/policies/subjects/framework.html.

DLF (Digital Library Federation) (2002) *More Access at Less Cost: the case for a digital registry,* www.diglib.org/about/moreaccess.htm.

Documenting the American South (DAS), http://docsouth.unc.edu/.

Driscoll, M. J. (1998) The Virtual Reunification of the Arnamagnaean Manuscript Collection. In Burnard, L., Deegan, M., and Short, H. (eds), *The Digital Demotic: a selection of papers from Digital Resources in the Humanities, 1997,* Office for Humanities Communication (OHC).

Eaves, M. (1997) Collaboration Takes More Than E-Mail, *The Journal of Electronic Publishing,* **3** (2), www.press.umich.edu/jep/03-02/blake.html.

EICTA (2002) *Delivery of Digital Content by Digital Rights Management Systems,* www.eicta.org/copyrightlevies/resources/additional_resources.html.

Ellison, T. (2001) *Special Collections Archival Procedure Manual,* http://swcenter.fortlewis.edu/tools/FLCArchivalProcedureManual.htm.

Ensworth, P. (2001) *The Accidental Project Manager: surviving the transition from techie to manager,* John Wiley & Sons.

Ester, M. (1996) *Digital Image Collections: issues and practice,* Council on Library and Information Resources.

European Commission (2000) *eEurope 2002: an information society for all Action Plan prepared by the Council and the European Commission for the Feira European Council,* http://europa.eu.int/informationsociety/eeurope/2002/action_plan/text_en.htm.

European Commission, The Information Society Directorate-General

(2003) *Coordinating digitisation in Europe. Progress report of the National Representatives Group: coordination mechanisms for digitization policies and programmes 2002*,
www.minervaeurope.org/publications/globalreport.htm.

The Evidence in Hand: report of the Task Force on the Artifact in Library Collections (2001) Council on Library and Information Resources,
www.clir.org/pubs/reports/pub103/contents.html.

Feeney, M. (1999) *Digital Culture: maximising the nation's investment; a synthesis of JISC/NPO studies on the preservation of electronic materials*, National Preservation Office, The British Library.

Fishman, S. (2001) *The Public Domain: how to find copyright-free writings, music, art and more*, Nolo Press.

Flecker, D. (2001) Harvard's Library Digital Initiative: building a first generation digital library infrastructure, *Spectra – a Publication of the Museum Computer Network*, **5** (1), 34–49.

Fleischhauer, C. (1996) *Digital Formats for Content Reproductions*,
http://memory.loc.gov/ammem/formatold.html.

Fox, M. J. and Wilkerson, P. L. (1998) *Introduction to Archival Organization and Description*, Getty Information Institute.

Frey, F. (1997) Digital Imaging for Photographic Collections: foundations for technical standards, *RLG Diginews*, **1** (3),
www.rlg.org/preserv/diginews/diginews3.html.

Frey, F. and Reilly, J. (1997) *Digital Imaging for Photographic Collections: Foundations for Technical Standards*,
www.rit.edu/~661www1/sub_pages/digibook.pdf.

Frey, F. and Süsstrunk, S. (1997) Color Issues to Consider in Pictorial Image Data Bases. In *Proceedings of the IS&T's Fifth Color Imaging Conference, Scottsdale, Arizona*, 112–15, The Society for Imaging Science and Technology,
www.imaging.org/store/physpub.cfm?seriesid=4&pubid=1

Frey, F. and Süsstrunk, S. (1999) Color Management Panel: do you know what color your pixels are? In *Electronic Imaging and the Visual Arts (EVA) Conference, The Museum of Modern Art, New York, May 20, 1999.*

Gaines, S. (2003) I'll just check my diary . . ., *The Guardian*, (5 June),
www.guardian.co.uk/online/story/0,3605,970300,00.html.

Garnett, T. and Gwinn, N. (2001) *Preservation and Digitization – Natural Partners?* Summary of Survey Results, IFLA Standing Committee on

Preservation and Conservation,
www.ifla.org/VII/s19/conf/consws01.html.

Gay, G. (2001) Co-Construction of Digital Museums, *Spectra – a Publication of the Museum Computer Network*, **5** (1), 12–15.

Geisler, G. et al. (2002). *Creating Virtual Collections in Digital Libraries: benefits and implementation issues*, Joint Conference on Digital Libraries.

Gertz, J. (1998) *Guidelines for Digital Imaging*, National Preservation Office, The British Library, www.bl.uk/services/preservation/gertz.html.

Gertz, J. (1999) Selection Guidelines for Preservation, *Joint RLG and NPO Preservation Conference Guidelines for Digital Imaging*, www.rlg.org/preserv/joint/gertz.html.

Gertz, J. (2000a) Selection for Preservation in the Digital Age: an overview, *Library Resources & Technical Services*, **44** (2), 97–104.

Gertz, J. (2000b) Vendor Relations. In Sitts, M. K. (ed.) *Handbook for Digital Projects: a management tool for preservation and access*, Northeast Document Conservation Center (NEDCC).

Geyer-Schulz, A., et al. (2003) Strategic Positioning Options for Scientific Libraries in Markets of Scientific and Technical Information – the economic impact of digitization, *JoDI – Journal of Digital Information*, **4** (2), http://jodi.ecs.soton.ac.uk/Articles/v04/i02/Geyer-Schulz/.

Gill, T. and Miller, P. (2002) Re-inventing the Wheel? Standards, interoperability and digital cultural content, *D-Lib Magazine*, **8** (1), www.dlib.org/dlib/january02/gill/01gill.html.

Goldman, K. H., and Wadman, M. (2003) There's Something Happening Here, What It Is Ain't Exactly Clear. In Bearman, D. and Trant, J. (eds), *Museums and the Web 2003: paper presented at Museums and the Web 2003, 19–22 March 2003, Charlotte, North Carolina*.

Greenberg, D. (2003) *Indexing Memory: The Shoah Foundation Archive of Holocaust Testimony*, presentation at NINCH conference 'Transforming Disciplines: Computer Science and the Humanities', 17 January, 2003, unpublished.

Greenstein, D. (2000) *DLF Draft Strategy and Business Plan*, Digital Library Federation, www.diglib.org/about/strategic.htm.

Greenstein, D. and Thorin, S. (2002) *The Digital Library: a biography*, Council on Library and Information Resources, www.clir.org/pubs/reports/pub109/contents.html.

Groen, F. (1999) Strategic Issues in Digitization Initiatives in Special

Collections. In *ARL Proceedings*, Association of Research Libraries, www.arl.org/arl/proceedings/134/groen.html.

Guthrie, K. (2001) Archiving in the Digital Age: there's a will, but is there a way?, *Educause Review*, **36** (6), 57–65, www.educause.edu/ir/library/pdf/erm0164.pdf.

Hall, V. and Albrecht, K. (1997) Review of the Conference on Fair Use and Proposed Guidelines, *VRA Bulletin*, **24** (1), 21–5.

The Hargrett Rare Book and Manuscript Library at the University of Georgia (2001) *Rare Map Collection*, www.libs.uga.edu/darchive/hargrett/maps/maps.html.

Harm, N. (2003) *Luna Imaging: a manufacturing model*. Paper delivered at NINCH Price of Digitization Symposium 2003, www.ninch.org/forum/price.report.html#nh.

Harnad, S. (2003) Online Archives for Peer-Reviewed Journal Publications. In Feather, J. and Sturges, P. (eds), *International Encyclopedia of Library and Information Science*, Routledge.

Harnard, S. (1995) A Subversive Proposal for Electronic Publishing. In Okerson, A. and O'Donnell, J. (eds), *Scholarly Journals at the Crossroads: a subversive proposal for electronic publishing*, Association of Research Libraries, www.arl.org/scomm/subversive/sub01.html.

Harper, G. (2001) *Managing the Risk of Copyright Infringement Liability*, www.utsystem.edu/ogc/intellectualproperty/riskmgt.htm.

Harrison, H. P. (ed.) (1997) *Audiovisual Archives: a practical reader*, UNESCO.

Hartlib Papers Project (2002), www.shef.ac.uk/~hpp/.

Harvard University Library (2001) *Guide to Image Digitization*, http://hul.harvard.edu/ois/systems/guide_images.html.

Harvard University Library (2002a) *Imaging Systems*, http://preserve.harvard.edu/resources/imagingsystems.html.

Harvard University Library (2002b) *Library Preservation at Harvard: Digitization*, http://preserve.harvard.edu/resources/digital.html.

Harvard University Library Digital Initiative (2003a) *Image Reformatting*, http://hul.harvard.edu/ldi/html/reformatting_image.html.

Harvard University Library Digital Initiative (2003b) *Text Reformatting*, http://hul.harvard.edu/ldi/html/reformatting_text.html.

Hastings, K. and Tennant, R. (1996) How to Build a Digital Librarian, *D-Lib Magazine* (November), www.dlib.org/dlib/november96/ucb/11hastings.html.

Hastings, S. K. (2000) Digital Image Managers: a museum/university collaboration, *First Monday*, **5** (6), www.firstmonday.org/issues/issue5_6/hastings/

Hazen, D., Horrell, J. and Merrill-Oldham, J. (1998) *Selecting Research Collections for Digitization*, Council on Library and Information Resources, www.clir.org/pubs/reports/hazen/pub74.html.

Heath, F. et al. (2003) Emerging Tools for Evaluating Digital Library Services: conceptual adaptations of LibQUAL+ and CAPM, *JoDI – Journal of Digital Information*, **4** (2), http://jodi.ecs.soton.ac.uk/Articles/v04/i02/Heath/.

HEDS (2003) *Costing a Digitization Project*, http://heds.herts.ac.uk/resources/costing.html.

Hedstrom, M. (1995) *Digital preservation: a time bomb for digital libraries*. Paper delivered at Symposium on Reconnecting Science and Humanities in Digital Libraries, Lexington, Kentucky, www.uky.edu/~kiernan/DL/hedstrom.html.

Hedstrom, M. (1998) The Role of National Initiatives in Digital Preservation, *RLG Diginews*, **2** (5), www.rlg.org/preserv/diginews/diginews2-5.html#feature2.

Hedstrom, M. and Ross, S. (2002) In Brief: EU(DELOS)-NSF Working Group on Digital Archiving and Preservation, *D-Lib Magazine*, **8** (9), www.dlib.org/dlib/september02/09inbrief.html.

Ho, C. (2002) CHANT (CHinese ANcient Texts): a comprehensive database of all ancient Chinese texts up to 600 AD, *JoDI – Journal of Digital Information*, **3** (2), http://jodi.ecs.soton.ac.uk/Articles/v03/i02/Ho/.

Hodges, D. (1999) Digital Imaging: towards international agreement on guidance, guidelines and best practices, *National Library News*, **31** (2), http://nlc-bnc.ca/9/2/p2-9902-05-e.html.

Howell, A. (1997) Film Scanning of Newspaper Collections: international initiatives, *RLG Diginews*, **1** (2), www.rlg.org/preserv/diginews/diginews2.html.

Hughes, C. A. (2000) Lessons Learned: digitization of special collections at the University of Iowa Libraries, *D-Lib Magazine*, **6** (6), www.dlib.org/dlib/june00/hughes/06hughes.html.

Hughes, R. (1992) *Nothing If Not Critical: selected essays on art and artists*,

Penguin USA.

Hyvönen, E. et al. (2002) *Cultural Semantic Interoperability on the Web: Case Finnish Museums Online* (sic), presentation at International Semantic Web Conference (ISWC), http://iswc2002.semanticweb.org/posters/hyvonen_a4.pdf.

ICOM (1997) *ICOM-CIDOC Multimedia Working Group, Multimedia Evaluation Criteria*, www.archimuse.com/papers/cidoc/cidoc/mmwg.eval.crit.html.

IFLA Manifesto on Open Access to Scholarly Literature and Research Documentation (2003), www.library.otago.ac.nz/pdf/ifla_manifesto_scholarly.pdf.

IFLA/UNESCO Survey on Digitisation and Preservation (1999), www.unesco.org/webworld/mdm/survey_rtf_en/intro_a.rtf.

IMLS (Institute of Museum and Library Services) (1999) *World Wide Web Resources for the Digital Imaging Lab*, http://courses.unt.edu/shastings/HastingsWWW/IMLS/resources.htm.

IMLS (Institute of Museum and Library Services) (2002) *Status of Technology and Digitization in the Nation's Museums and Libraries*, IMLS Public Report, www.imls.gov/reports/techreports/action02.htm.

Joint RLG and NPO Preservation Conference (1998) *Guidelines for Digital Imaging: selection criteria, guidelines, decision-making aids*, www.rlg.org/preserv/joint/selection.html.

Jones, T. (2001) *An Introduction to Digital Projects for Libraries, Museums and Archives*, http://images.library.uiuc.edu/resources/introduction.htm.

Jones-Garmil, K. (1997) *The Wired Museum: emerging technology and changing paradigms*, American Association of Museums.

JUGL (2001) *Seminar: Digitisation in Practice, Open University Conference Centre, London 9 January 2001*, Janet User Group for Libraries, http://bubl.ac.uk/org/jugl/.

Katz, R. (1999) *Dancing with the Devil: information technology and the new competition in higher education*, Jossey-Bass Publishers.

Katzenbeisser, S. and Petitcolas, F. (eds) (1999) *Information Hiding Techniques for Steganography and Digital Watermarking*, Artech House Books.

Keene, S. (1998) *Digital Collections: museums and the information age*, Butterworth-Heinemann.

Kenney, A. (1997) The Cornell Digital to Microfilm Conversion Project:

final report to NEH, *RLG Diginews*, **1** (2),
www.rlg.org/preserv/diginews/diginews2.html.

Kenney, A. (1998) Mainstreaming Digitization into the Mission of Cultural
Repositories. In *Collections, Content and the Web*, CLIR (Council on
Library and Information Resources), 1998.

Kenney, A. et al. (2002) Preservation Risk Management for Web Resources,
Virtual Remote Control in Cornell's Project Prism, *D-Lib Magazine*, **8**
(1), www.dlib.org/dlib/january02/kenney/01kenney.html.

Kenney, A. and Rieger, O. (eds) (2000) *Moving Theory into Practice: digital
imaging for libraries and archives*, RLG (Research Libraries Group).

Kesse, E. et al. (2001) *Caribbean Newspaper Imaging Project. Phase I: Imaging
and Indexing Model*,
http://web.uflib.ufl.edu/digital/collections/cnip/eng/CNIP1report.htm.

Kiernan, K. (1994a) Digital Preservation, Restoration, and Dissemination
of Medieval Manuscripts, In Okerson, A. and Mogge, D. (eds) *Scholarly
Publishing on the Electronic Networks: gateways, gatekeepers, and roles in the
information omniverse*, Association of Research Libraries, Office of
Scientific and Academic Publishing, 37–43.

Kiernan, K. (1994b) Scholarly Publishing on the Electronic Networks. In
Okerson, A. (ed.), *Proceedings of the Third Symposium*, ARL Publications.

Kiernan, K., Rhyne, C. and Spronk, R. (2001) *Digital Imagery for Works of
Art*, Mellon/NSF/Harvard University Art Museums, 2001,
www.dli2.nsf.gov/mellon/report.html.

Kiernan, K., Seales, B. and Griffioen, J. (2002) The Reappearances of St.
Basil the Great in British Library MS Cotton Otho B. x, *Computers and
the Humanities*, **36** (1), 7–26,
http://ipsapp007.lwwonline.com/content/getfile/4589/22/3/fulltext.pdf.

Kirschenbaum, M. (2002) Editor's Introduction: Image-based Humanities
Computing, *Computers and the Humanities*, **36** (1), 3–6, http://ipsapp007.
lwwonline.com/content/getfile/4589/22/2/fulltext.pdf.

Klijn, E. and Lusenet, Y. de (2000) *In the Picture: preservation and digitisation
of European photographic collections*, ECPA-report, 11,
www.kijkopinternet.nl/ecpa/epic/pdf/885.pdf.

Knoll, A. (2000) *ELAG 2000 Progress Report of the National Library of the
Czech Republic*,
www.stk.cz/elag2001/Reports/Czech_RepuNational_Library_of_the_C.
html.

Koelling, J. M. (2000) Revealing History, *Spectra – a Publication of the Museum Computer Network*, **20**, 9–14, www.mcn.edu/pdf/MCN_Spectra_Fall00.pdf.

Krämer, H. (2001) *Museumsinformatik und Digitale Sammlung*, WUV-Universitäts-Verlag.

Kravchyna, V. and Hastings, S. K. (2002) Informational Value of Museum Web Sites, *First Monday*, **7** (2), www.firstmonday.org/issues/issue7_2/kravchyna/.

Kuny, T. (1997) A Digital Dark Ages? Challenges in the preservation of electronic information, www.ifla.org/IV/ifla63/63kuny1.pdf.

Lauder, J. (1995) Digitization of Microfilm: a Scottish perspective, *Microform Review*, **24** (4), 178–81.

Lawrence, G. et al. (2000) *Risk Management of Digital Information: a file format investigation*, Council on Library and Information Resources, www.clir.org/pubs/reports/pub93/contents.html.

Lee, S. (2001a) *Digital Imaging: a practical handbook*, Neal-Schuman Publishers in association with Library Association Publishing.

Lee, S. (2001b) Digitization: Is It Worth It?, *Computers in Libraries*, **21** (5), www.infotoday.com/cilmag/may01/lee.htm.

Lee, S. (n.d.) *(Reactive) On-Demand Digitization Service Proposed Work-Flow*, University of Oxford, www.bodley.ox.ac.uk/scoping/ondd.pdf.

Leek, M. R. (1995) Will a Good Disc Last Forever?, *CD-ROM Professional*, **8** (November), 102.

Lenhart, A. (2003) *The Ever-Shifting Internet Population: a new look at internet access and the digital divide*, www.pewinternet.org/reports/pdfs/PIP_Shifting_Net_Pop_Report.pdf.

Lesk, M. (1995) *Preserving Digital Objects: recurrent needs and challenges*, http://lesk.com/mlesk/auspres/aus.html.

Lesk, M. (1996) *Mad Library Disease: holes in the stacks*, http://lesk.com/mlesk/ucla/ucla.html.

Lesk, M. (1997a) Digital Libraries: the revolution in scholarly information, *HEIA (Higher Education in the Information Age) Proceedings*, www.upenn.edu/heia/proceed/present/lesktrans.html.

Lesk, M. (1997b) *Practical Digital Libraries: books, bytes, and bucks*, Morgan Kaufmann Publishers.

Lesk, M. (2002) *How to Pay for Digital Libraries*, http://lesk.com/mlesk/derek02/derek2.html.

Lesk, M. (2003) *NINCH Symposium: 8 April 2003, New York City, The Price of Digitization: new cost models for cultural and educational institutions, a short report*, www.ninch.org/forum/price.lesk.report.html.

Levine, M. S. (2000) Overview of Copyright Issues. In Sitts, M. K. (ed.) (2000) *Handbook for Digital Projects: a management tool for preservation and access*, Northeast Document Conservation Center (NEDCC).

Levy, D. (2001) Digital Libraries and the Problem of Purpose, *Spectra – a Publication of the Museum Computer Network*, **5** (1), 8–11.

Lewis, J. P. (1999) *The Project Manager's Desk Reference*, McGraw-Hill Trade.

Library of Congress (1997) *National Digital Library Program (NDLP) Project Planning Checklist*, http://memory.loc.gov/ammem/techdocs/prjplan.html.

Library of Congress (2003) *Building Digital Collections: technical information and background papers*, http://memory.loc.gov/ammem/ftpfiles.html.

Library of Congress, Committee on Information Technology (2001) *LC21: a digital strategy for the Library of Congress*, The National Academies Press, http://search.nap.edu/books/0309071445/html/.

Library of Congress, National Digital Library Program and the Conservation Division (1999) *Conservation Implications of Digitization Projects*, http://memory.loc.gov/ammem/techdocs/conserv83199a.pdf.

Library of Congress, Preservation Reformatting Division (2002) *Selection Criteria for Preservation Digital Reformatting*, http://lcweb.loc.gov/preserv/prd/presdig/presselection.html.

Library Preservation at Harvard (2003) *Digital Initiatives*, http://preserve.harvard.edu/news/digital.html.

Lippincott, J. (1996) Networked Information in an International Context, *ARL Newsletter*, 185, www.arl.org/newsltr/185/networked.html.

Lohr, S. (2003) 'New Media': ready for the dustbin of history?, *The New York Times* (11 May), www.nytimes.com/2003/05/11/weekinreview/11LOHR.˜

Lossau, N. and Klaproth, F. (1999) Digitization Efforts at the Center for Retrospective Digitization, Göttingen University Library, *RLG Diginews*, **3** (1), www.rlg.org/preserv/diginews/diginews3-1.html#feature2.

Lossau, N. and Liebetruth, M. (2000) Conservation Issues in Digital Imaging, *Spectra – a Publication of the Museum Computer Network* (Fall), 30–7, www.mcn.edu/pdf/MCN_Spectra_Fall00.pdf.

Lusenet, Y. de (1999) Preserving Access to Information: the challenge of the future, www.ica.org/citra/citra.budapest.1999.eng/lusenet.pdf.

Lusenet, Y. de (2000) *Living Apart Together: conservation and digitization of historical photographs*, www.fmp.fi/fmp_fi/lusenet.htm.

Lyman, P. and Kahle, B. (1998) Archiving Digital Cultural Artifacts: organizing an agenda for action, *D-Lib Magazine* (July/August), www.dlib.org/dlib/july98/07lyman.html.

Marcum, D. (1998) Educating Leaders for the Digital Library, *CLIR Issues*, **6** (November/December), www.clir.org/pubs/issues/issues06.html#educate.

McKie, R. and Thorpe, V. (2002) Digital Domesday Book Lasts 15 Years Not 1000, *The Observer*, Sunday March 3, 2002.

McKitterick, D. (ed.) (2002) *Do We Want to Keep Our Newspapers?*, Office for Humanities Communication (OHC).

Menne-Haritz, A. and Brübach, N. (2001) *The Intrinsic Value of Archive and Library Material*, www.uni-marburg.de/archivschule/intrinsengl.html.

Miller, P., Dawson, D. and Perkins, J. (2001) Standing on the Shoulders of Giants: efforts to leverage existing synergies in digital cultural content creation programmes world-wide, *Cultivate Interactive*, **5**, www.cultivate-int.org/issue5/giants/.

Minerva Working Group (2003) *Best Practice Handbook*, www.minervaeurope.org/structure/workinggroups/goodpract/document/bestpracticehandbookv1.1.pdf.

Minnen, P. van (1995) *The Duke Papyri on the Internet*, http://scriptorium.lib.duke.edu/papyrus/texts/internet.html.

Minow, M. (2002) Library Web Pages: Identifying Public Domain Sources to Borrow From, *California Libraries*, **12** (5) (May).

Mintzer, F. C. et al. (1996) Toward On-line, Worldwide Access to Vatican Library materials, *IBM Journal of Research and Development*, **40** (2), 139–62, www.research.ibm.com/journal/rd/402/mintzer.html.

Mohr, M. (2002) Linking Chan/Seon/Zen Figures and Their Texts: problems and developments in the construction of a relational database, *JoDI – Journal of Digital Information*, **3** (2).

Moritz, T. (2003) *Toward Sustainability – margin and mission in the natural history setting*. Paper delivered at the NINCH Price of Digitization Symposium 2003, www.ninch.org/forum/price.report.html#tm.

Muller, C. and Beddow, M. (2002) Moving into XML Functionality: the combined digital dictionaries of Buddhism and East Asian literary

terms, *JoDI – Journal of Digital Information*, **3** (2),
http://jodi.ecs.soton.ac.uk/Articles/v03/i02/Muller/.

Mulrenin, A. and Geser, G. (2001) *The DigiCULT Report: Technological Landscapes for Tomorrow's Cultural Economy: Unlocking the value of cultural heritage*, Salzburg Research, on behalf of the European Commission,
www.salzburgresearch.at/research/publications_detail.php?pub_id=27.

Murch, R. (2000) *Project Management: best practices for IT professionals*, Prentice Hall.

Musea Project, Denmark (1997) *Standards for Cultural Heritage Information On-line – final report, conclusions and recommendations*,
www.portia.dk/musea/finalreport/10.htm.

National Library of Australia (2000) *Digitization Principles*,
www.nla.gov.au/libraries/digitisation/citwg_princ.html#p1.

National Library of Australia (2002) Management. In *PADI (Preserving Access to Digital Information) Thesaurus*,
www.nla.gov.au/padi/topics/73.html.

National Library of Australia (2003) *Digitisation Policy 2000–2004*,
www.nla.gov.au/policy/digitisation.html.

National Library of Canada (2001) *Selection of Materials for Digitization*,
www.nlc-bnc.ca/8/3/r3-409-e.html.

National Preservation Office (2001) *Managing the Digitisation of Library, Archive and Museum Materials*, National Preservation Office, The British Library, www.bl.uk/services/preservation/dig.pdf.

Networked Knowledge Organization Systems (NKOS) (2003) *Building a Meaningful Web: from traditional knowledge organization systems to new semantic tools.* The 6th NKOS Workshop at ACM-IEEE Joint Conference on Digital Libraries (JCDL),
http://nkos.slis.kent.edu/DL03workshop.htm.

NEWSPLAN: Diversity and Opportunity. Proceedings of the Fourth National NEWSPLAN Conference (2002),
www.bl.uk/concord/linc/pdf/newsplanconf-full.pdf.

New Zealand Digital Library Project, www.nzdl.org.

Nichols, S. G., and Smith. A. (2001) *The Evidence in Hand: report of the Task Force on the Artifact in Library Collections*, CLIR (Council on Library and Information Resources).

NINCH (National Initiative for a Networked Cultural Heritage) (2002) *The*

NINCH Guide to Good Practice in the Digital Representation and Management of Cultural Heritage Materials, www.nyu.edu/its/humanities/ninchguide/.

NOF-Digitise Technical Advisory Service (2002a) *The Digitisation Process,* www.ukoln.ac.uk/nof/support/help/papers/digitisation_process.

NOF-Digitise Technical Advisory Service (2002b) *Programme Manual,* www.ukoln.ac.uk/nof/support/manual/toc/.

Nowviskie, B. (2002) Select Resources for Image-based Humanities Computing, *Computers and the Humanities,* **36** (1), 109–31, http://ipsapp007.lwwonline.com/content/getfile/4589/22/7/fulltext.pdf.

Ober, J. and Lawrence, E. (2001) *The California Digital Library Acquires Unique Humanities Databases for the University of California from Alexander Street Press,* Press Release, 12 January, www.cdlib.org/news/press_releases/cdlasp.pdf.

Ockuly, J. (2003) *What Clicks? An interim report on audience research,* paper delivered at Museums and the Web 2003, http://archimuse.com/mw2003/papers/ockuly/ockuly.html.

OCLC Digitization and Preservation Resource Center (2003) *The Copyright Online Resource Kit,* http://digitalcooperative.oclc.org/copyright/.

Ogden, S. (ed.) (1994) *Preservation of Library and Archival Materials: a manual,* Northeast Document Conservation Center.

Okerson, A. and O'Donnell, J. (eds) (1995) *Scholarly Journals at the Crossroads: a subversive proposal for electronic publishing,* Association of Research Libraries, www.arl.org/scomm/subversive/toc.html.

Oppenheim, C. (2002) *Information Ownership, Copyright and Licences,* www.zbmed.de/eahil2002/proceedings/oppenheim-proc.pdf.

Orna, E. and Pettitt, C. (1998) *Information Management in Museums,* Gower.

Ostrow, S. (1998) *Digitizing Historical Pictorial Collections for the Internet,* Council on Library and Information Resources, www.clir.org/pubs/reports/ostrow/pub71.html.

Owen, C., Pearson, A. and Arnold, S. (2000) Meeting the Challenge of Film Research in the Electronic Age, *D-Lib Magazine,* **6** (3) (March), www.dlib.org/dlib/march00/owen/03owen.html.

The Oxford Text Archive (2000), http://ota.ahds.ac.uk/ota/.

PALMM (Publication of Archival Library & Museum Materials, State University System of Florida) (2002) *PALMM Guidelines and Procedures,* http://palmm.fcla.edu/strucmeta/standres.html.

Patterson, L. R. and Lindberg, S. W. (1991) *The Nature of Copyright: a law of users' rights*, University of Georgia Press.

Pence, D. (2003) *Ten Ways to Spend $100,000 on Digitization*. Paper delivered at NINCH Price of Digitization Symposium 2003, www.ninch.org/forum/price.report.html#dp.

Peterson, T. (1997) Putting Records First to Make Them Last. In Lusenet, Y. de (ed.), *Choosing to Preserve: towards a cooperative strategy for long-term access to the intellectual heritage*, European Commission for Preservation and Access (ECPA).

Preserving the Recorded Past (2003), *New York Times*, Editorial/Op-Ed, (30 January), www.nytimes.com/2003/01/30/opinion/30THU4.html.

Presto (2000) *European Project PRESTO, developing technology and processes to preserve European broadcast archives*, http://presto.joanneum.ac.at/Public/brochure.pdf.

Price, L. and Smith, A. (2000) *Managing Cultural Assets from a Business Perspective*, Council on Library and Information Resources, www.clir.org/pubs/reports/pub90/contents.html.

Pugh, M. J. (1992) *Providing Reference Services for Archives and Manuscripts*, Society of American Archivists.

Puglia, S. (1999) The Costs of Digital Imaging Projects, *RLG DigiNews*, **3** (5), www.rlg.org/preserv/diginews/diginews3-5.html#feature.

Raitt, D. (2000) Digital Library Initiatives across Europe, *Computers and Libraries*, **20** (10), www.infotoday.com/cilmag/nov00/raitt.htm.

Rayner, J. (2002) Experts Find Fault with New 1901 Census Website, *The Observer* (6 January).

Reddy, R. and StClair, G. (2001) *The Million Book Digital Library Project*, www.rr.cs.cmu.edu/mbdl.htm.

Reilly, B. F., Jr (2002) *Risk Management Aspects of Cooperative Collection Development Projects*. A Paper and Presentation at Aberdeen Woods, www.crl.edu/info/awcc2002/Reilly%20paper.pdf.

Renoult, D. (2000) Organising the Digitisation of Collections at a National or International Level: models for research library development, *Liber Quarterly*, **10** (3), 393–403, http://webdoc.gwdg.de/edoc/aw/liber/lq-3-00/lq-3-00-s393b403.pdf.

RLG (Research Libraries Group) (1992) *RLG Preservation Microfilming Handbook*, RLG.

RLG (Research Libraries Group) (2000) Guides to Quality in Visual

Resource Imaging, www.rlg.org/visguides.

RLG (Research Libraries Group) (2002) *RLG Worksheet for Estimating Digital Reformatting Costs*, www.rlg.org/preserv/RLGtools.html.

RLG (Research Libraries Group) (2003a) *Long-Term Retention of Digital Research Materials*, www.rlg.org/longterm/.

RLG (Research Libraries Group) (2003b) *RLG Guidelines for Microfilming to Support Digitization*, RLG.

RLG (Research Libraries Group), DLF (Digital Libraries Federation) and CLIR (Council on Library and Information Resources) (2002) *Tools for Digital Imaging*, www.rlg.org/preserv/RLGtools.html.

Resnick, D. (2000) The Virtual University and College Life: some unintended consequences for democratic citizenship, *First Monday*, **5** (8), www.firstmonday.dk/issues/issue5_8/resnick/.

Roderick, E. (1998) *More Than Just Pretty Pictures: a cost/benefit analysis of digital library holdings*, www.educause.edu/ir/library/html/cnc9804/cnc9804.html.

Rosenzweig, R. and Thelen, D. (1998) *The Presence of the Past. Popular uses of history in American life*, Supplements, http://chnm.gmu.edu/survey/.

Ross, S. (2000) *Changing Trains at Wigan: digital preservation and the future of scholarship*, National Preservation Office, The British Library.

Ross, S. and Economou, M. (1998) Information and Communications Technology in the Cultural Sector: the need for national strategies, *D-Lib Magazine* (June), www.dlib.org/dlib/june98/06ross.html.

Ross, S., and A. Gow (1999) *Digital Archaeology: rescuing neglected and damaged data resources*, eLib: The Electronic Libraries Programme, eLib Supporting Studies, www.ukoln.ac.uk/services/elib/papers/supporting/pdf/p2.pdf.

Rothenberg, J. (1995) Ensuring the Longevity of Digital Documents, *Scientific American*, **272** (1), 42–7, www.clir.org/pubs/archives/ensuring.pdf.

Rothenberg, J. (1998) *Avoiding Technological Quicksand: finding a viable technical foundation for digital preservation*, Council on Library and Information Resources, www.clir.org/pubs/reports/rothenberg/contents.html.

Rowe, J. (2002) Developing a 3D Digital Library for Spatial Data: issues identified and description of prototype, *RLG Diginews*, **6** (5), www.rlg.org/preserv/diginews/diginews6-5.html#feature1.

Royal Netherlands Academy of Arts and Sciences (2001) *Suggestions for Further Reading 'In the Picture'*, www.knaw.nl/ecpa/publ/bibliography.html.

Ruddy, S. (1999) *Planning Digital Projects for Historical Collections*, http://digital.nypl.org/brochure/planning.htm.

Sanett, S. (2003) The Cost to Preserve Authentic Electronic Records in Perpetuity: comparing costs across cost models and cost frameworks, *RLG Diginews*, **7** (4) (15 August).

Schiff, J. (2002) *Library Division Celebrates 20 Years of Restoration and Repair*, University of Michigan, www.umich.edu/~urecord/0102/Sep23_02/preservation.html.

Serenson Colet, L. (2000) *Planning an Imaging Project*, RLG CLIR and DLF Guides to Quality in Visual Resource Imaging, Research Libraries Group, www.rlg.org/visguides/.

Simpson, S. (1996) *The Virtualisation of Objects*, www.simpsons.com.au/documents/museums/papers/TheVirtu.pdf.

Simpson, S. (1998) *Digitisation of Museum Collections – a management issue*, www.simpsons.com.au/documents/museums/papers/Digitisa.pdf.

Sitts, M. K. (ed.) (2000) *Handbook for Digital Projects: a management tool for preservation and access*, Northeast Document Conservation Center (NEDCC), www.nedcc.org/digital/dighome.htm.

Smith, A. (1999) *Why Digitize?*, Council on Library and Information Resources, www.clir.org/pubs/reports/pub80-smith/pub80.html.

Smith, A. (2001a) *Building and Sustaining Digital Collections: models for libraries and museums*, Council on Library and Information Resources, www.clir.org/pubs/reports/pub100/contents.html.

Smith, A. (2001b) The Problem of Authenticity in Digital Libraries, *Spectra – a Publication of the Museum Computer Network*, **5** (1), 40–3.

Smith, A. (2001c) *Strategies for Building Digitized Collections*, Council on Library and Information Resources, www.clir.org/pubs/reports/pub101/contents.html.

Smith, S. (1998) *Digitising Collections: the redefining of museums*, paper delivered at Museums and the Web 1998, www.archimuse.com/mw98/papers/smith_s/smith_s_paper.html.

Smith, S. (2000) Cooperative Imaging: scans well with others. In Sitts, M. K. (ed.) *Handbook for Digital Projects: a management tool for preservation and access*, Northeast Document Conservation Center (NEDCC).

Snyder, H. and Davenport, E. (1997) *Costing and Pricing in the Digital Age: a practical guide for information services*, Neal-Schuman Publishers.

Staples, T., Wayland, R. and Payette, S. (2003) The Fedora Project: an open-source digital object repository management system, *D-Lib Magazine*, **9** (4), www.dlib.org/dlib/april03/staples/04staples.html.

State Library of Queensland (2001) *Digital Library Strategic Plan 2000–2003*, www.slq.qld.gov.au/planning/digital_2000/.

Stefano, P. de (2000) Selection for Digital Conversion. In Kenney, A. and Rieger, O. (eds) *Moving Theory into Practice: digital imaging for libraries and archives*, Research Libraries Group, 11–23.

Stinson, D., Ameli, F. and Zaino, N. (1995) *Lifetime of Kodak Writable CD and Photo CD media*, www.cd-info.com/CDIC/Technology/CD-R/ Media/Kodak.html.

Sukovic, S. (2002) Beyond the Scriptorium: the role of the library in text encoding, *D-Lib Magazine*, **8** (1), www.dlib.org/dlib/january02/sukovic/01sukovic.html.

Sullivan, R. (2002) Indigenous Cultural and Intellectual Property Rights – a digital library context, *D-Lib Magazine*, **8** (5), www.dlib.org/dlib/may02/sullivan/05sullivan.html.

Surface, T. (2002) *Digitopia Cooperative Activities for Digital Collections: national & global perspectives.* Paper presented at MLC/OCLC Users' Day, Tuesday 9 April , East Lansing, Michigan, www.mlc.lib.mi.us/workshop/oclcday02/surface_presentation/.

Tanner, S. (2001a) *DEF Digitisation Project Proposals – a Review*, HEDS, http://heds.ac.uk.

Tanner, S. (2001b) *From Vision to Implementation – strategic and management issues for digitising collections.* Paper presented at The Electronic Library: strategic, policy and management issues conference, http://heds.herts.ac.uk/resources/papers/Lboro2000.pdf.

Tanner, S. (2001c) *Planning Your Digitization Project: the technologies and skills.* Paper presented at the JUGL Conference, Open University Conference Centre, London, 9 January 2001, http://heds.herts.ac.uk/resources/.

Tanner, S. (2003a), correspondence.

Tanner, S. (2003b) Economic Factors of Managing Digital Content and Establishing Digital Libraries, *JoDI – Journal of Digital Information*, **4** (2).

Tanner, S. and Deegan, M. (2002) *Exploring Charging Models for Digital Cultural Heritage: digital image resource cost efficiency and income generation compared with analog resources.* A HEDS report on behalf of the Andrew W. Mellon Foundation, http://heds.herts.ac.uk/mellon/charging_models.html.

Tanner, S. and Lomax Smith, J. (1999) *Digitisation: how much does it really cost?.* Paper for the Digital Resources for the Humanities conference, http://heds.herts.ac.uk/resources/papers/drh99.pdf.

Tanner, S. and Robinson, B. (1998) *JISC Image Digitisation Initiative: feasibility study (final report),* The Higher Education Digitisation Service (HEDS), http://heds.herts.ac.uk/resources/papers/jidi_fs.pdf.

TASI (Technical Advisory Service for Images) (2002a) Deciding to Digitise, *Advice – Managing Digitisation Projects,* www.tasi.ac.uk/advice/managing/decide.html.

TASI (Technical Advisory Service for Images) (2002b) Managing the Project, *Advice – Managing Digitisation Projects,* www.tasi.ac.uk/advice/managing/project.html.

TASI (Technical Advisory Service for Images) (2003) *An Introduction to Making Digital Image Archives,* www.tasi.ac.uk/advice/overview.html.

Tennant, R. (1998) So Much To Digitize, So Little Time (and Money), *Library Journal* (1 August).

Tennant, R. (2000) Selecting Collections for Digitizing, *Library Journal,* **125** (19) (15 November), 26.

Thomas, S. and Mintz, A. (1998) *The Virtual and the Real: media in the museum,* American Association of Museums.

Turko, K. (1998) *Guidance for Selecting Materials for Digitization, Canadian overview,* National Preservation Office, The British Library, www.bl.uk/services/preservation/turko.html.

UNESCO, IFLA and ICA (2002) *Guidelines for Digitization Projects: for collections and holdings in the public domain, particularly those held in libraries and archives,* UNESCO, http://portal.unesco.org/.

United States Army Digitization Program (1997) *US Army Science and Technology Master Plan (ASTMP),* www.fas.org/man/dod-101/army/docs/astmp/c7/P7F5.htm.

University of Virginia Library (2003) *The Electronic Text Center,* http://etext.lib.virginia.edu.

Unsworth, J. (1997) The Importance of Failure, *Journal of Electronic*

Publishing, **3** (2), www.press.umich.edu/jep/03-02/unsworth.html.

Unsworth, J. (2000) *Scholarly Primitives: what methods do humanities researchers have in common, and how might our tools reflect this?*, www.iath.virginia.edu/~jmu2m/Kings.5-00/primitives.html.

Vaidhyanathan, S. (2001) *Copyrights and Copywrongs: the rise of intellectual property and how it threatens creativity*, New York University Press.

Varian (2002) *Smithsonian Researchers Use High-Tech Digital Imaging Device to Study Collections*: *a PaxScan image receptor from Varian Medical Systems speeds research and cuts costs*, Press Release, www.varian.com/com/020213.html.

Veltman, K. (2002) Paper at the workshop 'Envisioning our Digital Future', School for Scanning (SfS) organized by NEDCC, Koniklijke Bibliotheek, The Hague, 16 October 2002, unpublished.

Victoria's Virtual Library Digital Collection (2003) *Storage and Management – Local History Digitisation Manual*, www.libraries.vic.gov.au/downloads/Victorias_Virtual_Library_Digital_Collection/storage.htm.

Victorian Times – Victorian social conditions. A New Opportunities Fund Project, Business Plan, http://vt.cdlr.strath.ac.uk/Documents/businessplan4.htm.

Villa, P. (2000) *Looking at the Future: what strategic reviews are other national libraries undertaking to assess their future service requirements?* A study for the British Library's Policy Unit, www.bl.uk/concord/policy2.pdf.

Viscomi, J. (2002) Digital Facsimiles: reading the William Blake Archive, *Computers and the Humanities*, **36** (1), 27–48, http://ipsapp007.lwwonline.com/content/getfile/4589/22/4/fulltext.pdf.

Vogt-O'Connor, D. (2000) Selection of Materials for Scanning, *NEDCC Handbook*, www.nedcc.org/digital/iv.htm.

Washington State Library Digital Best Practices Resources (2003), http://digitalwa.statelib.wa.gov/newsite/projectmgmt/resources.htm.

Waters, D. (1998) Digital Preservation?, *CLIR issues*, **6** (November/December), www.clir.org/pubs/issues/issues06.html#digital.

Waters, D. (2003) *The Economics of Digitizing Library and Other Cultural Materials: Perspective from the Mellon Foundation*. Paper delivered at NINCH Price of Digitization Symposium 2003, www.ninch.org/forum/price.report.html#dw.

Webb, C. (2000) *Limitations and Pitfalls of Digitisation*. Paper presented at Pacific History Association conference, Canberra, www.nla.gov.au/nla/staffpaper/2000/webb5.html.

Webb, C. (2001) *Who Will Save the Olympics? The Pandora archive and other digital preservation case studies at the National Library of Australia*, www.oclc.org/events/presentations/2001/preservation/preisswebb.htm.

Weber, H. and Dörr, M. (1997) *Digitisation as a Method of Preservation? Final report of a working group of the Deutsche Forschungsgemeinschaft (German Research Association)*, translated by Andrew Medlicott, www.knaw.nl/ecpa/publ/weber.html or www.clir.org/pubs/reports/digpres/digpres.html.

Whitehead, R. (2001) *Leading a Software Development Team: a developer's guide to successfully leading people and projects*, Addison-Wesley.

Williams, D. (1998) *Selecting a Scanner*, Guides to Quality in Visual Resource Imaging, Guide no. 2, RLG/CLIR/DLF, www.rlg.org/visguides/visguide2.html.

Wilson, M. (2001) Correspondence.

Witten, I. H. (2003) Examples of Practical Digital Libraries: collections built internationally using Greenstone, *D-Lib Magazine*, **9** (3), www.dlib.org/dlib/march03/witten/03witten.html.

Witten, I. H. and Bainbridge, D. (2003) *How to Build a Digital Library*, Morgan Kaufmann.

Witten, I. H., Cunningham, S. J. and Apperley, M. D. (1996) The New Zealand Digital Library Project, *D-Lib Magazine* (November), www.dlib.org/dlib/november96/newzealand/11witten.html.

Wittenberg, K. (2003) *Sustainability Models for Online Scholarly Publishing*. Paper delivered at NINCH Price of Digitization Symposium 2003, www.ninch.org/forum/price.report.html#kw.

Wittern, C. (2002) Chinese Buddhist texts for the New Millennium – the Chinese Buddhist Electronic Text Association (CBETA) and its Digital Tripitaka, *JoDI – Journal of Digital Information*, **3** (2), http://jodi.ecs.soton.ac.uk/Articles/v03/i02/Wittern/

Zorich, D. (2003) *A Survey of Digital Cultural Heritage Collections and Their Sustainability Concerns*, Council on Library and Information Resources, www.clir.org/pubs/reports/pub118/pub118.pdf.

Zweig, R. W. (1998) Lessons from the *Palestine Post* Project, *Literary & Linguistic Computing*, **13** (2), 89–96.

Index